STEP BY STEP

A COMPLETE MOVEMENT EDUCATION CURRICULUM
FROM PRESCHOOL TO 6TH GRADE

by

SHEILA KOGAN

EDITOR
Frank Alexander

EDITORIAL ASSISTANT
Diane Alexander

ARTIST
Valerie Winemiller

Published by FRONT ROW EXPERIENCE, 540 Discovery Bay Blvd., Byron, Calif. 94514-9454

4090 BOOKS IN PRINT AS OF 1994

Copyright © 1982 SHEILA KOGAN

ISBN 0-915256-10-X

Published

by

FRONT ROW EXPERIENCE
540 Discovery Bay Blvd.
Byron, Calif. 94514-9454
United States Of America

All rights reserved. This material
may not be reproduced in any form
except upon written permission
from the publisher.

IN APPRECIATION

My first thanks go to Gertrude Blanchard who first took a chance on me and then taught me most of what I know. Mrs. Blanchard is a great teacher and a thought provoking mentor.

Enormous thanks to Bruce Cohen, who taught me to write and kept me going through that tenuous beginning.

Thanks to my friends, Lu, Marcia, Ruth, Deder and Pat, who helped so much along the way.

NOTE ON THIRD PERSON PRONOUN

I have used "he" to indicate both boys and girls. Combining both masculine and feminine pronouns proved too awkward. I chose the masculine pronoun because dance and movement have been traditionally feminine activities.

DEDICATION

to BB

ABOUT THE AUTHOR

Sheila Kogan received a degree in music theory and composition and a teaching credential from the University of California, Berkeley. She has an MS degree in Education with a concentration in Movement Education from the Dominican College of San Rafael, California. She has studied dance at the University of California in Berkeley, at the Shawl and Anderson Dance Studio of Berkeley, California, and at other California dance studios. For awhile she was a member of the Shawl and Anderson performing company.

Her most useful and inspiring teacher training came from Gertrude Blanchard of the Richmond Recreation Department in Richmond, California. Mrs. Blanchard provided the conceptual groundwork that later grew into a complete curriculum.

Sheila Kogan has taught for over twenty years in many different school environments with a great variety of children. She has taught elementary school in Chicago, Illinois; Montessori school in San Rafael, California; dance at California's Shawl and Anderson Dance Studio; and at California's world famous San Francisco Ballet. Since 1967, she has taught Movement Education to children in schools of the Richmond Unified School District in Richmond, California; in various private California schools; and at the University of California Extension and at the Dominican College in San Rafael, California. She has conducted workshops for Mills College in Oakland, California; for the El Paso School District in El Paso, Texas; for the University of Northern Iowa; for California's San Francisco Kingergarten Conference; for the California Polytechnic State University in San Luis Obispo; and for numerous state and school conferences.

Presently Ms. Kogan teaches Movement Education to kindergarten through sixth grades in the Richmond Unified School District, Richmond, California, and at Prospect School in El Cerrito, California. She teaches Movement Education and teacher preparation at the Dominican College in San Rafael, California, and conducts teacher workshops nationwide. (For workshop information, see the back page.)

It is this wide base of teaching experiences that makes Ms. Kogan's work realistic and applicable.

CONTENTS

INTRODUCTION --- 1
  IMPORTANCE OF MOVEMENT --- 1
    What Is Movement Education? --- 1
    Three Benefits --- 1
  ABOUT THIS BOOK --- 2
    The Goal --- 2
    Basis For This Book --- 2
    Span Of Material --- 2
    Conceptual Approach --- 2
  FOUNDATION OF A MOVEMENT PROGRAM --- 3
    Three Structures --- 3
    Structures Form The Basis For Activities --- 3
  A FEW WORDS ON GENERAL TEACHING TECHNIQUES --- 4
    Saying Exactly What We Mean --- 4
    Setting Standards --- 4
    Teaching Actively --- 5
  CONCLUDING --- 5
    To Beginning Movement Teachers --- 5
    What You Need To Start --- 6

Part 1
  THE FIRST CLASS --- 8
    ELEMENTS OF THE FIRST CLASS --- 8
      First Impression --- 8
      Organization Of The First Class --- 8
      Goal Of The First Class --- 8
      Organization Of The First Four Classes --- 9
    PERFECT SPOT --- 9
      Definition Of Perfect Spot --- 9
      Introducing Perfect Spot --- 9
      Children That Do Not Understand --- 11
      Facing Front --- 11
      Importance Of Perfect Spots --- 11
      Imperfect Spots --- 11
      Observations --- 12
    PERFECT SPOT GAMES --- 13
      Need For Perfect Spot Games --- 13
      Firecracker --- 13
      Other Perfect Spot Games --- 13
    INITIAL EXERCISES IN PERFECT SPOTS --- 13
      A Set Warm-Up --- 13
      Hello And Goodbye --- 14
      Teaching The Concept "Torso" --- 14
      Swordfish --- 15
      Blast Off --- 16
      Maybe I Don't, Maybe I Do --- 18
    OBSTACLE COURSE --- 18

  Use Of Obstacle Courses---18
  Beginning Obstacle Course---19
  Obstacle Course Test--19
  An Elaborate Obstacle Course--19
  Obstacle Course Additions---21
  To Make Life Easier---22
  Children's Own Obstacle Course--22
 CONCLUDING THE FIRST CLASS--22
  The First Few Weeks---22

Part 2
LOCOMOTOR MOVEMENTS---23
 INTRODUCING LOCOMOTOR MOVEMENTS---23
  Definition Of Locomotor Movements---23
  Introducing Locomotor Movements---23
  Introducing The Concept---23
  Initial Studies---24
  Structuring Locomotor Movements---25
 FREE TRAVELING STRUCTURE--25
  Definition--25
  Teaching It---25
  Precision---26
  Problems--26
 DIAGONAL STRUCTURE--27
  Definition--27
  Introducing The Concept---27
  Diagonal Lines Throughout The Room--27
  Setting It Up---28
 TEACHING LOCOMOTOR MOVEMENTS TO VERY YOUNG CHILDREN-------------------------29
  Why A Different Start?--29
  The Rocking Song--29
  The "Rocking Lesson"--30
 CATALOG OF LOCOMOTOR MOVEMENTS--32
  Walk--32
  Run---33
  Crawl---34
  Jump--34
  Hop---35
  Skip--35
  Gallop--36
  Side-Slide--37
  Roll--37
  Seat-Scoot--38
  Sliding On The Floor--39
  Kicks---39
  Leap--40
 LOCOMOTOR MOVEMENT STUDIES--41
  Importance Of Studies---41
  Teacher Taught Combinations---41
  Teacher Structured Group Problems---42

Part 3
WORKING TOGETHER--43
 FOSTERING FRIENDSHIP--43
  Need For Encouraging Friendship---43
  Touching--43

    Use Of Partner And Group Activities--43
  PARTNER ACTIVITIES--43
    Shake A Partner---43
    Nonlocomotor Movements With Partners--43
    Levels With Partners--45
    Directions With Partners--45
    Combining Levels And Directions With Partners-------------------------------46
    Bag A Partner---46
    Strictly Partner Movements--46
    Mirror And Shadow---48
    Lifting---48
  GROUP ACTIVITIES--50
    Necessity Of Groups---50
    Staying Together--50
    Group Movements---50
  TONE OF THE CLASS---51
    Importance Of Class Tone--51
    Promoting A Good Class Atmosphere---51

Part 4
  LEVELS--53
  INTRODUCING LEVELS--53
    Definition--53
    Introducing The Word And Concept--53
    Trying Them Out---53
    Nonlocomotor Movements--53
  NONLOCOMOTOR LEVEL STUDIES--54
    Stage 1---54
    Stage 2---55
    Stage 3---56
  LOCOMOTOR MOVEMENTS ON LEVELS---56
    Categorizing Locomotor Movements--56
  LOCOMOTOR LEVEL STUDIES---57
    Introducing Them--57
    Teacher Taught Combinations---57
    Teacher Structured Group Problems---57
  CONCLUDING--58
    Uses Of Levels--58

Part 5
  NONLOCOMOTOR MOVEMENTS--59
  INTRODUCTION--59
    Definition--59
    Introducing The Term--59
    Introducing The Concept---59
    Alternating Locomotor And Nonlocomotor Movements----------------------------60
  EXPANDING NONLOCOMOTOR MOVEMENT VOCABULARY--60
    Ways To Expand--60
    When To Use These Techniques--61
  INTRODUCING SPECIFIC NONLOCOMOTOR MOVEMENTS---------------------------------------61
    Framework---61
    Introducing "Shake"---62
    Introducing "Swing"---62
    Introducing "Contract And Stretch"--64
    Introducing "Strike"--65
    Introducing "Twist"---66

    Introducing "Bend And Straighten"--66
    Introducing "Spin, Turn, Or Twirl"--67
TWO PROBLEMS WITH NONLOCOMOTOR MOVEMENTS---68
    True Nonlocomotor Movements---68
    Dance---69
LOCOMOTOR PLUS NONLOCOMOTOR MOVEMENTS---69
    A Milestone---69
    Introducing The Idea--69
    Examples Of Combined Locomotor And Nonlocomotor Movements---------------------70
    Uses For Movement Combinations--70
CATALOG OF NONLOCOMOTOR MOVEMENTS--71
    Shake---71
    Swing---72
    Contract And Stretch--73
    Bend And Straighten---73
    Strike--74
    Twist---74
    Spin--74
    Falls---75
    Positions Of The Body---76
NONLOCOMOTOR MOVEMENT STUDIES--77
    Teacher Taught Combinations---77
    Teacher Structured Free Traveling Patterns-----------------------------------79
    Teacher Structured Group Problems--79

Part 6
AWARENESS OF SPACE--80
    DEFINITION OF SPATIAL AWARENESS---80
        Skills Necessary For Spatial Awareness------------------------------------80
        The Difference Between Direction And Floor Pattern-----------------------80
    DIRECTIONS--81
        Directional Skills--81
        Walk Down Your Front--81
        Nonlocomotor Movements Using Directions-----------------------------------81
        Locomotor Movements Using Directions--------------------------------------86
        More Difficult Locomotor Movements Using Directions----------------------88
        Beginning Direction Studies---88
        Mixing Directions With Other Concepts------------------------------------89
        Direction Problems--90
        Full Scale Direction Studies--91
    MIDDLE--92
        Introducing The Concept---92
        Measuring---93
        Middle Of Parts Of The Body---93
        Middle Of Planes--93
        Removing The Middle Marker--94
    FLOOR PATTERNS--94
        Definition--94
        Skills--94
        Floor Patterns: Maps--94
        Floor Patterns: Lines--102
        Floor Patterns: Additional Activities------------------------------------108
    ROOM DIRECTIONS---110
        Front, Back, Right And Left Sides Of A Room------------------------------110
        Body Directions Combined With Room Directions---------------------------110

SYMMETRY AND ASYMMETRY---111
  Why Include It With Floor Patterns?--111
  Introducing The Words--111
  Shapes---111
  Floor Patterns Using Symmetry And Asymmetry--------------------------------111
  Their Own Partner Patterns---112

Part 7
GIMMICKS---113
 WHERE WE ARE--113
 TRICKS OF THE TRADE---113
  Are You Alive?---113
  The Foam---114
  The Stage--115
  Alignment--115
  Turn Out---116
  Twirls---118
  Brain Catcher Game---118
  Rocking As A Relaxer---120
  Spaghetti--121

Part 8
PROPS--123
 WORKING WITH PROPS--123
  The Benefits And Dangers Of Props--123
  Formula For Using Props--123
  Uses Of The Formula--124
 BALLS---124
  Start With Balls---124
  Passing Out The Balls--124
  Free Time--125
  Guided Movements---125
  Studies--126
  Partner Work---126
  Other Uses---127
 SCARVES---127
  What Kind Of Scarves?--127
  Passing Out The Scarves--127
  Free Time--128
  Guided Movements---128
  Studies--128
  Partner Work---129
  Putting The Scarves Away---129
 ROPES---130
  What Kind Of Ropes?--130
  Chinese Jump Ropes---130
  Straight Ropes---131
 HULA HOOPS--132
  Hoops As An Individual Prop--132
  Hoops As A Patterning Prop---132
 BALLOONS--133
  Unblown Balloons---133
  Blown Up Balloons--134
 SCOOTERS--136
  What Are They?---136
  Free Time And Guided Movements---136

- Scooter Line —————————————————————————— 136
- Scooters With Partners ———————————————— 137
- PARACHUTE ——————————————————————————————— 137
  - Introducing The Parachute —————————————— 137
  - Ocean ——————————————————————————————— 137
  - Whooshing ——————————————————————————— 138
  - Hamburgers And French Fries ——————————— 138
  - Merry-Go-Round ——————————————————————— 139
  - Bag Them Up ————————————————————————— 139
  - Ms. Monster —————————————————————————— 139
  - Flying ————————————————————————————— 140
  - Rocks And Waves ——————————————————————— 140
  - Lifting ——————————————————————————— 141
  - Mushroom —————————————————————————— 141
  - Putting The Parachute Away ————————————— 142
- OTHER PROPS —————————————————————————————— 142
  - What Can Be Used As A Prop? ———————————— 142
  - Marbles ———————————————————————————— 143
  - Feathers ——————————————————————————— 143
  - Newspapers —————————————————————————— 143
  - Plastic Garbage Bags ——————————————————— 143
  - Chairs ————————————————————————————— 144
  - Costumes ——————————————————————————— 145
  - Props That Move--Beginning Abstractions ———— 145
- CONCLUDING ———————————————————————————————— 146
  - About Criticizing Creative Works ———————— 146
  - About Fun —————————————————————————— 147

Part 9
MOVEMENT AS AN ACADEMIC TOOL —————————————————— 148
- USING MOVEMENT TO TEACH SKILLS ————————————————— 148
  - Techniques Presented ———————————————————— 148
  - Ways That Movement Can Be Used ——————————— 148
- LANGUAGE DEVELOPMENT ——————————————————————— 148
  - Letters ——————————————————————————————— 148
  - Word Comprehension —————————————————————— 150
  - Spelling ——————————————————————————————— 163
- MATH ——————————————————————————————————————— 164
  - Numbers ——————————————————————————————— 164
  - Geometry —————————————————————————————— 165
  - Computations ————————————————————————— 166
- PATTERNING ————————————————————————————————— 168
  - Patterning Skills ———————————————————————— 168
  - Name Syllable Patterns ————————————————— 168
  - Beginning Linear Patterns--Color Paper Squares —— 168
  - Other Patterning Possibilities ————————————— 169
- CONCLUDING ——————————————————————————————— 170
  - The Academic Spirit ————————————————————— 170

Part 10
ADVANCED WORK ————————————————————————————— 172
- WHAT CONSTITUTES ADVANCED WORK ——————————————— 172
  - The Crux Of Advanced Work ——————————————— 172
- ADVANCED PHYSICAL CHALLENGES —————————————————— 173
  - Warm-Up ———————————————————————————————— 173

```
        Exercises----------------------------------------------------------173
        "Raising Our Standards" Speech------------------------------------174
        Coordination And Control------------------------------------------174
    ADVANCED CONCEPTS-----------------------------------------------------174
        Focus-------------------------------------------------------------174
        Dynamic Quality---------------------------------------------------177
        Falls-------------------------------------------------------------177
        Balance-----------------------------------------------------------179
    ADVANCED PATTERNS-----------------------------------------------------180
        The Partner Dance-------------------------------------------------180

Part 11
    LESSON PLANS----------------------------------------------------------183
        FRAMEWORK---------------------------------------------------------183
            General Structure---------------------------------------------183
            Variances With Reality----------------------------------------183
            Use Of Plans--------------------------------------------------183
        THE PLANS---------------------------------------------------------184
            Preschool/Grades K-1------------------------------------------184
            Grades 2-3----------------------------------------------------193
            Grades 4-6----------------------------------------------------205
        STATIONS----------------------------------------------------------216
            Use Of Stations-----------------------------------------------216
            Station Charts------------------------------------------------217
            Other Possible Stations---------------------------------------221

INDEX---------------------------------------------------------------------222
```

INTRODUCTION

IMPORTANCE OF MOVEMENT

WHAT IS MOVEMENT EDUCATION?
  Movement education works with the body and how it moves. This is an enormous scope. It includes work on strength, flexibility, agility, large and small muscle coordination, eye-hand and eye-foot coordination, spatial awareness, and grace of movement.

THREE BENEFITS
  There are 3 benefits of a movement program: 1) Movement training is necessary for children with motor problems. 2) Movement training is worthwhile for average or "normal" children. 3) Movement is an excellent tool to teach or reinforce academic skills.

  1) *CHILDREN WITH MOTOR PROBLEMS*
      There is mounting documentation that motor development is a major force in a child's academic, social, and personal development. Teachers have known it for years. The child that has motor problems has a lot of other troubles in the classroom. A child with motor problems might be withdrawn, aggressive, hyperactive, dull, awkward, or full of reversals. His language or math skills or both might be below grade level or he might do well academically but have trouble making friends. Not every child that has difficulties has motor problems, but motor development should be one of the first areas checked.*

  2) *"NORMAL" CHILDREN*
      For normal or average children a movement program may not be crucial but it is enormously beneficial. A good movement program is fun, exciting, challenging, and tiring. It is a place to let off steam, to get closer to friends or make new ones, to learn new and harder skills, to expand an already workable movement vocabulary, and to increase physical competency.

      In addition, average children need movement for, if nothing else, the exercise. Most children today are out of shape. They are not necessarily fat but they do not have the agility, strength, or endurance that they could and should have. Most children have weak stomach muscles, bad posture, and a tendency to stop any activity when they feel the least bit tired. I have, at 4 months pregnant, challenged entire classes to sit-up contests and won. This is disheartening.

  3) *TEACHING ACADEMIC SKILLS*
      Movement is a wonderful teaching aid. Children can make letters and numbers out of body shapes; they can learn the words "circumference," "radius," and "diameter"

---
*How do you find the time to test motor development? If there is not a specialist handy, here are the basics to check: 1) Can the child, first grade on up, walk backwards on a balance beam? 2) Can the child hop equally well, forward and backward, on either foot? 3) Can the child skip? 4) Can the child run and dribble a 6 inch ball? These 4 areas can be checked within 5 minutes. If a child has a lot of difficulties with one of these tasks, it is a good indication that he has motor problems.

while working with the parachute; and they can reinforce the concepts "under" and "over" by crawling under and climbing over tables. These are obviously excellent teaching techniques. Movement makes many abstract and forgettable concepts real and memorable.

In addition, a good movement program is chock full of more subtle academic skills. Learning a long movement pattern is excellent practice in memory, perseverance, and focus of attention; transferring a floor pattern (map) into a movement pattern fitting a particular room involves many visual and problem solving skills; creating a group pattern showing 6 ways of moving with a scarf promotes creativity and cooperation, as well as sequencing and memory. I envision a movement program in its broadest scope, where physical, academic, social, and personal skills are intertwined and developed.

ABOUT THIS BOOK

THE GOAL
The goal of this book is to encourage teachers to initiate or expand a movement program. The book will present a complete step-by-step curriculum for teaching movement to children ranging from pre-school to 6th grade. The program is directed to full classrooms in urban public schools; that is, too many children, too many divergent abilities, too little space, too little time, too little help, and too many extra problems. No previous training is necessary. Classroom teachers, special education teachers, dance and movement teachers, private school teachers, and children's center teachers will find the program very adaptable.

BASIS FOR THIS BOOK
This book is based 100% on experience. All activities have been used for at least 2 years and most have been tested for many years. All activities have been used in different classroom situations: lower-economic schools, middle-class schools, private schools, and dance studios. Whenever possible, I have asked other teachers to use these activities so that I am sure they are successful with different personalities and approaches.

SPAN OF MATERIAL
The material in this book will span 2 to 4 years of work depending on the age and sophistication of a class. Part 11 provides specific lesson plans for preschool, kindergarten and grades one to 6th. In addition, most teachers find that the program is self generating; that is, the movement ideas presented foster new ideas from the class and teacher. This program grows and adapts easily because it is based on a conceptual approach.

CONCEPTUAL APPROACH
Whenever possible a movement idea is presented in its broadest scope. Only after the general concept is grasped will an idea be exemplified in a specific way. For example, "contract" is taught as *any* "energetic curling up." It can be done with a hand, an arm, a leg, the torso, or the whole body in different positions. After the children understand and explore the full range of possible contractions, they learn a pattern that uses specific contractions.

This conceptual approach is crucial. It is like learning to read instead of simply memorizing lines. It opens up new worlds. First, knowing movement concepts allows children to understand movement patterns fully. A dance pattern is no longer an undifferenciated jumble of steps; it is an intelligible sequence of concepts. Children in my programs learn startlingly long and complex patterns. Second, the conceptual approach promotes greater creativity. Since the children are not bound by a rigid movement vocabulary, they are free to use and expand their imaginations. And third, teaching concepts opens up new horizons for the teacher. Concepts can be combined or expanded in any number of ways. New concepts are readily found in classroom work. Most importantly, the conceptual approach takes movement education out of the realm of an esoteric art form and brings it into the realm of a comprehensible curriculum.

FOUNDATION OF A MOVEMENT PROGRAM

THREE STRUCTURES

Every teacher has a lot of good ideas. What is needed to implement these ideas is a foundation of structures. There are 3 structures absolutely necessary for a sound movement program: 1) Perfect Spot, 2) Free Traveling Structure, and 3) Diagonal Structure. These provide the boundaries essential for maintaining control. As all teachers know, control is essential for any teaching to take place and for any teaching to be fun.

1) *PERFECT SPOT*

    Means the children situate themselves in the room with space all around. They are "far from everything, far from everybody, and facing front." A class should be able to get Perfect Spots in 10 seconds. Perfect Spots are essential for stationary movements, for work on laterality, and for relaxation.

2) *FREE TRAVELING STRUCTURE*

    Means the children can travel anywhere in the room, moving to a "sound" (drum, piano, whatever) and freezing immediately when the sound stops. The children move without bumping. Free Traveling Structure is necessary for learning and practicing locomotor movements, for warming-up, for working on stamina, and for working with props.

3) *DIAGONAL STRUCTURE*

    Means that a child lines up on one side of the room, moves on the diagonal, and lines up on the other side of the room as illustrated in the diagram. The child, or small group, begins moving on the diagonal without having to be told to start, for example, each group starts when the group ahead reaches the end of the diagonal. The Diagonal Structure is essential for learning difficult locomotor movements, for working on locomotor patterns, for precision of locomotor movements, and for testing.

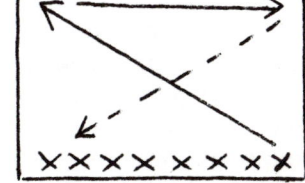

STRUCTURES FORM THE BASIS FOR ACTIVITIES

These 3 structures, Perfect Spots, Free Traveling Structure, and Diagonal Structure, are taught in the first 4 to 8 weeks. If you use nothing else from this book, I strongly recommend that you do use the 3 basic structures. They will allow your year to flow smoothly and enjoyably. They form the foundation for the rest of the movement program. All subsequent activities depend on these structures for ease of instruction and control. For example, when introducing balls, each child is given a ball and allowed some free time with it. This would be totally chaotic if the class were not trained to move to the sound and stop when it stopped (the Free Traveling Structure). It is the firm underpinning of these simple structures that provides a basis for the freedom of other activities.

A FEW WORDS ON GENERAL TEACHING TECHNIQUES

SAYING EXACTLY WHAT WE MEAN
   In this world of general sloppiness we need to be bastions of precision. "Watch," I say and I expect the children to be still and look, *not* for them to move with me. "Sit in your Perfect Spots" means the children sit in their spots; they do *not* lie down, stand up, or twirl. "Go to your Perfect Spots" is open-ended.

   Why am I stating the obvious? Because it is easy to forget and it is important. Clear thinking and clear talking are inseparable. It is hard to say which comes first, but it is easy to see that we can not have one without the other. So, we can no longer say "Get partner groups of 4," when we mean "Get partners" or "Get into groups of 4"; "Jump on one foot" when we mean "Hop"; "Do the movement backwards" when what is meant is "in the reverse order"; "Do you want to?" when there is no option;* "Can you?" when there is no question.

   It is a waste of time to speak clearly and not to demand results. I have stopped demonstrating a pattern to repeat "Watch!" 7 times before everyone stopped moving and actually watched. Groups of 3 means groups of 3 (except for a remainder) even if it breaks up a circle of friends. Certainly the line between precision and rigidity is a hair's breadth, but it is worth walking the thin line.

SETTING STANDARDS
   Just as we must demand precision of ourselves, we must also demand it of our classes. I was recently questioned whether my strict adherence to "perfection" did not stifle children's creative expression and lessen their feelings of self-worth. No. I do not believe in uniformity, but precision in movement structures, like getting Perfect Spots, is absolutely necessary for the functioning of the class. Further, precision in any subject is a measure of excellence toward which a child must strive. If everything is praised equally why should a child strain to grow? As long as the standard of excellence is clear and within the child's reach (not easily attainable but within a strenuous reach) then I think the work on precision can only benefit a child's sense of accomplishment and open up new areas of creativity.
----
* A note on "want": I do not use the word "want" unless I am prepared to have the children make an actual choice. If I say "Do you want to do this?" and they say "No" I do not do it. I have nothing against direct commands as long as they are honest commands: "We will do this. I expect you to do that. You are required to do this." To offer a choice and then take it away is not fair. To offer a choice and manipulate it away is completely foul play.

I think not enough is asked of our children. Observers are sometimes shocked by what I expect physically and intellectually from my classes. Once in a while I do make a mistake and have to say "This is too hard for us this year," but mostly the children come through. The pride that shows on their faces and bearings when they achieve what seemed unattainable, convinces me that it is worth the work for them and for me.

TEACHING ACTIVELY

Children learn best in proportion to how active they are in the learning process. Information superimposed on a child slips away easily; information discovered by the child remains and expands. Active learning is increasingly accepted in teaching reading, language arts, and math. It is also important in teaching movement.

Traditionally, physical education and dance have been taught in an authoritarian, perhaps even sadistic manner: "25 burpies...50 sit ups...8 grande battement..." This is fine for building muscles---only. My movement program has a broader scope. I want children to become physically stronger and I want them to think.

This comes down to some basic teaching principles. Whenever I am able to pose a question instead of simply providing information (which is often), I do so. "Are you sure you are far from everything?" rather than "Albert, move over here." "Where do you guess a diagonal line is on the ceiling?" "How else can you move and stay in one place?" "How can you move a balloon without touching it?"

This questioning technique works well for teaching concepts but obviously does not work for teaching specific movement patterns. In teaching patterns, I work as much as possible through imitation. Imitation is in itself a good developmental process because the children have to transfer what they see to their own bodies. As a last resort, when I am stuck or when I am teaching a very difficult movement, I physically help children rearrange arms, legs, hips, elbow.

Therefore, when I can teach verbally rather than imitatively, I pick the verbal. If I have to choose between imitation and direct manipulation of bodies, I pick imitation. Only if the children are having difficulty with a particular movement will I help individual children with actual body placement.

Movement has for too long been removed from the mind. Athletic people were always supposed to be stupid and just follow orders. But just as smart people are now becoming more aware of their bodies, the "era of the dumb dancer is over."

CONCLUDING

TO BEGINNING MOVEMENT TEACHERS

If you are beginning a movement program you are to be congratulated: you are brave. Teaching movement is different from other subjects. It seems that using one's body makes people feel vulnerable and exposed. Almost every teacher I have met has felt this way. Remember that you do not need to be graceful or even coordinated to teach an excellent movement program; also remember that the work will be worth it because the children will grow immeasureably and they will love it.

WHAT YOU NEED TO START

Essentially all that is needed to start this movement program is a room. Ideally the room should be large, clear of most furniture, warm, and clean. But I have worked most of my life in conditions that were less than ideal.

Because this movement program is based on concepts, equipment is not mandatory. With just a room, tambourine, paper, and crayons you can cover all the basic concepts: Perfect Spots, locomotor and nonlocomotor movements, levels, directions, floor patterns, plus partner activities and work on many academic skills.

The children wear no special clothing. I ask them to wear play clothes so that their parents will not mind them getting on the floor. Girls wear pants or shorts under skirts.

However, props are a wonderful and useful addition to any movement program. Most urban school departments have all or most of the equipment mentioned in this book available for loan to teachers. If not, many schools have some funds set aside for new equipment. If not, any money you spend is tax deductible. If money is limited, this is what equipment I would get in order of importance. *The size and type of equipment is almost completely your preference.* When it does matter I have noted it.

1) Balls, enough for at least half your class. For primary grades I prefer 6 inch balls; for intermediate grades 3 inch balls are fine. Balls are used for warm-up, partner work, sequences, obstacle courses, and stations.

2) One or more pieces of foam rubber approximately 2 feet by 2 feet by 4 inches for the foam jump. (Try to accumulate 10 pieces.)

3) A parachute, approximately 12 feet in diameter, for parachute activities.

4) Balance beam. A balance beam is expensive to buy but easy to make. One sanded or painted 4 inch by 8 foot plank, resting on the floor, will do. If you can have blocks raising it off the ground, that is better. Simply cut out a 2 inch by 4 inch section from 2 wood blocks (I used blocks measuring 12 inches by 6 inches by 4 inches) and place the ends of the board in the grooves. The balance beam is an important element in obstacle courses, stations, and games such as the In and Out Game.

5) Some old bicycle tires, preferably in different sizes. These are used in obstacle courses, stations, and games.

6) A few mats. Almost any kind will do. It is nice to have some soft and some stiff mats. I greatly prefer mats that are light enough to move easily. Also mats that attach one to the other make life easier. Mats are used in obstacle courses, stations, and games.

7) Six or more scooters. Scooters are used individually, with partners, and in obstacle courses.

8) Scarves, enough for one per child. Almost any size and type of washable material will do. Young children have an easier time with 2 foot square, sheer, head scarves. Scarves are used for sequences and for costumes.

9) Ropes, at least enough for half your class. Chinese jump ropes and straight ropes (I prefer ropes without handles, about 6 feet long) are equally useful. It is nice to have both types. Ropes are used for warm-up, coordination work, partner activities, sequences, and games.

10) Balloons. Size is not as important as durability--the thicker the better. Also, round balloons are a little easier to handle than long ones. Balloons are used for coordination work and sequences.

11) Onion bags, enough for at least half your class. Bags are used for partner and coordination work.

12) Hula hoops, enough for half your class in as many colors as possible. Hoops are used for patterning, obstacle courses, games, and coordination work. (Hula hoops would be a higher priority if bicycle tires were not available.).

13) More of everything and anything else that caught my fancy.

PART 1
THE FIRST CLASS

ELEMENTS OF THE FIRST CLASS

FIRST IMPRESSION
"Hello, welcome to movement class. Sit down, take your socks and shoes off,* put your socks *in* your shoes, and put them way *under* your chair. When you're done, come sit on the floor near me."

Not too many words; not much time to worry.

The children gather near me on the floor. I introduce myself succinctly ("My name is Ms. Kogan and this is movement class.") and immediately set them moving.

ORGANIZATION OF THE FIRST CLASS
In the first class I introduce 3 activities: 1) Perfect Spot (a method of spacing them out in the room), 2) initial exercises done in Perfect Spots, and 3) an obstacle course.

The activities are done in this order or just as easily rearranged: obstacle course, Perfect Spot, initial exercises. The decision to start with Perfect Spot or with the obstacle course is based on a snap judgment of how rambunctious the particular class is. If they look apathetic and inhibited I start with the obstacle course; if they look wild and fight-prone I start with Perfect Spot. More often than not it does not matter and I start with what I want. What I want most is the first class to be orderly and fun. Of the 2, orderly is more important.

GOAL OF THE FIRST CLASS
The first class is a barrage of new ideas, experiences, and impressions. What the children actually learn about movement is less important than the tone set for the class. If the children begin to believe, after the first class, that movement is a subject like reading or math, then you are set; if they think it is going to be recess for an hour, then you need to start over.

This movement-is-a-subject tone is crucial. If it comes down to a fast choice between not allowing a child to join or allowing the child to join on his terms, e.g., will not take off his shoes or will not spit out the gum, I recommend not letting the child join. Movement is naturally fun. When the child sees all the other children crawling under tables and rolling down mats, he will join, especially if he is given a chance to save face. "I want you to join us now. When you get those shoes off there is a spot for you right here."

---
* The children work barefoot because shoes can be slippery, treacherous, and dirty. Socks alone, of course, are dangerously slippery. Plus that, children have better sensory awareness and control when barefoot.

Harsh? Perhaps. But don't you remember your favorite teachers? The ones that were strict but fair. The ones that you did not initially like but grew to respect.

ORGANIZATION OF THE FIRST FOUR CLASSES
The next 3 or 4 lessons are quite similar to the first.* We review Perfect Spot, do more preliminary exercises, and maybe do another obstacle course. Additional time in these beginning lessons is given to locomotor movements, which are covered in Part 2. (Also in Part 2 is a totally different beginning class for pre-school children: "Teaching Locomotor Movements To Young Children.") Part 1 will deal with the techniques needed for a basic first class: Perfect Spot, initial exercises, obstacle course.

PERFECT SPOT**

DEFINITION OF PERFECT SPOT
Good for: 1) Spatial awareness.
2) Classroom control.
3) Safety in doing large movements.

If children just came into a room and started moving, the result would be chaos and bruises. Children need a space of their own. Their Perfect Spot is a space in the room where they can move freely and safely, where I can see them and they can see me. As I define Perfect Spot for the children, it is where "you are far from everybody, far from everything, and facing front."

INTRODUCING PERFECT SPOT
I have taught Perfect Spot in many ways. (I will later describe some early trials with spacing.) The most effective teaching method is through the concepts "near" and "far." When introducing these concepts I use large cards with "near" and "far" printed on them.

---

* A nice introduction for the 2nd or 3rd class is Jump Your Name. Children up to about grade 4 like it. I say "I want you to tell me your names but in a special way. Shout your name *in the air!* I'll show you what I mean." I stand and jump, shouting my name at the high point of the jump. "Would you like to do it?" Usually children do want to. If some do not, I pass them. If the children find jumping and shouting their name very easy, ask them to shout their names 2 times, then 3 times, while in the air. Or ask them to jump and turn in the air while they shout their name.

Jump Your Name is essentially a nice, friendly, non-scary way to start movement class. In addition, the game points out a great deal about a class. Who were the children that were too afraid to try it? Who shouted their names at top volume? Who whispered their names? Who got the timing of shouting while in the air and who did not? Who landed on their seat rather than their feet? You will learn a lot about a new group of children, even their names.

** The term "Perfect Spot" comes from Gertrude Blanchard.

USING PRINTED CARDS

"Why signs?" I was asked by a kindergarten teacher. Even if the children cannot read yet, the card focuses their attention and makes the lesson more formal, that is, more the way a reading or math lesson would be introduced. For those children who can read, the sign brings another sense into play. My basic teaching principle is simple: the more senses involved the better; the more specific the concept the better. Therefore, I use the cards and very specific concepts, "near" and "far."

"NEAR"

Hold up a card with the word "near." Have the children come near you. (In rambunctious classes I add a rule, "You can only move when the tambourine sounds." Therefore when I ask the children to come near me, they start when the tambourine sound starts and stop when the sound stops. Even if the children are not precise, this prevents me from getting trampled.) Have the children go "near" a wall, then "near" a chair, then "near" a table, then "near" a classmate, the floor, the ceiling, a door, the piano, a desk, and so on.

"FAR"

Do the same with the word "far": "far" from me, "far" from the walls, the floor, ceiling, door, piano, stage, "far" from anybody. "Far" is the harder of the 2 concepts for young children. I am very fussy at this point: "Are you really 'far' from that wall? You are too near him; go 'far' from *any* body."

COMBINING "NEAR" AND "FAR"

When each of the concept words is clear, start to combine them. For example, go "near" a wall and "near" a classmate; go "near" a chair but "far" from me; go "far" from the piano but "near" a chair; go "far" from anybody and "far" from the ceiling.

FINDING PERFECT SPOTS

Finally, "I am going to tell you 2 things to go 'far' from and this is going to be hard! Are you ready? Go 'far' from *everybody* and 'far' from *everything*. There you will have your Perfect Spot. When you have it, sit down." (See illustration.)

The first few times, I go around and shake hands (or feet) with children who found Perfect Spots: "Congratulations! You found your Perfect Spot. How great!" The children love the handshake and it reinforces the term Perfect Spot.

I teach Perfect Spot this way to 5 and 12 year olds; despite its formality children find it fun. Plus that, it works.

CHILDREN THAT DO NOT UNDERSTAND

What happens to non-Perfect Spot children? If a child is next to something, like a chair, I will say, "Are you 'far' from *every*thing?" The child usually realized his mistake and finds a Perfect Spot (I then shake his hand). Often children are oblivious of what is in back of them. They need to be reminded to *look around* and be sure they are far from everything. If a child is totally lost, like under a table, I will gently drag him by the legs: "Let me give you a ride to your Perfect Spot. See, now you have room all around you." Usually totally lost children are just frightened, since Perfect Spot is one of the first lessons in movement class. They generally pick up the idea as soon as they relax a bit.

If more than 3 or 4 children are lost, start *completely* over. More likely than not this new start needs to be more formal, more academically oriented. Movement class is not physical education; it is education through the physical. To learn through movement the children need to follow your instructions precisely. Go slowly. If the children go near a table when you have asked them to go near a chair, correct them. If they start to run wildly around the room, stop everything. Perhaps make a competitive game out of it: "Only the children that listen will be able to play; if you do not follow the instructions you will be out of the game." You probably will not need to do that; simply your attitude of *This Is A Subject* will convey itself to the children and they will treat movement respectfully.*

FACING FRONT

After the children understand how to space themselves in a room (it might be 15 minutes; it might be a week), I add the final ingredient of a truly Perfect Spot: facing front. I designate one wall of the room as front and ask the children to align themselves so that they face it completely. "Face straight front, the way the floor boards go." I physically help children who do not understand. It is important that they face the front *wall* and not the teacher, so that they do not end up angled in a semi-circle. For the next few weeks I am extremely fussy that the children face absolutely straight front and I will stop whatever I am doing to correct even a slightly angled child. With all the children facing the same way, 1) right and left are easily checked and later work on laterality is simplified, 2) it is safe to do large movements like kicks, and 3) you are able to move around the classroom without the children constantly turning to face you.

IMPORTANCE OF PERFECT SPOTS

Perfect Spot is invaluable not only for freedom of movement and safety, but also as an important step in spatial awareness and self-discipline. A child that can and does find his Perfect Spot has already made great strides in defining his body in space and in taking responsibility for himself.

I do not think I can emphasize the importance of Perfect Spot enough. It is one of the basic structures necessary for future movement activities. Movement is a natural chaos producer. But chaos is not freedom. I know you want your children to be uninhibited; however they will not develop this freedom in an unstructured class. It is hard to be

----
* Let's pause for a brief testimonial. I asked a teacher friend to follow my instructions with her kindergarten class. After trying Perfect Spot the first time she said the children went crazy: "I was scared and stopped and we did something I was used to doing... but I was determined, so the 2nd time I did exactly the same thing except I had a 'get tough' attitude. I insisted they do *exactly* as I wanted and I slowed down until they did. This movement doesn't mean move; it means move with a purpose. It worked, and worked well."

nice, to experiment, to play with children if they are unruly. The class needs to be orderly and manageable, and you need to feel comfortable. You need to be able to say "get your Perfect Spots" and know that within 10 seconds your entire class is there. Only then are you free to improvise and only then are the children free to experiment and create.

IMPERFECT SPOTS

The method of teaching Perfect Spot conceptually through "near" and "far" works dramatically well; it was discovered after many years of trial and mostly error.

The first time I introduced Perfect Spot, I said to my class that their Perfect Spots were places where they could extend their arms, spin, and not touch anyone. I demonstrated spinning with extended arms and the children started spinning with extended arms. The children would not stop spinning. They spun faster and faster, crashed into one another, fell down, started fighting...that was the first dance class I ever taught!

I concluded the children did not have an awareness of space around them. With a great deal of effort I made name cards for all the children and taped them down around the room in Perfect Spots. I did this for each class! It was totally exhausting picking up and putting down all those name cards. (This brings me to a rather strange theory: if an activity takes too much work and is drudgery for you, it is probably irrelevant.) The children then simply had to find their own name and they had a Perfect Spot. This was easy. We practiced several times and then removed the markers. What do you guess happened? The children remembered exactly who they were next to but had no idea of how far away from each other they had been, e.g., Yolanda remembered that her name card had been between Yvette and Robert, so she stood next to Yvette and Robert and that was that.

In order to teach general spacing within a room, I decided we needed to scale it down so the children would understand the concept as a whole. I placed a large piece of paper on the floor and said, "This is our room." (This unfortunately was before I discovered room representations which you will discover in Part 6.) I gave each child a small rock and asked him to place it in the "room" so there was plenty of paper showing around it. The result? There were a few rocks on the paper, some were spaced and some were not; however, most of the children became so enamored with their rocks they would not give them up at all.

As they say in story books, that was when I sat down and thought for a long time. I came up with a basic question from by Montessori training: What *pre*-concepts are the children lacking in order to understand the concept Perfect Spot? It became clear. They needed to know how near and how far they were from other people and things. That is how I came to a workable method of teaching Perfect Spot.

OBSERVATIONS

From this process, I have come up with several observations: 1) To work, any teaching method must be right for you. What is right for you may not be right for another teacher. 2) A workable teaching method must be comfortable and relatively easy. 3) What did not work once may work later. 4) What did not work once may have to be scrapped. (To know what should be kept and what should be scrapped is the tricky part.) 5) Teaching is hard work.

PERFECT SPOT GAMES

NEED FOR PERFECT SPOT GAMES
Good for: 1) Practice in finding Perfect Spots.
             2) Speed in finding Perfect Spots.

Once the children have worked with "near" and "far" and understand Perfect Spot, it is good practice and fun for young children to play some Perfect Spot games. These games are introduced in later classes and are essentially used to speed up the Perfect Spot process. In the first class it is enough they find their Perfect Spots once.

FIRECRACKER
Gathering the children in one corner of the room, I say, "We are one big fire cracker. I am going to light the fuse and when it pops you run and find your Perfect Spot as fast as you can. Pssssssss (I make the sound of a lighted fuse)...Pop!" The children run and find any Perfect Spot. I discourage set spots, that is, a specific child always sitting in the same place; each time we find Perfect Spots it is in new places.

I use this game to work for faster Perfect Spots. The next round of Firecracker I say, "It took about 20 seconds to find your Perfect Spots. Do you think you could do a 10 second Firecracker?" Then a 4 second Firecracker? In a typical game we play 3 Firecrackers, each time getting our Perfect Spots faster.

OTHER PERFECT SPOT GAMES

BALLOON POP
"You are all balloons floating around the room, when I touch you, 'pop' to a Perfect Spot."

BLIND MAN'S SPOT
This is *only* for gentle, rather mature classes. With the children gathered around, I tell them to "see," that is, sense, if they can find a Perfect Spot with their eyes *shut*, while crawling or walking slowly.

INITIAL EXERCISES IN PERFECT SPOTS

A SET WARM-UP
The exercises that follow are all done in Perfect Spots. They are the first ones the children learn and they become part of a warm-up for the beginning classes. These initial classes, perhaps the first 4 weeks, are set and quite repetitive. Later, as the children become less frightened of the idea of movement class, as they get to know me, and as they learn new concepts and movements, I become more flexible in class structuring and less repetitive in movement choices.

HELLO AND GOODBYE
   Good for: 1) Feet and ankle warm up.
              2) Stomach and back strength.
              3) Coordination.
              4) Concept word: opposite.
              5) Concentration (a good first exercise).

Children sit on the floor with their arms and legs straight in front of them. In the "Hello" position their feet and hands are flexed; that is, toes and fingers are pulled hard toward the ceiling. (See illustration #1.)

In the "Goodbye" position hands and feet point down; that is, toes and fingers are pulled hard toward the floor, while arms and heels remain stationary. (See illustration #2.)

In the first stage of this exercise simply alternate the "Hello" and "Goodbye" positions. Watch that the foot moves distinctly and with energy.

The 2nd stage of Hello and Goodbye uses opposites. First, both feet say "Hello" while both hands say "Goodbye"; they switch back and forth. Secondly, one hand and one foot say "Hello" while the other hand and foot say "Goodbye." (See illustration #3.)

They switch back and forth slowly and then in more complicated rhythms. For example:
♩ ♩ ♫ ♩   Each note is a switch in position.

Finally, one foot says "Hello" while that hand says "Goodbye"; the other foot says "Goodbye" while that hand says "Hello." In other words everything is in opposites. Switch everything!

In the last stage the torso is included. (See "Teaching The Concept 'Torso'" on page 14 for teaching that word.) With the hands and feet saying "Hello," the torso stretches tall, reaching for the ceiling. (See illustration #4.)

With "Goodbye" hands and feet, the torso lies back so that the body is fully extended on the ground. (See illustration #5.)

The "Goodbye's" are done slowly to increase muscular control and then more quickly, with a loud "Oh, goodbye!" said as if angry. Of course the children join me in shouting the "Hello's" and "Goodbye's." This exercise is a fun way of doing sit-ups.

TEACHING THE CONCEPT "TORSO"
   Good for: 1) Learning body part.
              2) Isolation of movement.
              3) Expanded movements.

I introduce "torso" by a process of elimination: "Shake your arm so hard...(the children and I all shake an arm violently) that it flies away! (The arm circles back as if it had flown off and then returns to the side of the body.) Shake your other arm so hard (same movement process)...that it flies off! Shake your leg so hard...it flies away! Shake your other leg so hard...it flies away! Shake your head and neck (head gently shakes; if done too hard it could cause strain and headaches)...until it flies off!" (Head rolls back as if it had flown off, then unobtrusively comes back to place.)

"We have gotten rid of our arms, legs, heads, and necks. What is left?"

Children will usually answer, "Stomach." "Our bodies." "Seat." "Waist."

"That's right. What is left is the *middle* part of our body and that is called our 'torso.'"

PATTING TORSOS

After we practice saying the word "torso," extending it, saying it quickly, changing the syllable accent, I ask the children to pat their own torsos all over and say the word as they do so. This is simply to associate the name with the place.

Here we come to a policy decision. Whether you touch your breasts and lower abdominal area or you do not, the children will giggle. They giggle if you touch and they giggle if you avoid touching. I believe that too many people are alienated from their own bodies and that this distance usually stems from experiences in childhood. One movement teacher brazenly touching her own breasts will not sway this tide of alienation, but prim avoidance may reinforce it. I am not terribly uninhibited; I have quite a bit of trouble with this. But I very strongly want to impart to my children that the body, every part of it, is respectable and beautiful.

So, without making a fuss or commotion about it we all gently pat our torsos, front, side, back, from shoulders to hip joints, while saying the word "torso."

MOVING TORSOS

"Now that you know where your torso is, let's see how many different ways your torso can move." The children will come up with some ideas, for example, wiggling or shaking, twisting, bending, and straightenings. You might also suggest curl up or contract and stretch (even if it has not been officially taught), bouncing, circling the torso around, and swinging. It is best if just the torso initiates the movements. Arms and other parts of the body might follow, but we are finding ways the torso can essentially move on its own.

After this lesson if you ask what "torso" means, 9 out of 10 children will pat their middles and wiggle when they answer.

SWORDFISH
Good for: 1) Leg stretch and strength.
           2) Abdominal control and strength.
           3) Balance.

The children sit on the floor with their legs straight in front of them. One leg lifts "straight as a swordfish," that is, very stretched, toes pointed, knees straight. (It is possible to ask specifically for right or left legs to reinforce those terms.) This "swordfish leg" proceeds to "swim," that is, it moves about, crosses the body, and then stretches wide to build up strength and flexibility.

"Suddenly the mean old fisherman catches the swordfish"; the child grabs the leg with both hands behind the knee. (See illustration #1.)

"The fish then says, 'Let me go! Let me go! Let me go! Free.'" For each of the 3 "Let me go's" the leg does tap-tap-stretch (touching the floor for each tap and lifting straight up for the stretch.)
It is done to this rhythm:

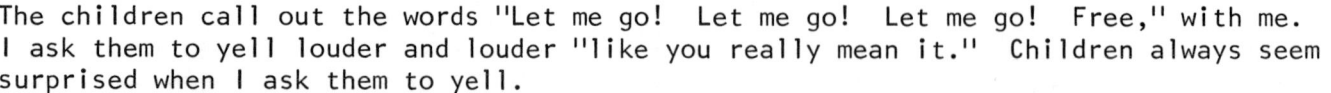

```
    ♩         ♩         ♩
   tap       tap      stretch
  "Let       me        go!"
```

For the word "free" the hands let go of the leg. The leg stays rigid for a few seconds and then is lowered. (See illustration #2.) This process is repeated with the other leg.

The children call out the words "Let me go! Let me go! Let me go! Free," with me. I ask them to yell louder and louder "like you really mean it." Children always seem surprised when I ask them to yell.

Next, both legs become "swordfish." I have the children lean on their elbows, rather than lie flat, to avoid backstrain. The "swordfish legs" do the same thing as the single leg: they "swim" with knees straight and toes pointed.

Sometimes the "swordfish become friends" (legs move parallel, closed together); sometimes they "have a fight" (straight leg scissors). "But they make up and are friends again" (parallel legs), "and that is when the fisherman catches both of them!" The children sit up quickly and grab both legs *behind* the knees. "The swordfish says, 'Let *us* go! Let us go! Let us go! Free.'" As with the individual leg, both legs do tap-tap-stretch for the words "Let us go!" That means that the children must balance on their seats each time their legs stretch up; this is difficult and fun. (See illustration #3.)

Before they lower their legs on the word "free," see if the children can hold the balance on their seats with their arms outstretched.

BLAST OFF
   Good for: 1) Total body conditioning.
                  2) Physical challenges.*

There are 3 stages. Each stage proceeds through a count down, "10, 9, 8, 7, 6, 5, 4, 3, 2, 1, 0", and a "Blast Off!" For each stage, the count down is a downward stretch and the "Blast Off" is a balanced position.

---

* These challenges are especially important for slightly older children who are worried about doing "baby stuff." Younger children, however, like and are able to do most of these challenges too. Blast Off is appropriate for kindergarten to 4th grades.

STAGE 1

The children sit on the floor with the soles of their feet "clapped" together. They grasp their ankles (not toes because it twists the foot) and straighten their backs. To get their torsos stretched and tall I ask for "rocket ship straight" torsos. (See illustration #4.)

(Note on how to help children pull torsos up: Put your knee against the middle of the child's back and gently but firmly pull back the shoulders. If you have an especially bony knee, use the side of the knee. See "Alignment," Part 7, for overall posture correction.)

The child is ready to count down and "Blast Off." For the counts "10, 9, 8, 7, 6, 5, 4, 3, 2, 1, 0" slowly round the back down toward the toes so that on "0" ideally the child's "nose is touching his toes" or as nearby as possible. (See illustration #5.)

For the "Blast Off," the child puts his hand on the floor close to his seat, the other hand reaches forward; he plants his feet on the floor and stretches up. This makes a high bridge stretching the pelvic area and torso in general. The child comes down, twirls on his seat and does the same stretch on the other side. I then ask the children to lift one leg and balance on the remaining hand and foot. This one-hand/one-foot balance is difficult. The trick is to stretch hard, thereby lifting the weight up. (See illustration #6.)

STAGE 2

Children sit on the floor with their legs straight in front of them. Legs are "railroad straight" with toes saying "goodbye" and the torso is "rocket ship straight." (A body of mixed metaphors!) Children slowly round their backs down for the count down, "10.......0" ideally reaching their nose to their knees by "0." (See illustration #7.)

"Blast Off" for Stage 2 is a traditional bridge: arms twist back, knees bend, and the child pushes up into a back bend. The trick is in the hands twisting back; once that is achieved the bridge gets higher and higher with practice. (See illustration #8.)

It is important to insist on *gently* pushing up and even more important on gently coming down. When coming down I ask for one part of the body at a time: head, shoulders, waist, hips. In addition to preventing bruises, this slow rounding down is good for general control.

STAGE 3

Children sit on the floor with legs in wide stride. After turn out is taught (See "Turn Out," in Part 7) legs are turned out. Again children work to sit "rocket ship straight" (very difficult in this position) and they round down for counts "10.......0." (See illustration #9.)

At this point, with the children working to round their backs while in wide stride position, you will probably have to deal with at least one child whining, "I can't do it." I do not have a set procedure for dealing with that awful sound. Sometimes I just ignore it. Sometimes I have long talks with the children about the futility of the word "can't." Mainly I say, "Go as far as you *can*. Let it hurt a little to stretch you out but don't let it hurt too much."

"Blast Off" for this 3rd Stage is swinging the legs overhead, working to touch the ground behind the head with the toes, the yoga plough position. (See illustration #10.)

When they can do this I have the children hold their hips up with their hands, legs reaching for the ceiling, the shoulder stand. We then "bicycle on the moon."

MAYBE I DON'T, MAYBE I DO
   Good for: 1) Relaxed, lowered shoulders.
               2) Isolation.
               3) Coordination.

Children often confuse good posture with stiffness. The confusion is especially noticeable in raised, tense shoulders. To unhitch this tension I do an exercise called "Maybe I Don't, Maybe I Do."

The children sit on the floor, soles of the feet clapped together, knees out, hands holding ankles. This is the stage 1 position for Blast Off and I frequently do this exercise right before Blast Off. I ask the children to get "rocket ship straight" or sometimes simply ask them to pull up their torsos.

Pulling my shoulders way up to my ears, I say, "I don't know." (Children imitate gesture and words.) Usually I ham it up with exaggerated facial gestures of "not knowing." Shoulders pulled way down go with the statement "Yes I do!" This alternation between "I don't know" and "Yes I do!" is repeated several times. From there, one shoulder goes up while the other stays down: "Maybe I do." "Maybe I don't; maybe I do." The children say the "maybe's" as they alternate shoulders up and down. The "maybe's" are repeated a few times, then one final "I don't know" (shoulders way up) is followed by an emphatic "Oh yes I do!!" (shoulders way down).

Whenever those shoulders begin to get tense after this, ask for "Oh yes I do!" shoulders.

OBSTACLE COURSE

USE OF OBSTACLE COURSES
   Good for: 1) Tone of the class.
                2) Teaching initial rules.
                3) Testing.
                4) Teaching relationship words.

An obstacle course is often the first activity I present to 4th to 6th graders. At this age children are often swaggeringly timid. They come in full of bluff and bravado because they have not the slightest idea what movement is about. They are not sure if it is going to be "sissy," if they are going to make fools of themselves, if they will be able to do it, if their feet are going to stink when their socks come off. An obstacle course leaves little time for worrying, is certainly not sissy, and *is* most definitely fun. Also, it acquaints children with the room as a moving space and sets a nice tone for the class.

In addition, obstacle courses can be: 1) sneaky ways of getting your rules across, for example, no gum during class, the stage is used only for performing perfected patterns; 2) quick pre-program tests, telling you the general mental and physical coordination level of your class; and 3) fun ways of teaching relationship words like "over," "under," "between," "around," and so forth.

BEGINNING OBSTACLE COURSE
Here is an example of a relatively simple course:

In this course, the children are told what to do rather than given written instructions. As I tell the instructions I point to the appropriate object; sometimes I demonstrate.

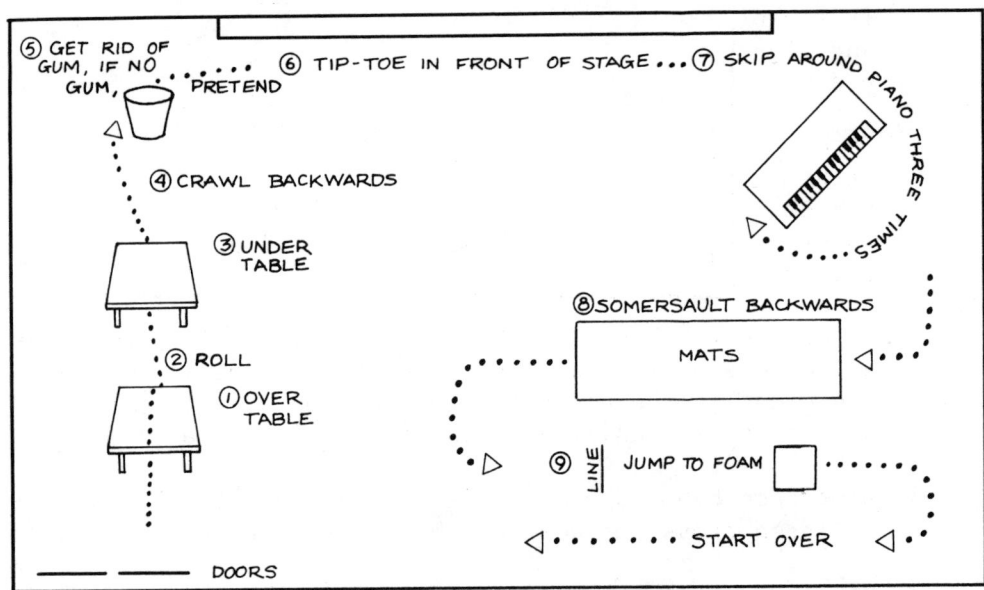

OBSTACLE COURSE TEST
The "beginning obstacle course" example on the right is a typical first day obstacle course. From it several things will become clear. 1) You can see how generally coordinated the children are. Did they leap easily over the table or clutchingly crawl over? Could they do a backward somersault? How far could they jump? 2) You will have a clear idea of the mental state of your class. How many instructions did they remember the first time through? The 2nd time? How precisely did they do the 3 times around the piano? Were they comfortable with the words "over," "under," "between," "around"? Obstacle courses tell a lot. I use an obstacle course like the one above at the beginning of the year for observation and generalized testing. Later in the year obstacle courses are used as teaching devices.

AN ELABORATE OBSTACLE COURSE
A number of summers ago I worked for the Richmond Recreation Department in Richmond, California, in a program called Noah's Park. There, with enormous amounts of equipment available, some of the greatest obstacle courses of all time were created. On the next page is a course a fellow staff member, Dan Cieloha, and I developed. All instructions were written. They were taped where the numbers are indicated on the course. A description of this obstacle course follows the diagram.

The instructions for the "elaborate obstacle course" as diagramed on the right is as follows:

1) Child goes through cloth tunnel. (Staff member makes it shake and wiggle.)

2) Three paths are set up by taping color

papers to the backs of chairs; each piece of paper indicates a step. Red is the hardest with several chairs between steps, blue is medium hard with 2 chairs between steps, and green is the easiest with steps on adjacent chairs. The children pick their path and follow it, walking on the appropriate chairs.*

3) A balance beam is placed like a plank across the aisle separating rows of chairs. The children cross the beam, with a staff person to help, if needed.

4) Mats are set on the inclined aisle (this is an auditorium), and the children somersault down the mats.

5) Hula hoops are arranged in a color pattern; for example, one red, followed by 3 blues, followed by 2 yellows, etc. Each color represents a movement: jump in the red, hop in the blue, step in the yellow. The children have to figure out the resulting movement combinations.

---

* "Gad, isn't that dangerous?" asks my teacher friend, Pat. It is a curious thing about "dangerous" activities. In 12 years of teaching, no one has gotten hurt on the "dangerous" activities. In the case of the chair paths, we warn the children to step on the outside of the chair so that it will not collapse on them. It has worked fine, especially since a child does not have to choose the hardest path unless he wants to. Children almost never elect to do something that is too dangerous for them. If they want to do something (not out of bluff but genuinely want to), they are usually ready to do it. And I believe that danger-within-reason is important for children (adults too). It gives them a feeling of exhilaration, a sense of excitement and challenge. Why be limited by our preconceived limitations?

6) Children somersault backwards uphill on mats placed in a 2nd aisle.

7) Children walk on the chairs, under the parachute.

8) Here are several large rubber balls with handles, called "Hoppities." The children sit and bounce on them out the door.

9) Out on a little porch area the children try their hand at balancing a plate (plastic) on a pole and spinning it.

10) The children bounce on a trampoline-like contraption, called a "Jumpin' Jiminy," and shoot "baskets" (tennis balls thrown into a waste paper container).

11) The children lie on their tummies on scooters (square skateboards) and have to follow the path marked by the tape.

12) The children run and leap off a large foam "mountain," ready to start the whole course again.

OBSTACLE COURSE ADDITIONS

I consider an obstacle course like the preceeding one on page 20 almost a work of art. Unfortunately, most schools do not have the staff or equipment to do a course like the "elaborate obstacle course." Still, ordinary materials are available to make your course slightly more intricate. Many tire stores give away old tires. Tires are wonderful to jump in, crawl through, and roll on. Hula hoops are great as movement markers, for example, hop, jump, step, step-hop; or the hoops can be used, for a short time, in their intended around the waist circling. Large boxes, available from furniture stores, are perfect to crawl through or be given a ride in. Sometimes obstacle courses can have surprise textures. In a box with a lid, make a small opening for a hand; put a bowl in

it filled with cold, cooked spaghetti in water or fill it with hardened jello. The children stick their hands in as part of the course. (Have a damp towel handy.) Gruesome! Of course tables and chairs are standard for going over and under, and large objects, like pianos, are great for going around. Mats can be used for all sorts of rolls, cartwheels, crawls, and leaps. Even the stage can be used as part of the course: put the balance beam one or 2 feet from the edge of the stage and have the children pretend they are a thousand feet high as they cross the beam; with double or triple thick mats on the floor, have the children jump as far as they can off the stage. (For a slightly more elaborate obstacle course see diagram on page 21.)

TO MAKE LIFE EASIER

If objects in the course need to be in specific places, use masking tape to mark the spot. In the preceeding course, for example, on page 21 at number 4, the placement of the chair legs are marked so that the chairs remain a foot apart. At number 7 on page 21, the place for the waste basket is marked by a taped "X." The children are instructed, "If you mess anything up, put it back."

The children are also told when to begin on their own. For example, "When the person in front of you finishes the hula hoops, you start." Even if the children are not very precise yet, this self-starting mechanism frees you from a needless task and keeps the children's spacing more proportionate.

Finally, use a record or piano to keep the obstacle course moving. The children are instructed, "When the music stops, freeze, no matter where you are." Again, even if they are not precise this offers some control to stop the movement without a lot of commotion.

CHILDREN'S OWN OBSTACLE COURSE

Later in the year the children put obstacle courses together themselves. A group of 4 or 5 children sets up a course for the rest of the class. Later on another group will do their own course and so on until everyone has had a turn. A basic rule is that each group has to be able, and willing, to go through their own course before they ask anyone else to try it.

CONCLUDING THE FIRST CLASS

THE FIRST FEW WEEKS

We have begun. The children are acquainted with Perfect Spot, they have done a few preliminary exercises, and they have perhaps tested an obstacle course. The children see that movement class will be controlled fun and they have a sense of the structure and tone of the class. All we need are locomotor movements (Part 2) and we are set for the next few weeks.

PART 2
LOCOMOTOR MOVEMENTS

INTRODUCING LOCOMOTOR MOVEMENTS

DEFINITION OF LOCOMOTOR MOVEMENTS

Locomotor movements are those that "go somewhere." Traveling through space (running, skipping, jumping, rolling, walking, leaping) is at the heart of most dance, at the heart of most children. In addition to being one of the most fun parts of movement class, locomotor movements are essential for muscular growth, endurance, and coordination. They are a central part of any movement program.

There are millions (at least thousands) of locomotor movements available. Most of these are variations on basic steps. A catalog of basic locomotor movements, their leading variations, and some patterns combining several movements, is at the end of Part 2.

INTRODUCING LOCOMOTOR MOVEMENTS

I introduce locomotor movements during the 2nd or 3rd class. I begin with the word. As with most definition work, I teach the *sound* of the word first and then its *meaning*. The children and I sit gathered on the floor. I say the word "locomotor" slowly and have the children say it after me. We play with the syllables, "looooooooooocomotor, loco-mooooooooooootor, lo/co/mo/tor, locomotor (very fast), loco/motor," until the word is familiar.

I point out that our word has a "motor" in it and ask the children for examples of things that have motors. This method of teaching the meaning of "locomotor" is effective but it can be dangerous! Usually children will say, "cars, trucks, motorcycles." This is great because they all "go somewhere." However, you might have one child who says "washing machine." There is nothing to do but say that *"locomotor"* uses its motor to go somewhere. You can bypass the whole thing and simply tell the children the definition, but you will also be bypassing some fun and a useful memory tool for this long word.

INTRODUCING THE CONCEPT

We then combine the word "locomotor" with locomotor movements so that the word is associated with the activity. I ask the children to stand on one side of the room.

"Locomotor means going somewhere. We are going to go somewhere, from this side of the room to the other. How can we go?"

"Run. Walk. Jump. I don't know. Skip. Run."

"Great," I say, "Let's start with walk. We will do the locomotor movement walk to the other side of the room. Walk and say the word 'lo/co/mo/tor' as you go. Do it as if you were angry so I can hear you." We all stomp across the room, shouting lo/co/mo/tor (one syllable per step).

"What different locomotor movement can we do going back to the other side of the room?" (I use the entire phrase "locomotor movement" every time I refer to a movement in space; for example, "Let's do the locomotor movement run," or "You did a wonderful locomotor movement skip," until the children are at ease with, perhaps sick of, the word "locomotor.") As the children think of possible locomotor movements, we do them across the room while saying the word "locomotor." Jump (2 feet together) and hop (one foot) are done with the word broken into even syllables, as with the walk: lo/co/mo/tor. Locomotor movements skip and gallop bring an uneven rhythm to play:

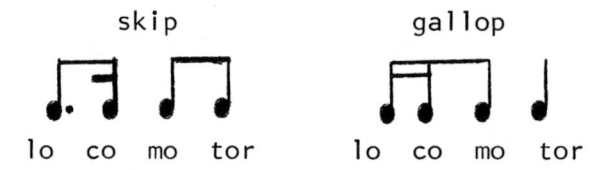

skip gallop

lo co mo tor   lo co mo tor

The movements roll, crawl, and slide on the floor are jumbled rhythmically.

I ask, "How else can we go from this side of the room to the other?" until the children come up with most of the basic locomotor movements: walk, run, hop, skip, jump, gallop, crawl, roll, and slide on the floor on tummy or back. If the children do not think of these movements, I gently prod: "How does a ball go downhill? How does a baby get somewhere? How does a horse move?"

The locomotor movement run is the most fun and I save it for last. I ask the children to "run so fast that you go from this side of the room to the other just in the time it takes to shout 'locomotor' *once*." I demonstrate, running and shouting "loocoomootooor," completing it at the same moment I arrive. Each child tries it out. Hearing the word 34 times pretty well ingrains it! As a finale, we all charge and shout at once. There is no doubt that at the end of this introduction the word "locomotor" and the idea of moving in space are firmly associated.

INITIAL STUDIES

Most often I conclude a beginning lesson on locomotor movements with a simple study. For example, I might have the children do a different locomotor movement for each side of the room: skip along one side of the room, crawl backwards along one side, roll on one side, and run on one side. I do a simple study like this even with older children (4th to 6th grade) making the locomotor movements harder: skip backwards on one side, jump and turn on one side, roll with your knees to your chin, and run the last side.

Here are a few more initial locomotor movement studies:

1) Any visible mark can help establish a pattern. For example, "Start at the double doors; side-slide to the piano; hop to my desk; run to the stage; and slide on your back (pushing with just your legs) to the double doors, ready to start again."

2) Have a long piece of tape marking the middle of the room. "Start on one side; run to the middle, fall down and roll to the other side; jump back to the middle, fall down and crawl to the original side."

3) An initial study can use the diagonal lines in a room before teaching the concept "diagonal." For example: "Run to the corner where the piano is." or "Run to the corner near the side door." Have the children run one diagonal line, jump across the side of the room, skip the opposite diagonal line, and hop across the other side. The children move on the 2 diagonals at the same time with "no disasters!"

Even at this early stage the children are asked to remember the study by themselves. I call it out or do it with them the first time and then we practice it until the children can do it "perfectly" alone.

STRUCTURING LOCOMOTOR MOVEMENTS

In the next class, perhaps 2, we continue to do locomotor movements going from one side of the room to the other. Soon, however, it is time to structure.

As natural as locomotor movements are to movement class, they are natural chaos producers. Even more than stationary movements, locomotor movements need to be ordered for safety and control. Structuring locomotor movements comes in 2 parts: 1) being able to start and stop in a Free Traveling Structure, and 2) learning the concept "diagonal" and setting up the Diagonal Structure. Each of these structures is valuable for different uses.

FREE TRAVELING STRUCTURE

DEFINITION
Good for: 1) Warm-up activities.
2) Introduction of major concepts.
3) Partner activities.
4) Work on endurance.

Free Traveling Structure means the children move to a sound (piano, tambourine, record, whatever) and stop exactly when the sound stops. They move freely about the room but do not jostle or bump into each other. Since everyone is moving at once, you can see if a class has a general idea but not specific foot work.

TEACHING IT
Here is the full progression for teaching the Free Traveling Structure. Not all classes need the entire sequence.

STEP 1
The children are gathered on the floor around me. I have a drum or tambourine. "I'd like to see you shake your hands, but wait until I say 'start'; when I say 'stop,' freeze. Start...stop. Great!"* Now instead of me saying the start and stop, the tambourine will do it. When your hear the tambourine, shake your hands, when it stops, freeze. Good."

---

* If it is *not* great, stop. If your class is young (preschool through 2nd grade), giggly, and not following your instructions exactly, jump to the section on teaching locomotor movements to the very young. The technique presented there is effective for giggly, rambunctious classes as well as inhibited, scared ones. If your class is older (3rd grade on up) and is not following your directions, consider being tougher, more demanding, putting some children out, and yelling.

STEP 2

With the idea of "start" and "stop" extablished, we do different *stationary* movements to the sound: bounce heads, wiggle shoulders, open and close mouths, spin on seats, make sounds, and wiggle hips. At this point, I am extremely strict that no one starts before the sound and no one continue after it. I hold the freeze long enough to have it firmly established: "Are your fingers frozen? Are your eyelids frozen? Your teeth? Hair?...."

STEP 3

We begin doing *locomotor* movements using "start" and "stop." Jump is a good transition movement. For example, "Jump where you are during the tambourine sound. Good. Now you may jump anywhere in the room. What do you do when the tambourine stops? Right, freeze." We do a number of basic locomotor movements, jump, hop, skip, gallop, walk, and run.

STEP 4

Using one locomotor movement, I play with the length of sound. Sometimes I let the tambourine sound for a long time, sometimes for a series of extremely short sound durations. For example, doing the locomotor movement run I have the tambourine sound for 15 to 20 seconds, freeze, sound 12 seconds, freeze sound 2 seconds, freeze, 4 seconds, freeze, and so on. Children love this listening game.

As I said, not all classes need the entire progression. Some mature, attentive classes can jump right to the final step or final 2 steps.

PRECISION

I strongly recommend strict starts and stops. Since the tambourine sound is the only structure here, the childrens' beginnings and endings need to be visible, clear, and precise. The structure needs to be completely under your control. Further, since Free Traveling Structure is one of the earliest taught foundations of movement class, the tone set here will carry into many other activities. My motto: better strict and a little petty than slack and later sorry.

PROBLEMS

Two common complaints about Free Traveling Structure are children falling and children bumping into one another.

It is an amazing thing about accidents, most need not happen. Falling and bumping are largely self-controlled. In my classes, I place the responsibility fully on the child. "I want you on your feet. If you fall down again you will not be able to run with us." And it works. Of course, it takes a snap decision to judge which fall or bump is real and which is not, but most teachers have an excellent eye.*

---

* Two alternatives: Some teachers find it preferable to allow children to fall and bump (playing "bumper cars") and then to clearly stop the activity. Although I agree with the theory, this has not worked well for me. Other teachers use the idea "Carry your Perfect Spot with you." I think that this is OK but not technically correct. A Perfect Spot is one that is far from everyone. When moving in the Free Traveling Structure, the object is not to stay far from people, but to move freely without hurting one another. This is a minor point; if it works, use it.

If the children are working on fast movements like run or leap I ask the class to move in a track-like circle around the room. Otherwise, I do not direct the Free Traveling organization.

DIAGONAL STRUCTURE

DEFINITION
Good for: 1) Perfecting locomotor movements.
2) Working on locomotor patterns.
3) Testing.
4) Safety.

The Diagonal Structure means that a class lines up at one side of the room, moves diagonally across the room, and then lines up at the other side. This structure is the basic plan for moving across the floor safely, visibly, and orderly. The Diagonal Structure is to running what Perfect Spot is to exercising: invaluable!

INTRODUCING THE CONCEPT
I start by teaching the concept "diagonal." Holding a piece of paper with a diagonal line drawn on it, I say, "This kind of line is a *diagonal* line." I point to another corner on the paper and ask, "Where would I have to go to make the same kind of line, a diagonal line, from this corner?" The 2nd line is not visibly drawn but marked (a finger tracing the line) by the children. We turn the paper over and find the diagonal lines on the back. This is done a number of times, enough so that most children have a turn finding one diagonal on the paper.

Most children, 4 years old and up, understand the idea of diagonal lines easily. If a majority of the class has it, I go on to the next step; the rest of the class will pick it up with repetition. If most of the children are having trouble finding the diagonal lines on the paper, I start over and visibly draw the lines. In this case I do not go on to the next step. I re-introduce diagonal lines another day, until the children can mark the diagonal lines on paper without visibly drawing them.

DIAGONAL LINES THROUGHOUT THE ROOM
The next step is to mark diagonal lines throughout the room. I find any clear rectangle or square, point to one corner and ask, "Where do I have to go to make a diagonal line from this corner?" For example, we go to the chalkboard and I point to one corner, "Where do I have to go on this chalkboard to make a diagonal line?" The line is traced in the air, landing in the appropriate corner. We do the same with windows, doors, piano backs, table tops, whatever I can find that has a clear diagonal line. I move rather quickly from object to object and the class runs with me. The tone of the lesson is like a game.

We then move on to the larger diagonals in the room. "If I were standing at this corner of the ceiling, where would I have to go to make a diagonal line?" The children find both diagonals on the ceiling and then find both diagonals on the floor. At this point the concept "diagonal" is firmly established.

SETTING IT UP
   We are now ready to set up the Diagonal Structure. The children
line up on one side of the room either individually or in small
groups. They do a locomotor movement, usually run the first
time, on the diagonal, then walk across the opposite side of the
room and stop. (See diagram on the right.)

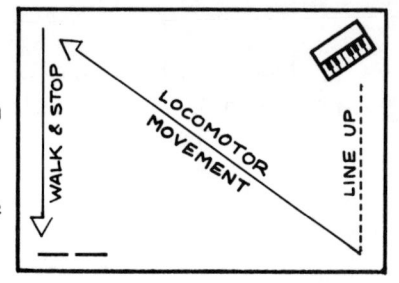

When everyone has had a turn on the first diagonal, the process is repeated on the cross
diagonal until each child is back at his starting place. (See diagram below.)

So that is the Diagonal Structure. Pretty simple, isn't it?
Here are a few refinements: perfect corners, cause and effect
starts, and group work.

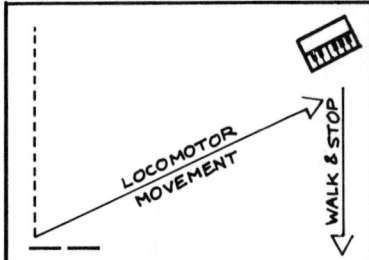

   PERFECT CORNERS
      From the beginning I am fussy that the children use the cor-
   ners fully. When one group begins moving on the diagonal,
   the children go all the way into the corner rather than round-
      ing it out. These "perfect" corners are necessary to utilize the full length of the
   diagonal and they make for a neater and more precise structuring.

   CAUSE AND EFFECT STARTS
      Cause and effect starts is any system where the children start across the diagonal
   without you shouting "Go!" The easiest cause and effect start is this: "When the
   group ahead gets to the *end* of the diagonal, you start." Another basic start is
   having subsequent groups begin when the group ahead crosses the middle of the diagonal. I have the middle marked with a large tape "X" until the concept "middle"
   is taught later in the year (see Part 6). In any case, any clear mark can be used
   for the cause and effect start.

   Generally for young classes I stick with the end of the diagonal as the signal for
   the next group to go. For older classes I like to be able to switch: the end of the
   diagonal is used as the signal when doing large, fast movement, like leaps, and a
   shorter distance is used for slower movements. These different cause and effect
   starts are established in the course of the first 5 or 6 weeks of movement class.

   Whatever the system, it is imperative that the children learn to watch and take
   responsibility for starting on their own. Easier said than done. "You are late!
   Come back, group one, and let's see if group 2 can watch and start at the right time.
   No, you're too early! Wait until they are *done* with the diagonal. Where are you
   group 3?"

   However, the effort needed to establish this self-maintaining cause and effect start
   is worth it. It lets the Diagonal Structure move at a constant flow, releases you
   from a needless task, and imposes a good self-reliance problem on the children.

   GROUP WORK
      The final element in a perfectly working Diagonal Structure is group work. Aside
   from the benefits of teaching and learning from others, group work is essential in
   a class of more than 10 students; 34 children waiting for one another to finish moving
   across the diagonal is not frequently workable.

Group work encompasses the childrens' ability to form their own groups and the groups' ability to stay together. The most important technique in getting children to form their own groups is patience. "Get into groups of 4," I say, and I wait. I have waited as long as 15 minutes! At least one or 2 groups will form. If I can no longer stand waiting I will start the locomotor movements across the diagonal with the first 2 groups. The others will join.

If there is an uneven division I say, "You are all in groups of 4 and there is a *remainder* of one." In order to remove any stigma to the idea of remainder, I continue, "Congratulations remainder, (I shake his hand), you get to join any group you want and that group will have 5." A remainder of 3 becomes the last group.

What about meanness? If children state a preference in choosing their groups, "We want Howard," I think that is fine. If there is obvious exclusion, "We don't want Howard," I come down hard with full authority: "That's mean. You will *not* act like that in my class. I do not care if you like Howard or not, but you absolutely can not act in a way that makes him feel bad." I do not use heavy handed authority much. I use it mostly when safety and meanness are at issue. In the long run the children appreciate this because if I will not let them be mean to Howard, I will not let Howard be mean to them.

In any case, everybody gets into their own groups including the youngest kindergarteners. Once the groups are formed, it is another story to keep them together. More on that in Part 3.

TEACHING LOCOMOTOR MOVEMENTS TO VERY YOUNG CHILDREN

WHY A DIFFERENT START?
Young children (pre-school to kindergarten) are often initially frightened of moving in space. Perhaps the space seems too big or unlimited. This fear comes out in different ways: "I don't wanna," tears, or sometimes uncontrolled giggling. I therefore introduce locomotor movements to very young children in a completely different way. We do not learn the word "locomotor" and we do not go from one side of the room to the other; we rock. Because it is safe and not threatening, this "rocking lesson" is an excellent first class for very young children.

THE ROCKING SONG

[Musical notation: "We are rocking, rocking, rocking. We are rocking, now we're still."]

The Rocking Song is an extremely valuable tool. In addition to being the crux of the following first class, it is a good quieter-relaxer (see Part 7), it can be used for leg and back stretches (see Part 5), and it is useful to reinforce the concept "level" (see Part 4).

THE "ROCKING LESSON"*
   There are 7 steps to this lesson. Go faster rather than exclude any steps.

   STEP 1
   Waste absolutely *no* time. As soon as the children are in the door, we sit on the floor cross-legged and sing the Rocking Song, rocking side to side. We do this once or twice.

   STEP 2
   If they look near tears I tell them, "'Still' means stop or freeze." If they look comfortable I take a minute and ask what they think "still" means. The children have already been freezing on the word "still" since they have been imitating me.

   STEP 3
   We rock in several different ways:

   a) Sitting with the legs straight ahead, we rock from side to side. The opposite leg lifts as the body leans sideways.

   b) Sitting with legs wide, we rock forward and back. For the rock back, the legs lift and the seat raises high in the air. (By this time the song is becoming quite familiar.) (See illustration at right.)

   c) "Let's make it harder," I say. We get on our knees and rock from side to side using hands to push the floor at either side.

   d) "Even harder," I say as I pantomime evil intentions. We stand and rock from side to side. Hands do not touch the floor. The opposite leg lifts off the ground as the body leans sideways and the "freeze" at the end is a one foot balance.

   STEP 4
   The Rocking Song is now completely familiar (we have sung it 6 to 10 times). The children and I sit down again. "Do you know what? We don't have to just rock to our song. We could, um, shake. When we shake we will sing 'We are shaking, shaking, shaking, we are shaking, now we're *still*.'"

   The tune and rhythm are *exactly* the same; just the one word is changed. We sing the song and shake while sitting. If the children look confident, I ask them to shake and jump in the air and then to shake while lying on the ground. We sing the song and shake, moving continuously from the air to the ground and back up.

---
* This is how the lesson came about: Several years ago I walked into a class of 15 preschool children coming to me for their first dance class. I had prepared what I thought was an excellent lesson. I planned Jump Your Name, Hello and Goodbye, and Swordfish all done near me, and beginning locomotor movements going across the room in partners. It was a disaster. Seven out of the 15, at one time or another during that horrendous half hour, began to cry. It was definitely one of those "Why did I ever go into this profession?" moments. Since then I have developed this lesson especially for that situation and it has worked well.

Generally, Step 4 is a process of changing the word "rocking" in the song to different *stationary* movements. The song is the same, the repetition seems to be quite soothing, but the movements change. Recommended beginning stationary movements: spinning (on seat), kicking (like a tantrum), bouncing (heads), wiggling (seats), jumping (in place). Any of these words fit rhythmically into the song. Before doing a new movement I ask the children how the song will go. Nine out of 10 have it down pat by now.

STEP 5

We are ready for the big step into locomotor movements. "You did jumping perfectly! We are going to jump again, but this time we will not stay right here, we'll jump *anywhere* we want in our movement room. Do you remember what to do for the word 'still'? Right, freeze."

So we sing and jump around the room. This simple transition starts the children moving on their own. If they are with you here, you have them. We do the song using walking, hopping, skipping, galloping, crawling, rolling, running, whatever. By this time they are shouting suggestions to me.

STEP 6

The next step introduces a more generalized start and stop structure. "This time when we skip to our song (the locomotor movement can be one already used or a new one) don't sing out loud. Sing the song silently to yourself as I beat the rhythm on the drum. Remember to freeze on the word 'still' even though we are not saying it out loud."

If you play the piano at all and can pick out the tune, that is better than the drum, but the drum rhythm works adequately. The children move and do *not* sing. They know rhythmically when to stop. We do this "silent tune" several times with different locomotor movements.

STEP 7

Finally, we are ready for the last step. "You are starting and stopping when you hear the sound so well that I am going to make it harder. I am going to play a different tune on the piano (or drum). Like with the song, you move when you hear the sound and when the sound stops, freeze." The children have already been doing this but only to one predictable rhythmic length. Now I play different length tunes and expect precise starts and stops.

There it is, a simple, incredibly repetitious lesson that is conceptually chock full. The tone of the class is set, the children have explored some nonlocomotor and locomotor movements, and they have begun the Free Traveling Structure. Most importantly, they have successfully survived their first movement class and so have you. The next lesson might repeat half of this first lesson. By then the children are ready to go on to other things.

CATALOG OF LOCOMOTOR MOVEMENTS

1) WALK

   VARIATIONS

   a) Directions: forward, backward, sideways, turning.

   b) Warming-up the foot:

   1- Tip-toe.

   2- Walk on heels. (Do this only for a few seconds otherwise it hurts.)

   3- Toe-toe-heel-heel. Alternate 2 tip-toe walks with 2 heel walks.

   4- Toe-toe-heel-heel-in-in-out-out. This is 2 tip-toe steps, followed by 2 heel steps, followed by 2 inside arch steps, and finally 2 outside arch steps. Difficult!

   5- Roll from heel smoothly to toe; balance. ("Like walking through molasses.")

   6- Roll from toe smoothly to heel.

   c) Emotions: angry (stomp), joyous, scared, sneaky, guilty, etc.

   d) Silly.

   e) Drunk.

   f) Heavy; light.

   g) High; low.

   h) Waltz walk: one low step, 2 high steps: low-high-high. This is a difficult movement but it is basic dance vocabulary. What makes the waltz walk so hard is its 3-ness, that is, if the right steps low, followed by left and right high, then the left foot has to step low to start the new waltz walk. Most mistakes are "fudges" so that the same foot can start the low step.

   I teach the waltz walk by asking for 4 low steps and 4 high steps; then 3 low and 3 high; then 2 and 2; then finally one low and 2 high steps, which is the waltz walk.

   For advanced students you can include waltz walk turns. The turn occurs on the 2 high steps. If the right foot has stepped low, the turn moves to the right; if the left foot steps low the turn moves to the left. The waltz walk turn can be done to one side, that is, alternating one straight ahead waltz walk and one turn waltz walk, or it can turn to each side.

   i) All time favorite: *Jazz Walk*. With rock music playing, ask for a walk that is jazzy, "cool," "bad," or whatever is the appropriate word of the moment.

   j) Environments: walk through glue (molasses, honey, etc.) walk on eggs and don't break them, through a jungle, feathers, stickers, whatever.

k) Twisted or crooked; straight.

l) Stiff, like a robot or soldier; limp, like a rag doll.

m) Leading part: have one part of the body lead the walk, elbow, stomach, chin, hip, foot, seat, etc.

n) Focus on different body parts: hand, knee, toe, elbow, etc.

o) Age: old, young, middle aged, teenager.

p) Noisily; quietly.

q) Like your teacher.

r) Weird.

s) Grapevine: side-step, cross the other foot in front, side-step, cross back.

t) Add nonlocomotor movements like swing in the arms, wiggle in the hips, shake of the head, contract and stretch, mouth opening and closing, etc.

u) Walk like a stereotyped male; like a stereotyped female.

2) RUN

VARIATIONS

a) Fast.

b) Jog.

c) Slow motion.

d) Run with knees up.

e) Run long steps.

f) Alternate 4 knees up runs with 4 long step runs.

g) Tiny, mincing run.

h) Directions: forward, backward, sideways, turning.

i) Lean the body forward; lean it back.

j) With a partner, hold both hands and run twirling your partner; run and twirl in a group.

k) Add nonlocomotor movements: shake the hands, wiggle the shoulders, strike the arms, etc.

l) Prance. (Not exactly a run, but that is the closest categorization.) Legs move as if pushing a ball with the front of the foot.

3) CRAWL

   VARIATIONS

   a) Regular or "baby" crawl.

   b) Directions: forward, backward, sideways, turning.

   c) Backward stretch crawl: stretch leg completely straight back and step backwards. (See illustration #1.)

   d) "Spider crawl": hands and feet on the floor (knees not on the floor), seat high. (See illustration #2.)

   e) "Crab crawl": hands and feet on the floor, tummy towards the ceiling, seat off the ground. (See illustration #3.)

   f) "Inch worm crawl": hands and feet move separately. Leaving the feet in place the hands move forward as far as possible; the hands then remain in place and the feet catch up. (See illustration #4.)

   g) Add nonlocomotor movements: wiggle in the hips, shake the head, contract and stretch. Contract and stretch is especially good to do in the baby crawl position. The contracted torso is like a "mad cat," that is, rounded back with knees remaining on the floor; a straight back is like a "table"; and a stretch or arched back is like an "old horse." I often call out the descriptions as the children are crawling: "Mad cat...Old horse...Table."

   h) "Bridge crawl." A difficult and strenuous crawl. Make a "bridge" (a back bend) and "simply" walk. (See illustration #5.) Attempt this only with children who have good, high bridges and only after they have thoroughly warmed-up their backs.

4) JUMP (two feet together)

   VARIATIONS

   a) Directions: forward, backward, sideways, turning. Sometimes try full turns.

   b) Big, high jumps.

   c) Little, fast jumps.

   d) "Jump so that your heels hit your seat. Ouch!"

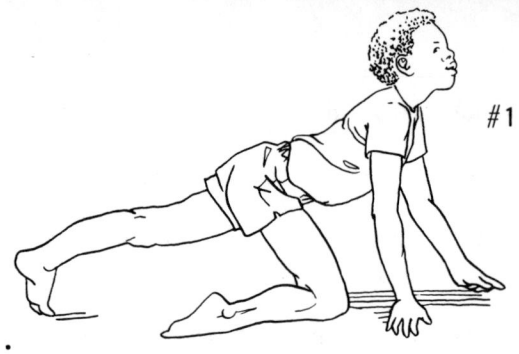

e) Long jumps: "Can you make it to the end of the diagonal in just 7 jumps?"

   f) Tuck jump: legs bend in the air, knees reach as close to the chest as possible.

   g) Straddle jump: legs stretch as wide as possible in the air.

   h) Side to side jumps: legs jump side to side while torso remains relatively stationary. Good to do over the balance beam.

   i) Hopscotch: alternate one jump with one hop, that is, jump-hop on right jump-hop on left.

   j) Add nonlocomotor movements: twist head, contract and stretch, wiggle shoulders, etc.

5) HOP (one foot*)

   VARIATIONS

   a) Directions: forward, backward, sideways, turning.

   b) Hold the raised leg with a hand.

   c) With a partner, hold each other's raised leg.

   d) Add nonlocomotor movements: shake the raised leg, swing arms, contract and stretch, twist head, etc.

   e) Alternate with jump for hopscotch.

   f) Change hopping foot every 4 beats.

6) SKIP (step hop**)

   VARIATIONS

   a) Directions: forward, backward, sideways (cross leg in front and back), turning.

---
* Do not forget to hop on the other foot. Hop is the preparatory movement for all the more difficult locomotor movements. If a child can hop well on either foot, he will be able to skip, gallop, side-slide, and leap easily and gracefully. Further, hop is excellent for general strength and coordination.

** Skipping is not sacred. Teachers are sometimes overly concerned with teaching a child to skip. Since a skip is an alternating hop, a child must first be able to hop easily on either foot. If a child can do that, it is simple to nudge him into a skip: "Hop on one side...Hop on the other side...Change sides...Change sides...Change, change." The "changes" get closer and closer together until they are one hop apart. In addition, I hold the child's hand and swing his arm in a strong upward rhythm as we skip together.

b) Add nonlocomotor movements: swing arms, twist head, contract and stretch, etc.

c) Skip for height; for distance.

d) Silly skips.

e) Link elbows facing a partner and skip; switch elbows faster and faster.

f) One-legged skip: a skip on one side only, that is, step-step-hop. (See illustration #6.) The one-legged skip is an extremely valuable element in the movement vocabulary: it is fun, it is easily varied, and it readily combines with many other movements. I teach this locomotor movement to 3rd grade on up.

I teach the one-legged skip by demonstration: "I am going to skip but only one leg will come up." I hold my right pant leg above the knee and do a few one-legged skips. "See, I take an extra step so that this is the only leg that comes up."

Most children pick up the movement best this way. They get the idea and, because they are not entangled in specific foot work, they soon swing into a high, free, energetic one-legged skip. If a child is having a great deal of difficulty, I will privately go through "Step right, step left, hop left, etc."

When the one-legged skip is first taught, the "skipping" leg, that is, the leg that is high in the air during the hop, is bent in front of the body (like an ordinary skip). After the children are at ease doing the one-legged skip, the skipping leg can be varied. It can be straightened in front of the body as in illustration #7.

It can be bent to the side of the body as in illustration #8.

The leg can be extended back, either bent or straight as in illustration #9.

These different leg positions can be mixed. For example, doing 3 consecutive one-legged skips, the leg is straight front for the first skip, bent side for the 2nd, and extended straight back for the 3rd. The same leg is in the air for each position.

7) GALLOP (step-together, one leg leads, the other joins)

VARIATIONS

a) Height: a gallop can be done very high if the back leg pushes hard off the floor.

b) Distance.

c) Alternate leading leg: 2 gallops with the right leg leading, 2 with the left leg leading; one gallop with the right and one with the left (a polka).

d) Add nonlocomotor movements: swing arms, shoulders up and down, bounce head, open and close mouth, etc.

e) Alternate gallops and skips: one gallop, one skip. Very hard.

f) If a gallop is done sideways it is a side-slide. Alternate gallops and side-slides.

8) SIDE-SLIDE (step-together done sideways)

VARIATIONS

a) Changing sides: one side-slide with the right side leading, one with the left side leading; change sides while traveling in one line.

b) With a partner, hold both hands in front of the body and side-slide.

c) With a partner, link elbows back to back and side-slide. If children are having trouble with this, it is probably because they are not going sideways. If they try to go forward, one child ends up dragging the other on his back.

d) Add nonlocomotor movements: swing the arms, raise and lower shoulders, contract and stretch, turn head, etc.

9) ROLL

VARIATIONS

a) Log roll. The body is stretched straight while rolling. The force for the log roll comes from an energized stretch of the torso. To stay *on* the mat (rather than angle off) the arms and legs must stretch equally.

b) Add nonlocomotor movement contract and stretch to log roll.

c) Cat or tuck roll: knees are bent to chest. The knees stay together, close to the chest, throughout the roll. (See illustration #10.)

d) Alternate one log roll and one tuck roll.

e) Forward roll or somersault. The children *stand* on the mats, put their hands *flat* down *near their feet*, tuck their heads *way under their feet* and roll. The knees bend but the seat remains as high as possible. The crucial part of these procedures is placing the head back toward the feet; only the *back* of the head touches the mat. (See illustration #11.)

If a child tries to roll over the top of his head he will get "stuck" and perhaps hurt his neck.

A forward roll can be done with the legs in various positions. These are the basic gymnastic terms: bent legs are called "tucked," straight legs together are called "piked," and straight legs wide apart are called "straddle." Of these 3 leg positions, the "piked" is the most difficult, requiring a great deal of stretch and strength. It is interesting to combine different forward rolls: one tucked forward roll, followed by one piked, and one straddle.

The legs do not have to remain in these standard gymnastic molds; they can assume almost any position. For example, the legs can lunge (one leg bent and the other straight), the knees and feet can flex, or the legs can shake during the roll.

Further, a forward roll can be done at different speeds, from super fast to slow motion.

f) Backward roll. This is much harder than a forward roll. The elements necessary for a backward roll are 1) the hands must twist back, palms flat, fingers pointing toward the shoulders, in order to *push* the floor, and 2) there needs to be some rolling momentum. I ask the children to start in a standing squat position (rather than sitting). They sit back, throw their legs over head and push with their hands, all in one continuous flow.

Once a backward roll is accomplished, it can be done with the legs in the same positions as the forward roll: tucked, piked (that means rolling over and pushing up onto straight legs; very hard!), and straddle. Or the legs can be varied in any way.

g) One-knee back roll. This is great! The one-knee roll is easier than the standard backward roll (many children learn how to do a standard back roll after mastering this roll), it can be done on the floor without a mat, and it is pretty.

The one-knee back roll starts from a sitting position. The child rocks back and lifts his hips and legs high (feet to ceiling). *One* knee bends getting as close as possible to the floor by the shoulder, while the other leg *remains lifted high*. (See illustration #12.)

This position, one knee bent and one leg straight, is the crucial point of success. Most children want to bend both legs, so I often hold the leg that is to remain straight. (See illustration #13.)

After the leg positions are clear, simply push gently with the hands and roll on to the bent knee. (If needed, instructor helps as shown in illustration #14.)

The roll is *over the shoulder* rather than over the back of the head. The ending position is on 2 hands and one knee with the other leg straight back. (See illustration #15.)

10) SEAT-SCOOT (seat sliding on the floor)

VARIATIONS

a) Directions: forward, backward, sideways, turning. (When doing a turning seat-scoot make sure the children actually get somewhere and do not just spin in one spot.)

b) Seat-scoot using only hands (feet are lifted); using only feet.

c) Walk on the seat. Legs are kept straight, hands are crossed on the chest. This is the old-fashioned hips and seat slimming exercise found in women's magazines. (At one time a movement teacher I know used this seat walk as punishment: "If you fool around once more you'll have to seat walk all the way to the side of the room and back." It worked OK except that the only way this movement is hard is if the legs are kept straight and the arms crossed, and that generally requires direct supervision.)

    d) With a partner, sit facing each other, hold each other's ankles and go somewhere.

    e) With a partner, sit back to back, elbows linked, and go somewhere.

    f) Add nonlocomotor movements: twist head, contract and stretch, shake, etc.

11) SLIDING ON THE FLOOR

VARIATIONS

    a) Slide on stomach.

    b) Slide on back.

    c) Slide on side.

    d) Slide on the back using only feet to push.

    e) On the back, slide in different directions: forward, backward, sideways, turning. If the children are unsure of directions while lying down, ask them to sit up for a minute to see how they would go sitting up. Then do it lying down.

    f) Slide ride. In partners, one child lies down, hands behind head, the other child holds his ankles and gives him a ride. Of course, they switch. A couple of notes on this ride: 1) Unless the lying down child is obese, the other child can pull him. If I hear "He's too heavy," I insist, "But you are strong enough to pull him." 2) If the class tends to be rough with one another, I have them practice lifting and lowering ankles gently before they are given the OK to give each other a ride.

12) KICKS

VARIATIONS

    a) Little kicks. The body hops with each kick so that, as one leg returns, the other kicks out. These little kicks can be done to the front, side, or back of the body. An interesting study is 4 front kicks, 4 back kicks, and 8 side kicks, then 2 front, 2 back, 4 side.

    b) Directions. The little kicks above can be done front, back, or side, and, in addition, the body as a whole can move in each of the 4 directions: forward, backward, sideways, turning. You can have a directional field day. "Kick your legs to the front and move forward...Kick your legs to the front and move backward...Kick your legs to the back and move forward...Kick your legs to the back and move sideways... Kick your legs to the side and move turning."

c) "Kick the habit." Children take a running start and click heels in the air. (See illustration #16.) This is hard. Once they get it children beam with accomplishment.

d) Hitch kick. The legs kick high to the front, touching in the air, while remaining straight and pointed.

e) Can-can kicking. Just for fun, ask groups of 3 to 20 to link arms at the shoulders and can-can.

f) Karate kick. Children do their versions of karate kicks. Ideally we work for that double kick where both legs are high in the air at the same time. At this moment of writing, the karate mania is just beginning to wane. For a while karate kicks structured into movement class was the only way I could reduce the karate eruptions all over the school.

13) LEAP (a step in the air*)

VARIATIONS

a) Directions: forward, sideways, and turning. A turning leap is actually a ballet *tour jete*, but if you keep that to yourself the children will be able to do it.

b) Vary the number of steps preceeding the leap: 3 steps and a leap, 2 steps and a leap, one step and a leap, no steps just leaps.

c) Stag leap. The front leg brushes straight to begin the leap, then bends sharply to touch the back knee for a second while the child is in the air.

d) Double bent leap. Both legs bend in the air. This is like a stag leap with the back leg also bent.

---

* A leap ideally has legs stretched straight like "doing the splits in the air." It is a glorious movement. Beautiful leaps are often what bring ballet crowds to their feet shouting "Bravo!"
I used to be scared of teaching leaps outside of the dance studio. I have since realized my mistake. Now if you were to ask the children I teach what their favorite locomotor movement is, 9 out of 10 would probably say "leap." The leap is not as hard to teach as it is cracked up to be. "A leap is a step in the air." I demonstrate. "The legs stay straight in the air. Take a few running steps to build up your speed so you can get very high." Most children pick up the leap that easily.
If a child cannot get the idea from example, I go through this process: take some little steps and then a big step, little-little-little-big. Make the big step get bigger and bigger until it is in the air.
For young children I ask that they take a running start and "leap" to touch the ceiling. I demonstrate. However, I do not concern myself or them with the leg position; I just want the rush of speed and the burst of energy. Later they will get the leg position.

LOCOMOTOR MOVEMENT STUDIES

IMPORTANCE OF STUDIES

Children love studies. Actually, children love to dance. Without handicapping them with that word, they love to learn set, repeatable, patterns. "Hey, Mom, watch what I learned in movement class." "I've almost got that pattern. I've just got to get that leap right." "I've been practicing this. Watch." "This pattern is ready for the stage."

You know how children love "productions," class plays, assemblies, projects that are completed. Studies are micro-productions; they are visual goals. Beyond that, studies are excellent for memory work, for precision and control, for coordination, and often for group work and problem solving.

In order for studies to accomplish their goals, the children must be able to perform them *by themselves*. Generally, I do a study once with the class, call it out a few times, and then help them practice it until they are proficient by themselves.

Following are 2 types of culminating locomotor movement studies: teacher taught combinations and teacher structured group problems.

TEACHER TAUGHT COMBINATIONS

1) Kick front 2, back 2, side 4, run 4 beats, kick in the air ("kick the habit").

2) Prance 4 times, jump-hop, jump-hop. Prance 4 times, jump-hop, jump-hop. Repeat going backwards. One group starts going forward as the group ahead starts going backwards. The backwards group beckons the forward with a "come here" finger.

3) This is one of my favorite locomotor studies. Step-hop on right foot; step left and "kick the habit"; step right and turn in the air landing on both feet. Again step-hop on right foot; step left and "kick the habit"; end with 3 little runs and leap.

   In rhythm the pattern goes: step-hop, step kick, step turn. Step-hop, step kick, run-run-run-leap. The quality is small and light. The pattern fits Scott Joplin's "The Entertainer" from *The Sting* album.

4) Waltz walk, one-legged skip, hitch kick, and step-leap are all done in a 3 beat rhythm. Therefore, they fit together nicely and are an almost unending source of pattern ideas:

   a) Waltz walk, one-legged skip, waltz walk (if possible, turn), step leap.

   b) Waltz walk, waltz walk, one-legged skip, step-leap.

   c) One-legged skip, one-legged skip, run-run-run-leap, hold in a balance.

   d) Hitch kick, one-legged skip, hitch kick, step-leap.

   e) One-legged skip with the leg extended straight front, waltz walk, one-legged skip with the leg extended straight back, waltz walk backwards.

TEACHER STRUCTURED GROUP PROBLEMS

1) The class is in groups of 3 to 5 children, ready to move on the diagonal: "Talk to your group and decide on one locomotor movement to do to the middle of the diagonal and a different one to do from the middle to the end." (If the class knows "level," ask for the 2 locomotor movements to be on 2 different levels.) I insist that the group has to work together. They must make a clear decision and all the group members must do the same 2 locomotor movements.

2) In groups ready to move on the diagonal: "Pick 4 locomotor movements. Do one for this diagonal, the 2nd across the side of the room, the 3rd on the crossing diagonal, and the 4th for the last side of the room." (If the class knows "level," ask for each locomotor movement to be on a different level.)

When the patterns are set, I ask subsequent groups to start when the group ahead of them has gotten to the middle of the diagonal. This means that a number of groups will be going at the same time, crossing each other's diagonal. "No disasters!"

3) "Somehow, fit in 3 different locomotor movements on one diagonal line." Older children might be asked to fit in 5 to 7 different movements.

4) "Pick 5 different locomotor movements, on 5 different levels, and fit them in some way in the room. For example, start at the door and skip to my desk, roll from the desk to the cabinets, leap from the cabinets to the piano, and so forth. See what design you end up making in space." (This is an excellent forshadowing of floor patterns, Part 6.)

5) "I will give you 30 beats, that is, I will count from one to 30. Within that time you do 4 different locomotor movements. Make sure your group stays exactly together."

6) I have a large stack of small cards with different locomotor movements printed on each. The children are divided into groups, and each group receives a packet of cards (3 to 7 cards depending on the children's ages). The groups arrange the cards in a sequence and do the appropriate movements to different points in the room. For example, they run to the corner, hop to the chair, etc.

7) Again, distribute a packet of cards, each naming a different locomotor movement. In addition, give each group 5 cards with numbers printed on them. A group might therefore end up with "run, jazzy walk, roll, skip, kick," and "9, 3, 3, 4, 5." The children arrange the movements and the numbers in any sequence they want, and then must perform each movement for its corresponding number. For example, given the above sequence, the group has to run 9 steps, take 3 jazzy walk steps, roll 3 times, skip 4 times, and kick 5 times. I ask for no stopping between changes in movement. I do not attempt to keep a steady beat, but do ask the groups to stay together. This is difficult.

PART 3
WORKING TOGETHER

FOSTERING FRIENDSHIP

NEED FOR ENCOURAGING FRIENDSHIP
One of the major goals of movement class is encouraging children's good feelings for themselves and others. An important part of this good feeling is having friends. Learning to make friends is as valuable as any intellectual or physical pursuit. Movement can do a great deal to foster friendships by 1) offering specific partner and group activities, and 2) creating a tone of friendship and cooperation in the class.

TOUCHING
Partner and group activities usually involve touching one another. Children want and like to touch, but often transfer physical warmth into teasing, fighting, and giggling. I think it is important that children get the okay to touch and feel close to one another. The movement activities in Part 3 promote appropriate touching.

USE OF PARTNER AND GROUP ACTIVITIES
During the first 6 weeks of movement class I will use several or all these partner and group activities any number of times, depending on how much the class needs it. Throughout the year we come back to a few of these activities just for the fun of it, or if there is an influx of new children. Generally, the partner activities are used as lesson warm-ups in the Free Traveling Structure, and the group activities are used as part of the locomotor movements in the Diagonal Structure.

PARTNER ACTIVITIES

SHAKE A PARTNER
This is essentially a name learning activity; therefore, I use it mainly in the first 2 weeks of class.

"When you hear the piano sound (as always, any sound will do) do the locomotor movement I call out. When it stops, freeze, and I will give more instructions." The piano sounds and I call out "Jump." With the children frozen, I continue: "Find a partner and shake your partner's hand. Make sure you know the name of the person whose hand you're shaking...Good!...Shake your partner with 2 hands...Shake so hard you are jumping each other up and down...Great!...Let go of your partner's hands."

Again the piano sounds. This time I might ask for skip. The children do the locomotor movements individually, that is, without a partner. "Get a *different* partner and this time shake feet with your partner...Yes, you and your partner's feet have to touch, and, just like your hands went up and down when you shook hands, your feet have to stay touching and go up and down...Know the name of your partner...Shake *both* feet." (Impossible to do without sitting or lying down.)

Since the children are already sitting or lying down, the next locomotor movement might be seat-scoot, roll, or crawl. The locomotor movements are not actually important in themselves. They serve as a nice rest from the touching and good energy release.

"Get a different partner...Know your partner's name...Shake heads...Yes, of course they have to touch!...Go up and down like you did for the hands...Great!"

The next locomotor movement may be run. "This time find a different partner and shake seats...Know your partner's name."

Shake A Partner, therefore, simply alternates individually done locomotor movements with a partner shake. The threat of the shake is reduced because it is done for a short time and the children continuously find new partners.

SUGGESTED PROGRESSION

Locomotor Movement	Partner Shake
1) Jump	Hands
2) Skip	Feet
3) Roll	Heads
4) Hop	Elbows
5) Run	Seats
6) Any locomotor movement they want.	Any 2 different body parts, that is, foot to shoulder, knee to hip. At the end of the shake, ask the children to hold their position and go somewhere together.

NONLOCOMOTOR MOVEMENTS WITH PARTNERS

This is similar to Shake a Partner. The children do an individual locomotor movement and then get a partner to do a nonlocomotor movement. The structure is again Free Traveling, and the children switch partners each time. Doing nonlocomotor movements with a partner works better if the concept "nonlocomotor" has been introduced, but it is not imperative.

SUGGESTED PROGRESSION

Locomotor Movement	Nonlocomotor Movement
1) Skip	Swing: "Hold both hands and do large, vigorous swings."
2) Hopscotch	Contract and stretch: "Contract with your partner into one tight ball, not 2 separate little contractions, but one big one. (Children have to hug each other or fold over one

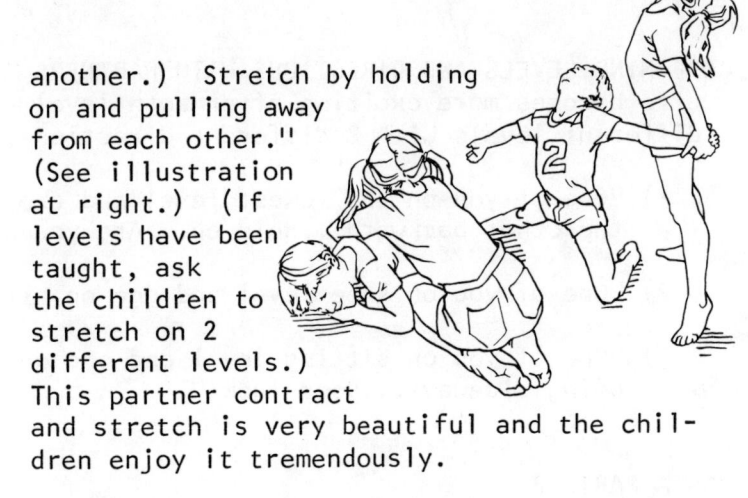

another.) Stretch by holding on and pulling away from each other." (See illustration at right.) (If levels have been taught, ask the children to stretch on 2 different levels.) This partner contract and stretch is very beautiful and the children enjoy it tremendously.

Another possibility is contract and stretch in opposites. When one person is contracted, the other is stretched. They switch faster and faster. The partners must hold on to each other at all times.

3) Leap-------------------------------Strike: "Face your partner and *without touching* do the nonlocomotor movement strike. Look mean! Strike arms, legs, elbows, torsos, heads, and hips."

4) Gallop-----------------------------Bend and straighten: "Bend and straighten in opposites, holding on to each other at all times."

LEVELS WITH PARTNERS

The children get a partner and hold hands as they move on the level I call out, "Move on the knee level." Both children get on knee level and do a locomotor movement; they then switch partners. "Move on air level...make sure you're holding onto each other." The children move on all levels, lowest, sitting, knee, standing, and air, and switch partners between each level change.*

I then ask for partners to move on 2 different levels, while holding on. "Move together, with one person on the lowest level and one on air level...Hey, don't let go...Now one person on standing level and one on sitting level."

Finally, I ask the children to pick their own 2 different levels, hold on, and move. For example, 2 children might pick sitting level and air level. When I say "switch," the child that was on air level goes to sitting level and the sitting child goes to air level. I switch faster and faster until the whole thing breaks down in laughter.

DIRECTIONS WITH PARTNERS

Reinforcement of the concept "directions" parallels the work just described with levels. The children hold on to each other by one hand and go in the direction I ask: forward, backward, sideways, turning. I then ask for 2 different directions: "One of you go forward and one of you turning...Hold on to each other...One sideways and one backwards." And so forth. Finally they pick their own 2 directions.

----

* When changing partners I sometimes throw in a trick: "Change partners but hold on to somebody at all times. You can not let go completely." This is fun and silly and can be used at any partner change.

COMBINING LEVELS AND DIRECTIONS WITH PARTNERS
   Life becomes more exciting after both level and directions are introduced. I mix 2
different levels with 2 different directions.   Examples:

   1) "One of you on the lowest level and one on standing level; one going forward and
      the other backward...Hold on...Are you getting somewhere?...Switch."

   2) "One of you on knee level and one on air level; one going sideways and one turning."

   3) "One of you on sitting level and one on air level; one going backwards and one
      going sideways...Good luck!"

BAG A PARTNER
   For children that are reluctant to touch each other or who consistently transfer physical
warmth into fighting or giggling, I have discovered a wonderfully sneaky partner prop:
burlap bags.**

The bags are also fun for children at ease with partner work.

I give each child a bag to explore freely. After 5 or 10 minutes I move
away from the persistent 2-legs-in-the-bag jump by offering other suggestions: "Put one leg and one arm in the bag and move somewhere...Great!...
Now put in 2 legs and one arm...How about one head and 2 arms..." A hard
combination is one leg and a head in the bag (see illustration at right);
I ask children to do it sitting down, and, when they feel confident, attempt it
standing and moving somewhere.

The next step is to take away half the bags; those without bags find partners like
magic. I call out combinations of body parts for the 2 children to put in the bag:
"Put one of each of your legs in the bag...One of each of your arms in the bag...All
4 arms...Both heads...All 4 legs." At the end I often ask one partner to put one leg
and a head in the bag while standing and for the other partner to carefully lead him
around the room. Of course they switch.

The power of the bags is that they offer an excuse for closeness. "It's not me, it's
the bag that is forcing me to be close to you." Most of the time, children simply forget to be shy.

Other props, like balls, ropes, the parachute, and scooters also foster friendships and
cooperation. These are described in Part 8.

STRICTLY PARTNER MOVEMENTS
   The following movements can only be done with a partner. These partner activities can
be done in the Free Traveling Structure (except for Give Your Teacher A Heart Attack
which must be more carefully controlled), or they can be done on the diagonal.

I use the Free Traveling Structure for calm classes and the Diagonal Structure for rambunctious classes. The benefits of the Free Traveling Structure are that it saves time
and the children can change partners. However, it is not worth risking the Free Traveling Structure if there is any doubt that someone may get hurt.

** Onion, potato, and peanut bags are sometimes available at old-fashioned grocery stores.
   If not, they can be easily sewn.

If we are using the Free Traveling Structure, I use a number of these partner movements as a lesson warm-up. If I decide to use the Diagonal Structure they become part of the locomotor movements done on the diagonal.

1) Side-slide. Partners stand facing one another. They hold both hands and side-slide.

2) Back to back side-slide. Partners stand back to back. They link elbows and side-slide.

3) Sitting down and getting up. Partners stand back to back, link elbows and sit down. They remain in that position and, with hands *not* touching the floor, they get up. (The trick is to push *against* your partner rather than lean forward.)

4) Flipping. Partners stand facing one another and hold both hands. They both go under their arms and end up back to back. (See illustration #4.) To teach the flip, ask the children to lift one arm, thereby forming a "bridge." *Both* children go "under the bridge" *at the same time*, twisting their arms around, and end up back to back. To return, they form a bridge and both back under it at the same time; they end up front to front again. Once the children get the idea, they can flip over and over in one continuous circular motion.

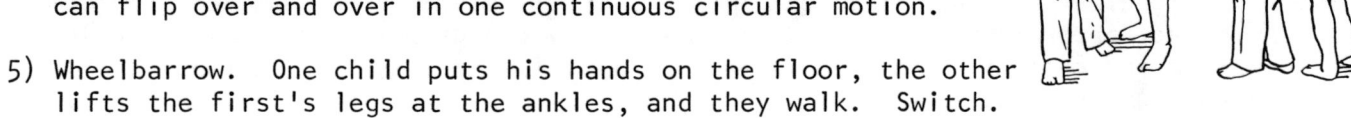

5) Wheelbarrow. One child puts his hands on the floor, the other lifts the first's legs at the ankles, and they walk. Switch.

6) Dragging. One person lies down on his back, hands behind his head. The partner lifts his ankles (not pantlegs because they can come off) and takes the lying down person for a ride. Often I begin this activity with the children practicing lifting and gently lowering their partner's legs. If they demonstrate gentle lowering they get the okay to begin the ride. Of course, switch positions.

7) Partner spin. Partners stand facing each other, hold on with 2 hands, and spin. The spin works best, that is, fast and exciting, if the children keep their feet close together, take little steps, and lean back.

   This partner spin, simple as it is, demonstrates a great deal about a child: Does he let himself get spun? Does he do all the spinning? Does he look like a straw in the wind? Often I find myself shouting, "Come on, Harry, pull your own weight! Don't let Robert pull you around, pull him!" Deep insight or not, the partner spin is a lot of fun.

8) Partner roll. "Get a partner and hold each other by 2 hands. Lie down and *without letting go of either hand*, roll."

   This initial roll is hysterical. Children roll on top of one another, get entangled among each other, and generally cause small scale havoc. Someone, it might be you, introduces the "secret" of the partner roll: lie facing each other. This makes for an easy partner roll. (See illustration #8.)

   Note: If you have an extra child and do not want to do the roll yourself, have the child join a group by holding on to another child's feet.

   When the children can do this partner roll easily, ask them to do it with tucked legs, that is, knees bent to the chest. The legs remain in that position throughout the roll.

9) Partner seat-scoot. Partners sit on the floor facing each other. Each takes hold of the other's ankles and they "go somewhere."

10) Hopping partners. Partners stand side by side or front to front and both lift a leg. Each holds his partner's leg so that both children have to hop to get anywhere. Switch legs.

11) Give Your Teacher A Heart Attack. Let me first say that in 9 years of doing Heart Attack no one has gotten hurt. I, however, have nearly fainted. This partner activity needs extremely clear traveling lines: it can be done on the diagonal or across the room from one side to the other *with only one partner group moving at a time*.

#11

One child lies down and rolls. The other child leaps over the rolling child, turns, and leaps in the opposite direction over the still rolling child. The faster the child rolls the harder (and scarier) it is. (See illustration #11. Note, of course, that the leaping child does not land on the rolling child as it might appear in the drawing.)

I organize Heart Attack by having all partners start on one side of the room; I select partners to go when it is safe. They change positions in the middle of the room and continue to the other side. All children stay on the new side until everyone has had a turn.

12) Leap frog. One partner crouches while the other jumps over him. They immediately switch positions.

MIRROR AND SHADOW*
Most people have done Mirror in drama or dance classes, group therapy, or education courses. Two children face each other; one moves slowly and smoothly while the other, his mirror, attempts to follow the movements precisely. The mirror's job is to move *with* the mover and not as an afterthought. The mover's job is to make the movements slow, smooth, predictable, and feasible. The children do not touch or speak. (It is ideal if they look only in each other's eyes and sense the movement, but I do not stress this with children.) The mover and mirror change roles frequently.

Shadow is a fast moving, locomotor Mirror. One child follows the other anywhere in the room moving in whatever way the leader moves. The leader can move as fast and as "crazy" as he wishes. Of course, the partners change roles frequently. Shadow is an excellent activity to follow Mirror; the children can release all the energy contained in the sustained Mirror movements.

LIFTING
"I am going to show you a way to lift somebody so that you could lift me, or your Mom or Dad." This is an attention getting statement, and true too. Lifting is at the apex of partner work; it requires a good deal of sensitivity, mutual trust, and cooperation. Once mastered, it is a lot of fun (even learning how to lift is fun) and it gives many children a boost in their feelings of self-esteem and physical power.

----
* The brilliant idea of Shadow comes from Ruth Bossieux.

I do lifting in 2 stages: stage one is easy and can be done with very young children; stage 2 is harder and can be done with children 2nd grade and higher. It is better if stage one is mastered before going on to stage 2.

STAGE 1

Two children sit on the floor back to back. They slowly rock forward and back. As one child rocks forward, the other child leans back, resting completely on the forward child's back. The child that is forward slowly pushes up (lifting the back and head of his partner) and the process is reversed. It is simply a rocking forward and back done with a partner. When the children are doing this, check to see that they are going slowly and carefully and that the person leaning back lets go of his weight and truly rests his back and head.

Now they are ready for the stage one lift. Once child leans forward as before, the legs are in any comfortable position and the *hands are on the floor*, ready to brace the child if he should go farther forward than is comfortable. The leaning child pushes up on the back of the forward child so that his whole weight is resting on the other. They stay like this for a short while (10 or 15 seconds) and slowly reverse positions. (See illustration above right.)

If, 1) the children are around the same size, if 2) the lifted child, the one on top, truly relaxes straightens his legs and lets his head and arms go, and if 3) the lifting child, the one on the bottom, braces himself with his hands, then there should be no pain. The bottom child will feel a strong stretch, especially if his legs are in wide stride, but he should not feel any real pain. If someone does, stop; something is wrong. Two common mistakes: the top child is not resting evenly on the bottom child's upper back, or the bottom child's elbows are straight, that is he is not allowing any push forward at all; this puts too much strain on the elbows and back.

In addition to all the social benefits, this partner lift is a good stretching exercise for the back and legs.

STAGE 2

Now for the real thing: the stand-up lift. (See illustration below right.) Partners stand back to back. At the beginning, partners need to be about the same size (height is more a factor than weight). Later, as I claimed, size will hardly matter. The child that is going to lift does 3 things: 1) links elbows with his partner, 2) keeps his back upright and *bends his knees so that his seat is below the other child's seat* (This is extremely important. In fact, it is the crux of this whole process.), and 3) hinges up, that is, straightens knees and bends forward at the same time, thereby lifting the other child. The most important thing is that the lifted child be high enough up on the lifting child's back, so that his seat is on the latter's lower back. The other thing is that the lifted child relax; a tense, rigid body is almost impossible to lift. The top child needs to let go of his head, arms, and legs, breathe deeply, and enjoy. The lifting child also needs to relax and take the weight in his knees as well as his back. They hold this position for a short while and reverse.

Again this is a good stretch, but it should not hurt. If it does, something is wrong. Ten to one what is wrong is that the lifting child (the one on the bottom) did not bend his knees enough, so that he did not go low enough, so that the top child did not get placed high enough on his back. Start again.

When the children are just learning to do this standing lift, I have them all in partners, but only allow one partner group to try it at a time so that I can supervise them completely. I certainly would not want someone getting hurt, or even unusually scared, just when we were working on building trust. Once a partner group has it (both children able to lift and get lifted) then they can "work" on their own.

Watch out that the bigger children do not do all the lifting and the smaller ones just get lifted. Many bad feelings about their bodies come out here: "I'm too big." "I'm too fat." "He'll never be able to get me off the ground." If the child is actually large, I will lift him until the other children learn how to do it and are able to lift the child. If you have a bad back or for some reason cannot lift, why not show some older children how to do it and have them help you?

If you can, let some competent lifters lift you. The kids will love it, you might too.

GROUP ACTIVITIES

NECESSITY OF GROUPS
Groups are necessary for the Diagonal Structure and for group studies. Groups are also an important teaching device in that 1) children learn a great deal from one another, and 2) groups provide excellent practice in cooperation and compromise.

If the children have done some partner activities, they will probably feel at ease working in groups. However, some special group activities are fun and useful.

STAYING TOGETHER
When doing locomotor movements on the diagonal, it is important that the groups stay together. Young children might hold hands but that is not workable with large, free, locomotor movements. For these young children groups I ask them to be peanut butter cookies: "The 3 of you, without holding hands, are one cookie. Stay together. Don't fall apart or you'll be crumbs."

For older children I stress compromise: "You run a little slower, you run a little faster, and see if you can stay together." Since children have such divergent abilities, I am not too strict on this point.

GROUP MOVEMENTS
The following are some activities that specifically promote group unity. These are done on the diagonal.

1) Group spin. A group of children hold hands to form a small circle and spins. This obviously is a take off on the partner spin, but it is even more exciting done in a group.

2) Can-can. The group holds shoulders and does their own version of a can-can dance. If treated with enough silliness, even boys like this one.

3) Horse in the Corral. One member of a group of 3 gallops forward, while the other 2 people hold hands around him and side-slide.

4) Carrying. Any method of 2 people carrying a 3rd is fun and is often requested. The easiest carry: one person lies down on his back and the other 2 people carry one arm and one leg each.

More complex, is the Seat Carriage: each of the 2 carrying people holds his left wrist with his right hand. (See illustration #4a.)

Then they hold each other's right wrist in order to form a solid square between them. (See illustration #4b.)

The 3rd person gently gets on and gets a seated ride. (See illustration #4c.)

In all rides, every person in the group gets a turn. Rides take longer than you might expect, and they are noisy and a bit chaotic. I do not think there is much you can or should do about this; I am just giving a small forewarning.

TONE OF THE CLASS

IMPORTANCE OF CLASS TONE
   The most significant contributor to children working together is the overall feeling of the class. The tone a class projects, mirrors itself in the children. If the general feeling of the class is warm, caring, and trusting, the children are likely to display those qualities with each other. No partner or group activities can overcome an unfriendly atmosphere.

PROMOTING A GOOD CLASS ATMOSPHERE
   Inumerable factors make up the emotional quality of a class. I want to mention 2 elements that are important and are easily forgotten: 1) take the time to lavish praise, and 2) take the risk to show some humanness.

Most teachers are friendly and caring, but we sometimes get caught in the rigors of curriculums and the push and pull of schedules. It is very easy to fall into the trap of a perfunctory "good work" and that is all. I believe that we should praise more, and more enthusiastically, than we criticize. That means taking the time and energy to call home about a job well done, write a note about a new achievement, twirl a child in the air for displaying self reliance, shake hands for showing a sense of fair play. Of course, this lavish praise can only take place within a framework of sound discipline. This all takes a lot of energy, but I have found that the more praise is lavished the less criticism will be needed.

Although it is sometimes embarrassing, I think it is important to show some of our human side. That means apologizing when necessary, admitting mistakes, and revealing some feelings both good and bad. If we want children to care about each other we must teach them that there is a common bond between people and, as an example, that bond exists between teachers and students. If we show care and respect to each child and demand care and respect back simply because we are all human beings, then the children are likely to start treating each other a little better.

PART 4
LEVELS

INTRODUCING LEVELS

DEFINITION
Level means height. The ability to use, recognize, and differentiate vertical space is an essential element in movement vocabulary. Level is a simple yet extraordinarily useful concept.

INTRODUCING THE WORD AND CONCEPT
We begin in Perfect Spots. "I am going to teach you a new word: 'level.' I am not going to tell you what it means; you'll have to guess." With the children imitating me, I demonstrate the 5 basic levels: air level (jumping); standing level (one or both feet on the ground); knee level (one or both knees on the ground); sitting level (sitting); lowest level (lying down).* The children and I go up and down through these 5 levels several times.

"What do you guess 'level' means?" Usually children see that level means high and low or up and down. If they do not guess, even with a few hints, I tell them. Sometimes a child brings up the idea that level means even or unbumpy. When that happens, I agree: "Yes, you are absolutely right. That is another meaning of 'level.' In movement class I use 'level' to mean height, like different floors in an office building."

TRYING THEM OUT
After the children go through the different levels with me, I ask them to find the levels without me.. I call out levels nonsequentially: "Air level...lowest level..knee level... sitting level..standing level.".I go fast and often play with the difference from air level to lowest level. If we have the time, I tease the class by doing a different level than the one I call: "I am going to trick all of you! I am going to call out a level but *do* something different. You do the level you hear, not the one you see. Can you do it?"

NONLOCOMOTOR MOVEMENTS
Now that the idea of levels is clear, we do nonlocomotor movements using levels. We do shake, swing, contract and stretch, and twist on all levels. For example: "How could you contract on the lowest level? Right, you would have to get on your back or side... Good...Now stay down there and stretch...Contract sitting up...How about stretch...Make

---

* What about squatting level or tip-toe level, or high knee and low knee level? I realize that the 5 levels I have listed are arbitrary. There could easily be 8 levels or more. If a class can remember and use 8 or 10 levels, all the better. Just the same, if a class would do better with 3 levels to start (low, medium, and high) that is fine. The goal is for the children to differentiate and use vertical space.

sure your legs stretch while you are sitting...Contract and stretch knee level...How about standing level?...Who can figure out how to contract air level?...Right, you have to jump and tuck in the air...Can you stretch air level?...Yes, it is like a cheerleader yell...Great!"

If the concept "nonlocomotor" has been taught, I use the term while working with levels; if it has not been taught, we just do them. Teaching movement is a juggling process. I want to teach one concept but need another concept in order for the children to understand the first completely. The result is that I teach what is necessary at the time. For example, I usually teach "level" before "nonlocomotor movements." We do nonlocomotor movements on different levels but I do not use the term "nonlocomotor." Later when I teach "nonlocomotor" we use a study that includes levels. There are 2 factors to this juggling process: 1) use what you need even if it has not been taught; 2) do not consider that using an idea is the same as teaching it.

After exploring nonlocomotor movements on all levels, we begin combining movements into studies.

NONLOCOMOTOR LEVEL STUDIES

STAGE 1
  In these first studies we use only one nonlocomotor movement and the levels are kept in sequential order.

1) Shake on all levels. Shake down through all the levels and back up again without ever stopping the shake: 8 beats down and 8 up, 4 beats down and 4 up, 2 beats down and 2 up.

2) Swing on all levels. Do 4 swings on each level from highest to lowest: air, standing, knee, sitting, lowest. Change levels quickly so that there is no break in the swing rhythm. Do 2 swings on each level with no rhythmic break.

3) Combine study 1 and 2. Shake from highest to lowest level and back up. Swing 2 swings on each level from air to lowest. Shake from lowest to air level and back down.

4) Twirl on each level: air level, jump-turn; standing level, twirl on one foot; knee level, twirl on knees with or without hands; sitting level, spin on seat; lowest level, spin on tummy or back. Twirl through all the levels without ever stopping the movement

5) Contract and stretch on each level. Contract and stretch 4 times on each level. Change levels quickly so that the rhythm is unbroken. Contract and stretch 2 times on each level, one time on each level.

    Contract on one level and stretch on the next higher level; stay on that level to contract again, and change levels to stretch. For example: contract *lowest* level and stretch *sitting* level, contract *sitting* level and stretch *knee* level, contract *knee* level and stretch *standing* level, contract *standing* level and stretch *air* level.

6) Combine study 4 and 5. Twirl from air level to lowest level without a break in the movement. Do the above example of contracting on one level and stretching on the next higher level. Twirl again from air level to lowest.

7) For young children (up to 3rd grade) rock on all levels using the Rocking Song, page 29.

   LOWEST LEVEL
   The children lie on their backs and rock from side to side. For a more difficult lowest level rock, the children lie on their stomachs and rock forward and back. Do this back-and-forth rock with legs and shoulders lifted off the ground, arms free, or with hands holding ankles. This is very strenuous. Do it only a few times. (See illustration at right.)

   SITTING LEVEL
   Children sit with legs crossed and rock from side to side. For a more difficult sitting level rock, stretch the legs wide and rock forward and back. When forward, the head goes as close to the floor as possible; when rocking back, the legs lift, still wide and straight, and hopefully touch the floor in back of the head. This is an excellent leg and back stretch.

   KNEE LEVEL
   The children rock sideways. The seat is lifted and the hands help push from side to side.

   STANDING LEVEL
   The children stand with legs apart and rock from side to side. The hands do not touch the floor; each rock is a balanced tilt with the opposite leg lifted. On the word "still" the children stay in that one-legged balance and become "still on the inside" so they can stay balanced longer. (See illustration at right.)

   AIR LEVEL
   The rocking is done like standing level, but with an added hop. This hop, of course, makes the final landing balance much harder.

8) Waves. Starting on lowest level, smoothly roll, rise, twirl, and turn through all levels like a wave rising out of the ocean, and jump breaking on shore. Have the wave recede down through all levels back to the spot from which it started. The movement can be structured to beats, for example, 8 beats for the wave to break, 13 beats to recede back to the original spot.

   In these initial studies I use only one or 2 nonlocomotor movements, the level changes move sequentially from lowest to highest or from highest down, and the rhythmic structure is simple. Changing one or more of these factors makes the study more difficult.

STAGE 2
The next stage is to combine different nonlocomotor movements but to still keep the levels in sequence.

1) Shake air level; swing standing level; contract and stretch knee level; spin sitting level; kick legs in the air lowest level. Do each movement for 4 beats.

2) Air level, jump turn for 4 beats; standing level, strike for 4 beats; knee level, swing for 4 beats; sitting level, contract and stretch for 4 beats; lowest level, have a temper tantrum for 8 beats.

Children love this temper tantrum. They wiggle, kick, thrash, and shout. My only restriction is that they must stop exactly on beat number 8. (They must control the yelling in order to hear the counts, but I do count very loudly.) If the children do not abide by the sound structuring, I do not let them do it, at least for the time being. Children love the opportunity to have a safe tantrum.

3) Shake on the lowest level, 3 beats; bounce seat on the floor, sitting level, 3 times; twirl on knee level (use hands on floor to push off into the twirl, but try to complete the twirl without hands touching), 3 beats; twist standing level, 3 beats; use the momentum of the twist to jump turn all the way around, air level.

4) Karate kick, air level, beats 1 and 2; contract and stretch, standing level, beats 3 and 4; spin, knee level, beats 5 and 6; shake hands and feet balanced on seat, sitting level, beats 7 to 8; have a temper tantrum, lowest level, beats 1 to 8.

STAGE 3
The last stage is to combine movements and mix up the level sequence.

1) Jump once air level; melt to sitting level; spin and tuck legs under to end up on stomach; pull seat back and lift to knee level; lift one knee in order to plant one foot firmly on the floor and stand.

If done to counts, this is an 8-beat study: 1--jump, 2--melt, 3--sit, 4--spin and tuck legs, 5--end on stomach, 6--pull seat back to heels, 7--plant foot, 8--stand, ready to repeat.

2) Fluid levels. 1--sit and spin; 2--throw legs under to lie on stomach; 3--pull up to knees; 4--side fall (see Part 5); 5--roll to back; 6--rock back and then roll up to an instant sitting balance; 7--bend one knee on the floor, the other foot flat on the floor near it, stand; 8--jump and sit, ready to start again. This is ideally done smoothly, one movement flowing into the next.

LOCOMOTOR MOVEMENTS ON LEVELS

CATEGORIZING LOCOMOTOR MOVEMENTS
Locomotor movements generally break down into the following classifications: Air level locomotor movements are those that leave the floor: jump, hop, skip, gallop, side-slide, and leap. Standing level locomotor movements: walk, jog, run. Knee level: crawl. Sit-

----

* What if the children come up with movements that do not fit the level categories, for example, a crab crawl or walking on one's hands? The children love to try to stump me. I will either make an approximation, "Crab crawl looks pretty much like an up-side-down knee level to me." or I will throw my hands up, "I have no idea what level walking on hands would be, do you?"

ting level: seat-scoot. Lowest level: sliding on stomach or back, rolling. The children will figure out most of this categorization. I fill in the blanks if they leave some out.* (See asterisk notation at the bottom of page 56.)

LOCOMOTOR LEVEL STUDIES

INTRODUCING THEM

We begin by moving on the diagonal. I divide the diagonal in half, and we do one level for the first half and another for the 2nd. For example, we do standing level run to the middle, pretend to get tackled, lowest level roll from the middle to the end. This division of the diagonal into 2 locomotor movements done on 2 different levels is the first initiation into locomotor level studies. Following are some additional locomotor level studies.

TEACHER TAUGHT COMBINATIONS

1) Spider crawl, 4 beats; tuck (cat) roll, 2 beats, stretch on knees, 2 beats; repeat tuck roll, 2 beats, stretch on knees, 2 beats; low, mean looking walks, 4 beats; turning walks, 2 beats, stretch jumps, 2 beats; repeat turning walks, 2 beats, stretch jumps, 2 beats.

   The count is 6 measures of 4 beats. The quality is like the hunter and the hunted. The spider crawl and the low walks are done with a mean, aggressive, hunter look. The rolls and stretches, and the turning walks and jump stretches are done like a little hunted animal running away. After the children know the study very well, add appropriate sounds and have the groups begin 4 beats apart.

2) Leap, 4 beats; roll, 4 beats; run, 4 beats; balance in a one-legged shape, 4 beats.

3) Jump, 4 beats; walk, 4 beats; walk on knees, 4 beats; seat-scoot backwards, 4 beats; collapse to lowest level. There is no extra time for the level changes.

TEACHER STRUCTURED GROUP PROBLEMS

1) Make up a pattern using 5 different locomotor movements on 5 different levels.

2) Make up a pattern using one locomotor movement done on 5 different levels.

3) Going across the diagonal, use 3 different locomotor movements on 3 different levels in 20 beats.

CONCLUDING

USES OF LEVELS

Levels open up a gold mine of movement ideas. If a group of students brings you a deathly boring study, tell them to use level changes. If your locomotor movements are getting too repetitious, use level changes. If a pattern is too easy, use level changes. Sounds miraculous? It is.

PART 5
NONLOCOMOTOR MOVEMENTS

INTRODUCTION

DEFINITION
Nonlocomotor movements are those that stay in one place. Generally children do not like them as much as locomotor movements. The challenge in teaching nonlocomotor movements is to expand the children's thinking so that nonlocomotor movements become an exciting part of their movement vocabulary.

Like locomotor movements, nonlocomotor movements can be categorized into basic movements and variations. This catalog and studies combining movements is found at the end of Part 5.

INTRODUCING THE TERM
"You know what 'locomotor' means, right?* Good. Now I have a question for you: 'Non' means 'not,' so what do you guess '*non*locomotor' means?" (As I say the word "nonlocomotor" I shake my finger no.)

Even pre-schoolers will shout brilliantly: "Not locomotor." "Right. Now, what could 'not locomotor' mean?" Again, either immediately or with some prodding, they will conclude: "Not locomotor means not going anywhere." A tangle of negatives.

I then shift the emphasis from "not moving" to "moving but staying in one place." The final result of this definition work: nonlocomotor means moving in one spot.

INTRODUCING THE CONCEPT
"How in the world can you move but stay in one spot?" Some children understand immediately and some look up in blank dismay. This is a judgement crossroad. It is much better for children to figure out "logic" problems for themselves. I make a snap decision whether the children are simply not concentrating, in which case I will wait and prod, ("Come on. What can you possibly move while staying right here?") Whether they need a hint ("Maybe you figure out one part of your body that can move without the rest of you going anywhere."), or whether they are truly stumped ("I'll show you some ways to move in one spot and then you think of some different ways.")

Once they get the idea of how to move in one spot, I ask the children to think of many different nonlocomotor movements. They will mostly jump, hop, and run in place. I accept everything as long as it is in place. We try them all out saying the word "nonlocomotor" while moving.

---

* If the class is not completely at ease with the term "locomotor" do not go on. I teach nonlocomotor in relation to locomotor. If locomotor is unclear, the result is pure confusion.

ALTERNATING LOCOMOTOR AND NONLOCOMOTOR MOVEMENTS

The next step is to alternate locomotor and nonlocomotor movements, in order to make the distinction clear. This is done in the Free Traveling Structure.

"When you hear the piano, do a locomotor movement; when you hear the drum, do a nonlocomotor movement. What do you do when the sound stops? Right, freeze." I use this alternation to suggest nonlocomotor movements that they have overlooked; if the children do not understand a movement, I demonstrate it. I am not fussy about how the movements are done, but I insist that the nonlocomotor movements remain exactly in whatever place the child stopped.

SUGGESTED PROGRESSION

Locomotor (piano sound)	Nonlocomotor (drum sound)
1) Skip	Swing
2) Hopscotch	Spin on seat
3) Run	Shake
4) Leap	Strike
5) Any locomotor movement	Nonlocomotor movement with just arms
6) Any locomotor movement	Nonlocomotor movement with just torso
7) Any locomotor movement	Any nonlocomotor movement

EXPANDING NONLOCOMOTOR MOVEMENT VOCABULARY

WAYS TO EXPAND

We spend 2 or 3 lessons exploring the children's own nonlocomotor movements. Often children are limited in thinking of nonlocomotor movements; their movements are repetitive and halfhearted. Most often children will simply do locomotor movements in place, for example, running in place. (More on that later.)

At this stage I want to expand their thinking rather than impose new movements. There are 3 ways to increase nonlocomotor movement vocabulary without introducing specific movements: 1) suggest an isolated movement, 2) suggest a change of level, 3) suggest a change in size.

ISOLATED MOVEMENTS

"Isolated movements" means to move one body part while forcing the rest of the body to remain still. Isolation of movements is good for concentration and coordination. It takes a great deal of focused energy to lift one shoulder and not the other, to wiggle toes but not fingers.

"What ways can you move *just* your head?...Just your shoulder?...Seat?...Torso?... Move just your eyes and keep everything else still...Move just one leg, but don't let your arms or anything else move...Move just your hips...Pick one part of your body and move it...Pick 2 parts of your body and move them one after the other... First body part...Second body part...Can you move them at the same time?...Great!"

How precisely isolated these movements are, of course, depends on the age and ability of the children. As long as a child is concentrating, I am satisfied with the resulting movement.

CHANGING LEVELS

Changing levels quickly eradicates the stationary locomotor movement syndrome. A run in place done on the lowest level becomes something like a shoulder stand bicycle; a skip done on sitting level becomes a kicky, swingy movement. Further, changing levels makes the most ordinary movements more exciting. For example, nonlocomotor movement shake done while going from air level down to lowest level and back up, becomes exciting to watch and to do.

"Do a nonlocomotor movement on lowest level...Do the same thing on air level... What could you do on the knee level?...Sitting level?...Do a nonlocomotor movement and change levels without ever stopping the movement...Terrific!"

MOVEMENT SIZE

Most children do nonlocomotor movements all one size: medium. A change either way, smaller or bigger, enlivens most any movement.

"Do the nonlocomotor movement swing...Make it smaller and smaller until I can barely see the swing. (Children love to "trick" me by making the movement so miniscule as to be invisible. They tell me, "But I am moving! Look at my big toe.") Now make it huge so that the swing is your whole body...Bigger!...Bigger!"

WHEN TO USE THESE TECHNIQUES

These techniques, isolation, level changes, and size changes, are used initially when the children work on their own nonlocomotor movements, and later when they work on specific nonlocomotor movements. They fit into a lesson most easily as a warm-up activity. For example, alternate locomotor and nonlocomotor movements in the Free Traveling Structure:

Locomotor (piano sound)   Nonlocomotor (drum sound)

1) Skip-----------------------------------Isolated nonlocomotor movements: shoulder, head, hips, leg, torso.
2) Jump, then hop, then hopscotch---------Nonlocomotor movements changing levels.
3) Run, then run and leap-----------------Nonlocomotor movements getting smaller and smaller, then getting bigger and bigger.

INTRODUCING SPECIFIC NONLOCOMOTOR MOVEMENTS

FRAMEWORK

Following will be examples of how I introduce specific nonlocomotor movements. I often use studies within my introductions, therefore some initial studies will be included. Following that will be a catalog of nonlocomotor movements and more studies.

INTRODUCING "SHAKE"

The children are in Perfect Spots, sitting down.

"What does 'shake' mean?"

"Wriggling." "Shaking the rug out." "Giggling with my body." "Being tickled."

"Right. Those are great pictures!"

We then work with shake using the 3 techniques mentioned above: isolated movements, change of levels, and change of size. "Let's shake our hands...Now just our arms... Legs...Torso...Whole body...Harder!...Let's shake lowest level...Sitting level...Knee level...Standing...Can you shake air level?...Yes, you have to jump and shake at the same time to do it. Do a shake that is so tiny I can barely see it...Where did it go? ...Now shake so hard that it tingles...Harder!...Now look, I'm going to shake and change levels and never stop the shake (I demonstrate). You do it...Go all the way from air level through to lowest level and back up...Keep going...Great!"

Shake is easily understood and just as easily done. Therefore it makes a good first nonlocomotor movement. The only thing to watch is that the torso shakes along with the arms and legs. I usually conclude this introduction with a short study.

A beginning study might use shake within the Diagonal Structure. The children pick one locomotor movement to do the middle of the diagonal. In the middle they shake, going to lowest level and back up to air level without stopping the shake. Then they do a different locomotor movement to the end of the diagonal. Possible result: skip, shake, run.

INTRODUCING "SWING"

A "swing" is an arc shaped movement, usually with a release of tension at the low point of the arc. It is such a useful movement that I often introduce it 2nd. We work on isolated swings, whole body swings, and swings on different levels.

ISOLATED SWINGS

"Swing one arm...Both arms...Swing a leg...Switch...Swing your hands...Your head... Can you swing just your torso?...Swing your hips...Pretty jazzy!" These individual body swings can combine to make interesting studies by themselves:

1) Swing right arm, front to back, beats 1 and 2; swing left arm, front to back, beats 3 and 4; swing right leg front to back, beats 5 and 6; swing left leg, front to back, beats 7 and 8. Swing head, left to right, beats 9 and 10; swing torso and head, right to left, beats 11 and 12; swing hips, left to right, beats 13 and 14; shake whole body vigorously, beats 15 and 16.

2) Pick 4 parts of your body to swing. Swing each part for 6 beats. Remember your pattern.

WHOLE BODY SWINGS

"Can you swing so big that your whole body is swinging?...Bend your knees so that you touch the ground ...Good." At this beginning stage I work with 4 basic full body swings: front, crossed, side, and twisted. More full body swings are described in the catalog.

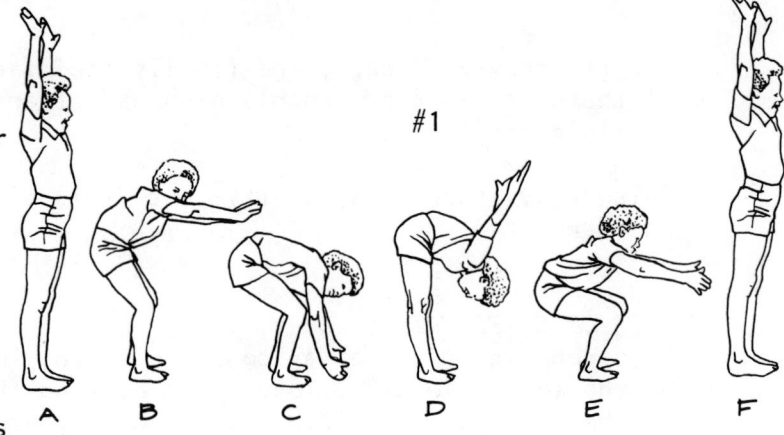

Front Swing

Children start standing with arms above the heads. Arms, head, and torso drop forward; hands touch the floor as the knees bend. The torso stays lowered as the arms swing back, knees straighten. That is one arc. To come back, the knees bend, hands touch the floor, and arms, head, and torso reach out in front and up. (See illustration #1.)

Crossed Swing

Children start standing with arms and legs wide apart. Torso and knees bend as arms drop to the ground. Knees straighten as arms cross in front of the body, but the torso remains bent. This is one arc. The arc is reversed as the arms uncross and drop, the torso and knees bend, and then straighten as arms end wide again. (See illustration #2.)

For young children, I do the crossed swing to this image: "Pick up a kitten," (first arc) "Let her go," (second arc). For older children I simply say "crossed swing and open."

Side Swing

Children stand, leaning to one side, arms over head. Everything (arms, head, torso, and knees) drops and straightens to the other side. That is one arc. The arc is reversed to the other side.
(See illustration #3.)

Twist Swing

Children stand with their arms held wide. Arms, torso, and head swing around to twist to one side and then to the other side. Ideally the hips work to remain facing front. In the twist swing, the arc shape of the swing is horizontal to the floor as opposed to the front, crossed, and side swings where the arc is vertical.

One of my favorite studies sequences the above 4 swings: 1) front swing and up, 2) crossed swing and open, 3) side swing and swing back, 4) twist swing and swing back. (The last twist swing spins around to start again.) We do 4 of each of the swings, then 2 of each, and finally one of each. When doing one of each swing see if the children can smoothly blend the transitions between swings so that the study is fluid and lyrical.

This study is not only pretty, but it is also an excellent body warm-up. I use it often.

SWINGS ON DIFFERENT LEVELS
"Who can figure out a way to swing on the lowest level?...Can you swing your legs on the lowest level?...Your whole body on the lowest level?...How can you swing on the sitting level?...How about with your legs wide on the sitting level?...How can we swing on the knee level?...Standing level?...Air level?" (Air level will be a swing and jump, going into the air at either end of the swing arc.) "Swing and change levels."

An interesting study results simply from doing a swing on one level and then changing levels and freezing in a "strange shape." The rhythm is swing 2-3, swing back 2-3, change le-vels and freeze. Go from air level down to lowest.

RELEASING SWING ENERGY
One difficulty with swings in general is letting go of the energy at the bottom of the arc. Children often want to stay in tight control, but that negates the flowing quality of the movement. To encourage the risk of letting go, I ask the children to shout "Blah" as they drop into a swing. This sound forces a quick exhalation, which forces a muscular release. The children, of course, think it is fun and anyone passing by will think it strange.

INTRODUCING "CONTRACT AND STRETCH"
Contract and stretch are my favorite nonlocomotor movements. "Contract" is a tight curling or rounding and "stretch" is a vigorous expanding or opening. They are a lot of fun to teach.

The children sit on the floor gathered around me. "'Contract' means to curl up tight like a fist (I close my hands into tight fists), and 'stretch' means to open wide, big, long, (I open my hands wide). Let's do the movements together and say the words at the same time."

The children and I contract and stretch different parts of the body. Each time, we shout out the word as we do the movement. We contract and stretch hands, arms, legs, faces, (Faces? Sure. Contract by squishing together your features and stretch by opening them wide.) necks, and torsos. Torsos curl as if "hit in the stomach" for contract and arch back for stretch. It is important to pay attention to the torso because children often neglect it.

After working with individual body parts the children contract and stretch their entire bodies. To get variety, I ask for different levels: "Can you contract on the lowest level?...Stretch on knee level?...Stretch one leg out while on knee level... Contract standing level and lift one leg off the floor...Stretch with that leg I lifted... Contract air level...Stretch air level...Wonderful!"

PUTTING ENERGY IN
"This is a grown-up idea," I say. "Look at my hand (I loosely close my hand). It is in a contracted *position* but this is not a *real contraction* because it is not tight and hard (I clench my fist extremely hard). The same goes for stretch (I show my hand open but not extended). This is a stretched *position* but it is not a *real stretch* because it is not pulled hard (I extend my hand completely). So when you contract your body let me see a real contraction, hard and tight and strong! Who can do that?...Great! Now let me see a real stretch, pull more, harder, pull your fingers, your toes, your nose, your eyebrows, your teeth... Fantastic! You look beautiful!"

INCLUDING "LIMP"
It is a good idea to introduce "limp" with contract and stretch in order to release the tension. I do not plan a formal introduction for limp; I just include it with the contract and stretch: "Do a hard contract...Do a huge stretch...Fine, now let everything go and hang limp...Make sure your head and neck let go too."

An introductory study uses contract, stretch, limp, and a locomotor movement. Contract on one level, change levels and stretch, and hang limp; then do a locomotor movement on any level. The rhythm is contract 1-2, change levels and stretch 3-4, hang limp 5-8, go somewhere 1-8.

PARTNERS
Contract and stretch are great to do with partners. I ask the children to contract not only their own bodies, but to contract with their partners so that they are like one ball. Partners usually hug or lean over one another. For the stretch, partners must touch and pull away. The sculptural designs are especially beautiful with the stretch if the partners use different levels, for example, one person stretches on the standing level while the other stretches on the lowest level; the standing child holds the other's foot.

This partner contract and stretch can be expanded into a group contract and stretch: "You and your partner combine with another 2 people and all 4 of you contract... Now all 4 of you stretch...Hold on...Can you get on 4 different levels and stretch... Beautiful...How about if a group of 4 combined with another group of 4, and all 8 of you contracted into one big ball...All 8 of you hold on to each other and stretch... Terrific!"

INTRODUCING "STRIKE"
A "strike" is a punch or hitting motion. It can be done like a boxer's punch or like a "Karate chop." The movement is hard and forceful. After telling the children the meaning of strike, I ask them to strike with their arms, legs (like Karate kicks), torsos (the whole upper body vigorously bends forward), elbows, shoulders, heads, and hips (a thrust to the side). Nonlocomotor movement strike is easy for children to understand. The only point to check is that they strike with energy and gusto.

A great study sequences these 4 strikes: 1) arms, 2) legs, 3) torso, 4) hips. Do 4 of each strike, 2 of each, then finally one of each. Striking each of the body parts once creates a nice jazzy rhythm: arm-leg-torso-hip.

INTRODUCING "TWIST"
   A "twist" is a stretch in 2 opposite directions. I hold up a large piece of paper wrapped around a book or rock, as if it were an enormous piece of candy: "You know how the ends of candies are twisted shut; to do that I have to turn this part (the center part of the candy) one way and the end of the paper the other way." I dramatically twist both sides. "That is all a twist is: one side goes one way while another side goes the other way."

We twist arms, legs, heads, hands, fingers, mouths, torsos. Arms and legs can be twisted singly from the joint socket, or can be twisted together like a pretzel. Twisting the torso is difficult for a number of children. To begin, I ask the children to lie down on their backs and roll their hips one way while their shoulders roll to the other side. Once they feel the movement lying down, we do it standing up.

After exploring the twist with individual body parts, I ask for several simultaneous twists: arms and legs, torso and head, fingers and toes, torso and arms, legs and head. We then try a few full body twists: "I hope you will be able to untangle yourselves!"

An introductory study sequences 3 twists and adds a shake: twist right arm and come back, beats 1 and 2; twist right leg and come back, beats 3 and 4; twist torso and come back, beats 5 and 6; shake out, beats 7 and 8; twist left arm and come back, beats 1 and 2; twist left leg and come back, beats 3 and 4; twist torso and come back, beats 5 and 6; shake out, beats 7 and 8.

   SPIRAL TWIST FALL
   A special use of twist is in the "spiral twist fall." This is a specific movement fall. (A "fall" in dance is a controlled lowering of the body. See Part 10.) It is a beautiful and extremely useful movement for older children (2nd grade and up).

The children start in Perfect Spots. They stand with their legs wide, facing the *back* of the room. Keeping the legs where they are, the children twist around so that they are facing the front of the room. The crux of the movement is that the *feet stay in place* but the torso, hips, and feet pivot around. When the torso is completely twisted (facing front) the legs bend (the back foot changes its weight to the top arch of the foot) until the person is sitting. The legs end up tightly crossed one over the other. (See illustration above right.)

The control for the spiral twist fall comes from pulling the weight forward onto the front thigh. Ideally, the movement is tightly controlled so that it can be done in slow motion and stopped at any point. It is most dramatic, however, when done quickly.

INTRODUCING "BEND AND STRAIGHTEN"
   A "bend" is a folding of 2 straight sides, like a book or a piece of paper. It is a hinge-like action. "Straighten" is an unhinging or aligning of the 2 sides. Of all the nonlocomotor movements, bend and straighten seem the hardest to do correctly.

I hold up a piece of cardboard: "Bend means folding 2 straight sides (I fold the cardboard). Straighten means putting the sides in one line (I straighten the cardboard).

That is pretty clear, huh? Now, I have a tough question for you: What is the difference between contract and stretch, and bend and straighten?"

The idea is that contract is a rounding or curling while bend is a folding of 2 straight sides. Stretch is an extended lengthening while straighten is purely an alignment of the 2 sides. If your class answers in any coherent form, congratulations! They understand a great deal about movement and about how their own bodies can move.

We bend and straighten isolated parts of the body, hinging from elbows, knees, wrists, ankles, arms hinging at the shoulder, legs hinging at the hip joint. These are relatively simple. The difficulty comes from the full body hinges. Usually a full body bend is done with the torso bending at the hip joint and *remaining straight*. The arms can remain by the side of the body or, harder, can reach front. If the children are having a lot of trouble, have them bend their knees, straighten their torsos forward, and then straighten their knees. This particular bend and straighten is excellent for back strength.

Another full body bend and straighten is done on knee level. The torso and hips remain absolutely straight while hinging back. This is excellent for strengthening the thighs. (See illustration at right.)

As the children pointed out to me, a straighten for this bend has to be falling flat on one's face.

A simple introductory study: bend and straighten the right arm, beats 1 and 2; bend and straighten the left arm, beats 3 and 4; bend and straighten the right leg, beats 5 and 6; bend and straighten the left leg, beats 7 and 8; bend and straighten the torso, beats 9 and 10; jump turning all around ready to begin again, beats 11 and 12.

INTRODUCING "SPIN, TURN, OR TWIRL"
To spin, the body rotates in space but remains in place. Children are familar with spinning so I do not make a special verbal introduction. "How many ways can your body spin?"

The children will immediately think of spinning of their seats. We also spin on different levels: stomach and backs, knees, feet, and in the air. Once the children have spun on all levels, ask them to turn and change levels without stopping the movement.

Turning from air level through to lowest level, without ever stopping, immediately creates a beautiful study. Specific beats for the turns completes the study. The beats can be kept the same, for example, 3 beats for air level turn, 3 beats for standing level, etc.; or each turn can get a different number of beats, for example, one beat for air level turn, 7 beats for standing level, 2 beats for knee level, 5 beats for sitting level, and 10 beats for lowest level. The movement should flow through each level change.

ONE FOOT STANDING TWIRL
A standing level turn can be done easily by taking little steps all around, or, with more difficulty, by balancing on the ball of one foot while twirling around. This one-foot twirl is dance studio work but most children enjoy trying it. Here are a few tricks to accomplishing this turn: 1) Step immediately up to the half-toe

rather than swooping up. 2) Keep the body aligned and stretched up (easier said than done). 3) Use less energy than you think necessary. 4) Keep the standing leg, the leg you are turning on, straight.

I do not attempt to teach a perfected one-foot twirl except in experienced dance classes.

FRACTION JUMP TURNS
   Air level turns (jump turns) are fun in themselves and are useful for working with fractions. The class stands in Perfect Spots. I show the traditional pie cut in fourths and ask the children what jumping in fourths would mean. Most children see that it means taking 4 jumps to get completely around. (If not, I tell them.) I demonstrate, exaggerating stiff, precise quarter turns: I jump to squarely face one side of the room, the back of the room, the other side of the room, and the front of the room. The children then do quarter turn jumps. For older classes, I include right and left directions: quarter turns to the right begin going right, to the left, go left.

Half turns are next. Children jump twice, first facing the back of the room and then jumping to face front. Again older children are asked to go to the right and left.

Full turns are complete turns in the air. These can also go to the right and left.

These fraction turns combine nicely into a pattern. The children stand in Perfect Spots: quarter turn, quarter turn, quarter turn, quarter turn, half turn, half turn, full turn. Older children do the pattern twice, once going to the right and once to the left. We work on going faster and faster while keeping the turns very precise.

ROTATION OR CIRCLE TURNS
   A different type of turn comes from individual body parts rotating or circling around. Arms, legs, the head, shoulders, upper torso, entire torso, and hips can all rotate from the joint. This kind of movement is good for limbering up and for isolation control. It creates a jazzy effect.

Combining a few of these rotating turns makes an interesting study: The children start standing. The head circles. When it reaches its starting point, the upper torso (waist up) rotates. Just as this circle is complete, the entire torso (hips up) rotates. This completed movement propels the entire body to twirl on one foot, back to starting position. There are no specific counts. The quality is loose, almost rag doll limp, and each turn propels the following one, like a pebble causing concentric circles in water.

TWO PROBLEMS WITH NONLOCOMOTOR MOVEMENTS

TRUE NONLOCOMOTOR MOVEMENTS
   Shake, swing, contract and stretch, strike, twist, bend and straighten, and turn are

the specific nonlocomotor movements we work on. Hopefully the children will incorporate some of these movements when creating their own nonlocomotor movements. Despite my persistent efforts, however, many children still think of nonlocomotor movements mainly as stationary locomotor movements. When asked to create a nonlocomotor movement, they will run or jump in place. It is then time for my "true nonlocomotor movements" speech.

"I have a grown-up idea to tell you. Running, jumping, hopping, skipping *in place* are *technically* nonlocomotor movements because they do not go anywhere, but they are not *true* nonlocomotor movements. What I mean is that running is *usually* a locomotor movement and it is the technicality of doing it in place that makes it become a nonlocomotor movement. The same goes for jumping, hopping, skipping, and so on. There are some movements, however, that are never locomotor movements by themselves. These movements are shake, swing, contract and stretch, strike, bend and straighten, twist, and turn. These are *true* nonlocomotor movements because they can not go anywhere by themselves. If you understand this, great! If you don't, don't worry about it."

DANCE
It is curious that working with nonlocomotor movements often brings up the word "dance." The word "dance" is one of the biggest bug-a-boos in teaching movement. I have had 2 kinds of disconcerting experiences with this word. In dance classes the children do beautiful dances with a prop or a movement problem and then ask me, "When are we going to dance?" The opposite problem occurs in schools where I teach perceptual-motor coordination. If I say something like "Now we are going to do the Fall Dance," the class gasps in horror as if I had said the word "sex."

I think the whole thing is ridiculous. I think it is unfortunate that children do not know when they have created a dance and just as unfortunate when children cannot move if they think they are dancing. What I do is use the word when it is appropriate and not use it when it is not. I call my school classes "movement classes" explaining that we do all sorts of movements: gymnastics, dance, physical education, and play. Later, when it is appropriate, I explain that a dance has a beginning, middle, and end, and usually is repeatable. If they create a dance I call it that. Generally I find that if I am relaxed with the word the children will eventually become relaxed with it too.

LOCOMOTOR PLUS NONLOCOMOTOR MOVEMENTS

A MILESTONE
It is a milestone when your children understand and feel comfortable with both locomotor and nonlocomotor movements because they have completed the ground work of their movement foundation. It is time to put them together.

INTRODUCING THE IDEA
"Do you know what locomotor movements are?"

"Yes."

"Do you know what nonlocomotor movements are?"

"Yes."

"Good. Pretend this is a locomotor movement (I lift one hand); this is a nonlocomotor movement (I lift my other hand). Who can figure out how to put a locomotor and a nonlocomotor movement together?" (I slap my hands together.)

The usual response is silent disbelief in the possibility. A few children will come up with an interesting solution: they do a locomotor movement, say walk, then stop and do a nonlocomotor movement, perhaps swing. So the result is walk-walk-walk-swing-swing-walk-walk, etc. I think this is excellent thinking and I praise the solution highly. However, I persist in asking for a locomotor and nonlocomotor movement going on *at the same time*.

Occasionally, I will attempt one hint before giving in and showing an example. "Remember, they do not have to be in the same parts of the body." Hopefully, someone will figure it out; that child is twirled, praised, and applauded.

EXAMPLES OF COMBINED LOCOMOTOR AND NONLOCOMOTOR MOVEMENTS

Here are some examples of combinations that work. The combinations are clearer if the nonlocomotor movement is done first and then the locomotor movement is added to it. I use the Free Traveling Structure to work on these.

1) Nonlocomotor swing your arms plus locomotor skip. Backwards?
2) Nonlocomotor swing your arms plus locomotor gallop.
3) Nonlocomotor shake your head "no" plus locomotor jump. Backwards? Sideways?
4) Nonlocomotor shake one leg plus locomotor hop on the other; change legs. Turning direction?
5) Nonlocomotor contract and stretch plus locomotor roll. (Contract while on the back and stretch while on the tummy.)
6) Nonlocomotor wiggle the shoulders plus locomotor seat-scoot. Backwards?
7) Nonlocomotor shake the head "yes" plus locomotor crawl. Sideways?
8) Nonlocomotor shake the hands plus locomotor run.
9) Nonlocomotor contract and stretch plus locomotor walk.
10) Nonlocomotor contract and stretch plus locomotor skip. (This is hard and is an excellent coordination problem.)
11) Nonlocomotor swing the arms cross and open plus locomotor side-slide changing sides.
12) Nonlocomotor strike plus locomotor walk. Change levels?
13) Nonlocomotor bend and straighten plus locomotor jump.
14) Nonlocomotor twist in the arms and torso plus locomotor skip.
15) Nonlocomotor twist in arms, rotating back and forth in the arm joint, plus locomotor jump with legs wide. (An African dance movement.)
16) Nonlocomotor wiggle in the hips plus locomotor walk.

USES FOR MOVEMENT COMBINATIONS

These locomotor and nonlocomotor combinations are wonderful warm-up activities for minds and bodies. At the beginning of class we do 3 to 7 of them, using the Free Traveling Structure. I am not critical of individual children, but check to see that the class as a whole has it; if not, I stop and demonstrate.

Locomotor and nonlocomotor combinations also provide an extra challenge used within a Brain Catcher Game (see Part 7). It makes this memory exercise a hundred times harder. For example, 1) nonlocomotor swing in the arms plus locomotor skip; 2) nonlocomotor contract and stretch plus locomotor roll; 3) nonlocomotor wiggle in the hips plus locomotor walk. This is a great deal harder to remember than 3 single movements.

Locomotor and nonlocomotor combinations can be used in concept combinations. It is always nice to see how much your class has achieved. If you have taught locomotor, nonlocomotor, floor pattern, direction, and level, try these instructions *strictly verbally.**

"Do the nonlocomotor movement shake in the arms, plus the locomotor movement walk, standing level, forward direction, in the floor pattern of a zigzag line." The thinking is hard but the result is easy. If the children get it, propose a toast, the children have understood a new language.

Here are a few more concept combinations:

1) Do the nonlocomotor movement swing in the arms plus the locomotor movement sideslide, obviously sideways direction, changing sides. Do the whole thing in a large circle floor pattern.
2) While doing the nonlocomotor movement wiggle with your shoulders, do the locomotor movement jump, air level, turning around direction. Do the whole thing in a circular floor pattern. (This combination emphasizes the difference between turning direction and circular floor pattern.)
3) Do the nonlocomotor movement contract and stretch plus the locomotor movement roll, lowest level, in the floor pattern of a straight line.
4) Do the nonlocomotor movement strike with your arms plus the locomotor movement run, standing level, backward direction, in a spiral floor pattern.

More of these concept combinations are in Part 6. If you understood them, congratulations! You have learned to read movement.

CATALOG OF NONLOCOMOTOR MOVEMENTS

1) SHAKE

VARIATIONS
   a) Isolated body parts: hand, arm, leg, torso, seat.
   b) Whole body. (Check that the torso is included.)
   c) Levels: air, standing, knee, sitting, lowest.
   d) Vibration. This is an extremely tight, quick, small shake, usually done in one part of the body like an arm or leg.
   e) Tantrum. This is a wiggling, kicking shake, usually done on lowest level. A tantrum is best accompanied by appropriate sounds.
   f) Size: small, big, growing, diminishing.
   g) Energy: limp, strenuous.
   h) Partners: shake hands, feet, heads, seats, elbows, etc.
   i) Combine with locomotor movements: roll, crawl, jump, hop, run, etc.
   j) Wiggle. Essentially the same as a shake. Generally a wiggle implies a slower shake usually in one part of the body, for example, "wiggle your hips."

---
* Say the instructions slowly and pause at the end of each phrase so that the children can visualize the movement.

2) SWING (an arc shaped movement usually with a release of tension at the low point of the arc)

VARIATIONS
   a) Isolated body parts: arm, leg, head, hips, hand, etc. Arms and legs can be swung either bent or straight.
   b) Front swing. Arms start above the head. Arms, head, and torso drop forward; hands touch the floor as knees bend. The torso stays lowered as arms reach back, knees straighten. That is one arc. To come back, the knees bend, hands touch the floor and every thing reaches up.
   c) Crossed swing. Arms and legs start wide. Torso and knees bend as arms drop to the ground and cross in front of the body; the torso remains bent. That is one arc. The arc is reversed as the arms uncross and drop; the torso and knees bend and then straighten as the arms open wide again.
   d) Side swing. Arms, head, and torso all lean to one side, arms are above the head. Everything drops and straightens to the other side. That is one arc. The arc is reversed. The side swing can also be done with hands clasped.
   e) Circle swing. This is like a side swing that continues around to outline an entire circle. The body leans to one side, arms overhead. The body drops and swings to the other side then reaches up and around to the original side. The circle swing can be done with isolated body parts (head, head and torso, arms, legs) or it can be done with the whole body. Arms can be clasped together or apart.
   f) Fan swing. This is a specific circle swing done with the leg. The child starts standing, legs together. The circling leg crosses over the other leg, opens wide, and returns to the starting position. The fan swing can be done lying down, resulting in a fan roll. The child starts lying on his back on the floor. The circling leg crosses the other leg, reaches up, and opens wide. As the leg returns to the side, the body rolls over.
   g) Figure eight swing. This is like the circle swing extended to a figure 8. The figure 8 can be done vertically with the arms and torso or horizontally with a leg.
   h) Twist swing. The child starts standing arms wide, feet and hips stable. The arms swing around to the back, twisting the torso. That is one arc. The arc is reversed to the other side. It is difficult, but better, if the hips work to remain facing front. For young children I sometimes use the image of a helicopter; we start slow and swing faster and faster.
   i) Body wave. I am not sure this is truly a swing but it is an arc shaped movement and comes closest to the swing category. The body wave is like a reversed front swing. The hips start by pushing forward, the waist then pushes forward, then the upper back, and finally the head. It is a ripple through the body. The arms meanwhile move in a circle: they start overhead, move forward, down, and back and up. The torso and arms flow together in one fluid movement. (See illustration #2i.)
   j) Size: huge, big, medium, small, tiny.
   k) Energy: limp, strenuous.
   l) Combine with locomotor movements: skip, gallop, jump, sideslide, walk, etc.
   m) Levels: air, standing, knee, sitting, lowest. Virtually all swings can be done on all levels.
      1) On the lowest level ask for swings of legs and hips as well as arms. Check that the swings do not deteriorate into shakes.
      2) A difficult swing on sitting level is done with the legs wide. The torso starts erect (a difficult position for most children), the hands clasp, the torso drops over one leg and swings to the other leg. (Try to reach forward at the midpoint of the swing.) The arc is reversed by swinging back to the original leg. This is a good stretch for the inner thigh.

3) A pretty knee level swing moves from sitting level to the knees. Start sitting with the right leg straight and the left leg bent or with both legs bent to the right. (See illustration #2m3a.)

Swing forward and left. Place the left hand near the seat and finish the swing by pushing up to the left knee, right arm continuing the movement up. At the high point of the swing the head reaches back and the hips push forward for a strong stretch of the entire torso. (See illustration #2m3b.) Of course, do the swing with the legs on the other side.

4) On standing level, check that the torso and head let go and drop into the swing.

5) For a good air level swing add a jump at both ends of a front swing. In other words, as the torso drops and the arms reach back, jump, and as the body straightens up, jump. Watch that the torso remains bent while doing the first jump. This air level front swing is an excellent exercise for the seat muscles.

3) CONTRACT AND STRETCH (Contract is a tight curling or rounding; stretch is a strenuous expanding.)

VARIATIONS
   a) Isolated parts of the body: arms, legs, torso, hands, face, neck, fingers.
   b) Combined body parts: arm and leg, hand and torso, torso and leg, etc.
   c) Whole body.
   d) Levels: air, standing, knee, sitting, lowest.
   e) Tempo.
   f) Size, that is, a partial rounding, full rounding.
   g) Dynamic quality: percussive, sustained.
   h) Energy: limp, strenuous. Unless otherwise specified, a contraction should have a great deal of energy.
   i) Partners:
      1) Contract together like a ball. Stretch apart holding on to each other, preferably on 2 different levels.
      2) Contract and stretch in opposites, that is, while one person contracts the other stretches.
   j) Combine with locomotor movements: walk, jump, skip, roll, and crawl.

4) BEND AND STRAIGHTEN (Bend is a hinge-like folding of 2 straight sides; straighten is an alignment of sides.)

VARIATIONS
   a) Isolated body parts: arm, leg, hand, finger, etc.
   b) Combined body parts: arm and leg, torso and knees, hands and feet (while sitting).
   c) Whole body: hinge from hip joint or from knees.
   d) Plies: a special bend and straighten. Plies come from ballet but are an integral part of all dance. Essentially plie means to bend and straighten the knees, but certain additional conditions make plies difficult. To be correct a plie must be done with 1) heels on the floor, 2) arches lifted, 3) torso perfectly aligned, 4) weight centered, usually between the big toe and 2nd toe, 5) knees pushed back, if the legs are in a turned out position, and 6) most important, energy---a plie is a burst of controlled energy. (See illustration #4d at the top of the next page.)

73

Plies can be done in any standing position, see #9, "Positions of the body" in this Catalog Of Nonlocomotor Movements. They can also be done sitting or lying down.
- e) Levels: air, standing, knee, sitting, lowest.
- f) Tempo.
- g) Dynamic quality: jerky, percussive, sustained.
- h) Combined with locomotor movements: walk, jump, hop. (On the whole, bend and straighten does not combine easily with locomotor movements.)

5) STRIKE (a punching motion)

VARIATIONS
- a) Isolated parts of the body: arm, leg, torso, hip, elbow.
- b) Combined body parts: arm and leg, arm and torso, elbow and hip.
- c) Levels: air, standing, knee, sitting, lowest.
- d) Size.
- e) Tempo.
- f) Combine with locomotor movements: walk, jump, crawl, etc.

6) TWIST (a stretch in 2 opposite directions)

VARIATIONS
- a) Isolated body parts: arms, legs, head, shoulders, torso.
- b) Combined body parts entangled: arms together, arm and leg, both legs.
- c) Whole body.
- d) Spiral twist fall: a specific whole body twist. The children start standing with legs wide. The feet remain in place but pivot as the torso twists completely around. The legs then bend to end up sitting in a tightly crossed position.
- e) Size; partial twist, full twist.
- f) Dynamic quality: percussive, sustained.
- g) Tempo.
- h) Levels: air, standing, knee, sitting, lowest.
- i) Combine with locomotor movements: walk, jump, hop, skip.

7) SPIN (turn or twirl)

VARIATIONS
- a) Isolated body parts turning or circling.*
- b) Whole body.
- c) Body part leading the turn, that is, a turn can originate with an arm, leg, head, torso, hip, elbow, whatever.
- d) Tempo.
- e) Levels: air, standing, knee, sitting, lowest.
- f) Partial or full turns.
- g) Dynamic quality: percussive, sustained, jerky.

---

* What is the difference between this and a circle swing? Just about nothing. This is one of the problems of categorizations. Generally, if the circle movement has a flowing, lilting quality, I call it a swing, if it is evenly controlled I call it a turn. Of course, we could always make up a new category just for circles. My point is that there is nothing sacred about these categories. They are simply a method of organizing movements in order to understand and use them more efficiently.

h) Combine with locomotor movements: walk, jump, hop, skip, leap.

8) FALLS (a controlled lowering of the body, see Part 10)

VARIATIONS
   a) Teeter-totter fall. Start standing very straight. The head and torso lower as one leg lifts, like a teeter-totter. Hands are in front of the body to help catch the fall. (See illustration #8a1.) When the head is as low as possible, place hands on the floor and walk down to tummy, that is, the foot stays in place and the hands walk forward until the body is lying flat. (See illustrations #8a2 and #8a3.)

   The important elements of this fall are 1) keep both legs straight, and 2) lower the torso *while* one leg lifts high.
   b) Back fall.
      1) Sitting back fall. This fall can start standing or on the knees. Pull the weight forward by reaching forward with the arms. Slowly, with control, lower seat to the ground and rock back to lowest level.
      2) One-knee back fall. Start standing level. The arms reach front to pull the weight forward. The body is gently lowered to one knee and one foot. (See illustration #8b2.) And then to sitting with one foot on the floor.

      From there the back can be lowered to lowest level. Reversing the one-knee back fall is a good way to get up.
   c) Side fall. Start on the knee level. To fall to the right side, lift arms overhead and reach to the *left*. (See illustration #8c1.) Keep the weight pulling left while lowering the seat to the right side of the feet. (See illustration #8c2.) After the seat is on the floor, place left hand to balance torso and lower right side to the ground. (See illustrations #8c3 and #8c4.) The process is reversed for the left side.

   This fall can also be done from standing level. The process is essentially the same as from the knees. Reach arms overhead and pull *left*; the body arches *right* as the right knee is lowered and as the seat is lowered to the right of the feet. The left hand aids the torso lowering to the ground.
   d) Spiral twist fall. Start standing with the legs wide. The feet stay in place but pivot as the torso and hips twist completely around. The knees then bend and the body is lowered to sitting.

e) One-leg side fall. Start standing, keeping the weight on the left leg, point the right foot diagonally forward. Put the right hand near the seat and stretch the left arm front. Look over the right shoulder at the right hand. This is the starting position. (See illustration #8e1.)

To fall, lift the weight up by *pushing the hips forward* and by stretching the left arm front. The forward push of the hips is crucial. Slide the right leg out while lowering the right hand to the floor. The left knee should *not* touch the floor at this point.

Once the right hand is on the floor, lower the seat and then the left knee to the final position. (See illustration #8e2.)

"But my right foot won't slide! It keeps sticking to the floor." Keep the weight on the left leg. The right foot has almost no weight on it until the very end. Further, keep the right foot sharply pointed for easier sliding.

"It looks scary!" Illusion. The fall is controlled by the right hand lowering to the floor, and it is not far from the floor to begin with. Before attempting the one-leg side fall I often have children practice just bending their knees and placing their right hand on the floor behind their seat. This is essentially the fall, except that one leg is kept straight while lowering. Do not forget to look at the right hand; this takes away some of the scariness. To fall to the other side, reverse all positions. This is a very dramatic fall. It looks like the person is falling into the splits. This is not so but the breath catching quality is there.

f) Lunge fall. A very simple fall. Start standing and take a long step forward, bending the front leg. This is a lunge position. Bend the torso and put the hands on the floor on either side of the front foot. This step and bend is done quickly. From the bent position it is easy to lower the seat to the ground, ending on sitting or lowest level.

9) POSITIONS OF THE BODY*

VARIATIONS
  a) Standing level positions.

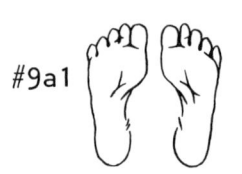

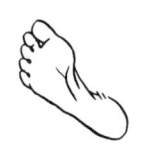

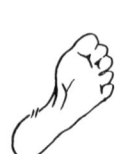

    1) Parallel feet: toes point straight ahead. (See illustration #9a1.)
    2) First position: heels touch, toes point diagonally out. (See illustration #9a2.)
    3) Second position: a step wider than first position. (See illustration #9a3.)

---
* These are not movements. These are some of the basic body positions common to most dance.

4) Third position: heel touching in-step, both feet turned out. (See illustration #9a4 on page 76.)
5) Fourth position: a step forward from third position. (See illustration #9a5 on page 76.)
6) Fifth position: heel touching toe, both feet turned out. (See illustration #9a6 on page 76.)
   b) Knee level positions:
      1) One knee and one foot on the floor.
      2) Both knees on the floor.
   c) Sitting level positions:
      1) Crossed legs (traditional "Indian Style").
      2) Soles of the feet clapped together.
      3) Triangle position: both legs bent to one side, toes of one foot touching knee of the other leg. (See illustration #9c3.)
      4) Both legs tucked tightly to one side. (See illustration #9c4.)
      5) One leg straight and one leg bent forward. (See illustration #9c5.)
      6) One leg straight and one bent back. (See illustration #9c6.)
      7) Wide stride: both legs straight and wide.
      8) Both legs straight and together.
      9) One leg bent and one foot on the floor. (See illustration #9c9.)
   d) Lowest level positions.
      1) Legs and arms together.
      2) Legs and arms wide.

NONLOCOMOTOR MOVEMENT STUDIES

TEACHER TAUGHT COMBINATIONS

1) Eight plus eight study. Children start in Perfect Spots, standing level, arms overhead.

   Front swing and up, beats 1 and 2; shake body down to sitting level, beat 3; spin on seat, beat 4; contract on lowest level, beats 5 and 6; stretch on knee level, beats 7 and 8.

   The children then have 8 more beats to run anywhere in the room, ending in their exact starting spot by count #8.

77

Once the children know this study well, it is fun to do both phases of 8 at the same time. Divide the class in half; half the class does the stationary 8 beats at the same time that the other half does the running for 8 beats. Repeat several times.

2) Swing and strike. Children start in Perfect Spots, standing level, arms overhead. Front swing and up, beats 1 and 2; strike one arm and then one leg, beats 3 and 4; side swing and back, beats 5 and 6; strike one elbow and then the hips, beats 7 and 8.

3) Isolated shakes. Children start in Perfect Spots, standing level, arms down. Shake the right arm, beats 1 and 2; shake the left arm, beats 3 and 4; shake the right leg, beats 5 and 6; shake the left leg, beats 7 and 8; shake the torso while turning around, beats 9 to 12.

4) Isolated contractions. Children start in Perfect Spots, standing level, arms down. Contract right arm and hold it there, beat 1; contract left leg and hold it there, beat 2; contract head and torso (while balancing on right foot), beat 3; stretch everything out, beat 4; contract left arm and hold it there, beat 5; contract right leg and hold it there, beat 6; contract head and torso, beat 7; stretch everything out, beat 8.

The quality is fast and percussive.

5) Swing and shake. Children start in Perfect Spots, standing level, arms overhead. Front swing and jump, beats 1 and 2; swing back up and jump, beats 3 and 4; shake down to sitting level, beats 5 and 6; spin once on seat and get up, beats 7 and 8.

6) Body wave warm-up. Children start in Perfect Spots, standing level, arms overhead. Front swing and up, beats 1 and 2; body wave swing, beats 3 and 4; front swing and up, beats 5 and 6; body wave swing, beats 7 and 8; roll torso down, ideally palms flat on the floor, beats 1 to 4; bend knees straighten the back forward parallel to the floor, arms stretched forward, beats 5 to 8. (See illustration at right.)

Straighten knees in illustration at right while holding back straight, beats 1 to 4; round the back from the base of the spine up, ending in a straight standing position, beats 5 to 8.

This is an excellent warm-up exercise for the back and legs. I use it often.

7) Fluid turns. This is one of my favorite studies. Children start in Perfect Spots, standing level, arms wide. Spiral twist fall to sitting level; spin on seat; throw legs under and spin half way around on stomach; lift up to sit in the triangle position; lift seat up and spin on knees; stand and spin on the standing level; jump turn.

Do not use counts for this study. The children do it on their own time, moving smoothly and fluidly.

8) The Monster Rises. Children start in groups ready to move on the diagonal. Run to the middle of the diagonal and freeze in a strange shape; drop limply to the floor; contract lowest level; start to shake (first small then getting bigger and bigger) and shake up to standing level, arms up; front swing and up, ending the swing in a stretched jump; leap to the other side of the diagonal.

TEACHER STRUCTURED FREE TRAVELING PATTERNS

1) Swing, return the swing, shake, and do a locomotor movement. The rhythmic structure is: swing-2-3, swing-2-3, shake-2-3, go-some-where. This is repeated over and over.

2) Add a contract and stretch to the above pattern: swing-2-3, swing-2-3, contract-2-3, stretch-2-3, shake-2-3, go-some-where. (You can extend the locomotor movement part for several measures.)

3) Waltz walk, 3 beats; waltz walk turn, 3 beats; spiral twist fall half way down, 3 beats; twist back up, 3 beats; side swing, 3 beats; swing back, 3 beats. Repeat.

4) Swing and return; twist; shake out; change levels and go somewhere. Repeat.

TEACHER STRUCTURED GROUP PROBLEMS

1) Pick 4 nonlocomotor movements, each one on a different level. Each nonlocomotor movement will get 6 beats. Remember your sequence.

2) Pick 5 different parts of the body. Do a nonlocomotor movement with each part. You may not repeat any nonlocomotor movements. Remember your pattern.

3) Pick 3 different nonlocomotor movements and 4 different locomotor movements. Alternate locomotor and nonlocomotor movements starting with the locomotor movements.

4) Within 20 beats, fit in 4 different nonlocomotor movements.

PART 6
AWARENESS OF SPACE

DEFINITION OF SPATIAL AWARENESS

SKILLS NECESSARY FOR SPATIAL AWARENESS
"Spatial awareness" is a battered phrase. Everybody is teaching it but few people know what it is. The phrase has fallen into the nebulous mire of jargon.

Awareness of space is actually a set of specific, somewhat mundane skills. These skills encompass a) how the child sees himself moving through space (direction), and b) how the child sees the space through which he is moving (floor pattern).

THE DIFFERENCE BETWEEN DIRECTION AND FLOOR PATTERN
Direction distinguishes which plane of the body (front, back, or side) is leading the body. I identify 4 directions: forward, backward, sideways, and turning. Floor pattern distinguishes the lines created by the body moving through space. A diagonal line, a circle, an intricate design are examples of floor patterns.

This distinction between direction and floor pattern is one I prefer to keep straight. Sometimes direction is used interchangeably with floor pattern: "Go in the diagonal direction." "Go in the direction of the stage." This is a different meaning of the word "direction" and it causes confusion. When a child brings up this confusion, I demonstrate: "Look, I can move on a diagonal *line* in the forward *direction*, I can go on the same diagonal line in the backward, sideward, or turning directions, or I can move in all 4 directions on this line. The diagonal line is from here to there; the direction is which part of my body takes me there."

Children confuse themselves with space. When running across a room most children have no thought of the line they have created nor do they perceive that a distinct plane of their body has led them.* Understanding and being at ease with the body moving in different directions, and understanding and visualizing the spatial design a movement creates, are keys to a greater control of individual movement and to an expanded movement vocabulary.

Direction and floor pattern, each with their own underlying skills, constitute my definition of spatial awareness.

---
* In fact, after you introduce directions a number of children will not know how to move forward.

DIRECTIONS

DIRECTIONAL SKILLS
Before a child can move clearly backwards he must know with certainty where his back is, from the back of his head to the bottom of his heels. Before a child can feel at ease with right and left, he must clearly sense 2 separate sides running the length of his body. Before children can move in different directions, they must be introduced to the planes of their own bodies. Therefore, the directional skills are:

1) The child knows where his front, back, and sides are.

2) The child can move clearly forward, backward, sideways, and turning directions.

3) The child can distinguish right and left sides on his body.

WALK DOWN YOUR FRONT
Good for: 1) Introducing front, back, and side.
           2) Leg stretch and arm strength.

Work on directions begins by finding front, back and side. We do this with Walk Down Your Front. For children that are uncertain of right and left, I do Walk Down Your Front and the following exercises without mentioning right and left. As they mirror me, I ask for "this hand" and the "other hand." After right and left are introduced I do these exercises again, using the proper terms.

Children stand in Perfect Spots. The "face front" component of Perfect Spots is crucial here. The first few times we do this exercise the children and I do it together, with the children imitating me. Later, the children follow my verbal instructions.

We start standing with hands on top of our heads. "Walk down your front," I say. Hands walk, step by step, down the front of our bodies, touching every part of the front. I ask that knees be kept straight.

Reaching the feet, I ask, "What is at the front of your feet?"

"Toes," they decide.

"Glue the front of your feet as you keep walking front."

Keeping the toes in place and the knees straight, our hands walk forward on the floor until the body is completely stretched out in push-up position (weight on hands and toes, everything else lifted off the floor).

I then say, "Walk *up* your front." (Warning! Do not, as I did the first time, say, "Walk *back* up your front." Complete confusion.) If done correctly, that is, legs straight, toes in place, body stretched as much as possible, this is an extremely good strengthening exercise.

After *walking* down and up our fronts, we *run* down and up our fronts.

"Walk down your back." We begin at the back of the head and walk down. Arms and hands must shift around to keep going below the shoulders. Knees are kept straight until hands reach the heels. We then glue the heels, bend the knees, and keep "walking." The body will end outstretched, seat off the ground.

"Walk up your back...Run down your back...Run up your back."

Children enjoy this exercise. If you have the time and inclination, do different locomotor movements down and up the front and back, for example, the hands can skip, hop, tiptoe, stomp, tickle.

After front and back, we move to the sides. (Reminder: if the children are shakey on right and left, simply ask for this or that mirrored side.) "Raise your right arm." Since the children are in Perfect Spots, it takes only a few seconds to check every arm. The left arm is kept down, "glued to it's side." We begin with our right hands on the top of our heads and slide down our right sides. Check that the children slide strictly down their sides and do not waver to their fronts. Slide all the way down to the right foot.

"Glue the side of your right foot and keep sliding to your right side." This is tricky. Ideally, the body ends in a side balance on the right hand and foot, everything else off the ground. For young children, I ask for a side balance with the body resting on the floor; later we attempt the harder balance.

"Slide up your right side...Raise your left arm...Slide down your left side...Slide up your left side."

"Do you know where your front is? Do you know where your back is? How about your right side? Left side?" Ten to one the children will be touching the appropriate place as they shout, "Yes."

NONLOCOMOTOR MOVEMENTS USING DIRECTIONS

After Walk Down Your Front we do stationary exercises that use directions. It is important the children feel how to move forward, backward, sideways, and turning with nonlocomotor movements before they attempt directions with locomotor movements.

1) Bouncing torso. Bounce the torso 8 times to the front, 8 to the back, 8 to the right side, and 8 to the left side, 8 times turning (circling around). Then bounce 4 times in each direction, 2 times in each direction, one time in each direction done 4 times. Go faster and faster with the one's. (You probably remember this one from your high school gym classes.)

2) Kicking. Kick legs (alternating right and left leg) 8 times to the front, 8 times to the back, 8 times with the right leg to the right side, 8 times with left leg to the left side; 4 times in each direction; 2 times; one time in each direction done 4 times.

3) Shaking hands. Shake hands in front of your body, shake hands in back, shake the right hand to the right side, shake the left hand to the left side, shake hands all around. Combine directions, for example, one hand shake in front of the body while the other hand shakes in back, one hand in back and one to the right side.

4) Looking. Look in front of you; keeping the body facing front, look in back of you; look to the right; look to the left; look all around.

5) Hip thrust. Push your hips to the front; pull your hips to the back; push your hips to the right side; push your hips to the left side; swing the hips all the way around. Go faster and faster.

6) Jumping. This is good for future locomotor movements using directions. Jump 4 jumps front, 4 jumps back, 4 jumps to the right, 4 to the left, 4 turning. (End the last turning jump facing front.) Then 2 jumps in each direction; one in each direction. Go faster and faster.

7) Stretches.
   a) Stretch front: arms and torso reach forward. Ideally the back is parallel to the floor with the spine working to remain as straight as possible.
   b) Stretch back: head and neck reach back, back arches. Arms can either stretch overhead or hands can rest on hips. Ideally the back arches high, in the upper spine, rather than only in the lower back. Watch that the stomach stays tucked in.
   c) Stretch to the side: arms above the head; head, arms, neck and torso all strenuously pull *diagonally* to the side rather than falling to the floor. Hips remain straight, not thrusting to the opposite side. Stretch right and left.
   d) Swing torso all the way around ready to start again.

8) Rolls. On mats, roll once front (forward somersault). Roll back (backward somersault). Roll once to the right (log or cat roll) and one to the left. Spin on the knees ready to start again.

9) Tantrum legs. Children sit in Perfect Spots. Ask them to have a temper tantrum with only their legs. Legs kick, shake, push, hit the floor. Have the tantrum with the legs in front, in back (they have to lie down on their stomachs), to the right (they sit up and balance on the left hip), to the left, and all the way around. How about adding the appropriate tantrum sounds?

10) Combinations:
    a) Bounce torso to the back while you shake your hands to the front.
    b) Jump forward while you look backwards.
    c) Kick alternate sides as you bounce your torso front and back.

11) Strike. Strike with different parts of the body to the front: arms, legs, elbows, head, torso. Strike back: legs, seat, arms, elbows. To the sides, strike elbows, legs, hips. Then pick a different strike to do in each direction. For example:
    a) Strike one arm to the front, one leg to the back, one elbow to the right, and one hip to the left.
    b) Strike torso front, elbows back, hip right, leg left.
    c) Strike head front, seat back, leg right, arm left.

    Whatever sequence you or the children pick, push it to go faster.

12) Sequential patterns. Just as the strike patterns above used different strikes in each direction, any of the above movements can be combined in a directional sequence. Examples:
    a) Bounce torso to the front; look to the back; kick right; kick left; jump turn.
    b) Sitting down, have a "leg tantrum" with the legs in front. Cross the legs "Indian Style" and strike elbows to the back. Open the legs wide and stretch right then left. Spin on seat.
    c) Jump front; kick one leg back; hip thrust to the right; stretch left; turn around.
    d) Shake hands in front; strike seat back; look to the right, kick left; turn around.
    e) Step hop front; one-knee back roll back; while remaining on knee level kick right; stand and turn; end with a hip thrust to the left.

f) Reach up; reach down; clap right; clap left; shake around.*

MIRRORED MOVEMENTS
   Ninety percent of the time I mirror what I ask the children to do; 10 percent I do it with the children, that is, my back to them. It would be a rare day indeed that, facing them, I would bounce to my left while the children bounced to theirs. The only time would be as a game, in which the objective was to see if they could stick to their own direction while I moved the seemingly opposite way.

   "You are not being honest with the children," said a stern 6th grade teacher. Why not? If a child figures out the mirror and complains that I am going to the "wrong" side, I congratulate him: "You are absolutely right. I am doing it like a mirror facing you so that it *looks* the same."

   The child who figures out the mirror is way ahead and the child who does not, needs it. As long as I am honest with the child who figures it out, I think I am playing fair.

TEACHING RIGHT AND LEFT
   Frankly, I do not think "right" and "left" are earthshaking concepts. They are simply terms. Children need to memorize these terms for report cards and other activities.

   As a child I could never keep them straight until my mother unwittingly bought me a ring. It was put on my right hand. My grades suddenly showed I knew "laterality." I remembered that "ring" starts with "r" and that therefore this must be my right hand. Years later, after the ring had to be sawed off my finger, the only way I knew my right was to feel where my precious ring had been.

   My point is that "right" and "left" are only words. I am not de-emphasizing true laterality, but this is more than right and left. True laterality is knowing clearly where the side of the body is, knowing the entire area that is side, knowing where side is at all times, knowing that there are 2 different sides, and knowing how to move distinctly sideways. That one side is called Herman, Right, or This and the other is called Sam, Left, or That is secondary.

   Tying a yarn "bracelet," marking a letter on the hand, putting a small piece of tape, all are fine beginnings to sensorially memorizing the right hand. I certainly recommend a little turquoise ring.

   When I am faced with an entire class that needs introduction to the terms "right" and "left" I follow this procedure: The children stand in Perfect Spots. "The arm that is closest to the chalkboard side of the room (I mirror the children) is your right arm. Raise your right arm." I check every arm quickly.**

---
* Add 2 diagonal stretches and this becomes a great cheerleader pattern. Reach up, reach down, clap right, clap left, stretch diagonally right (right arm stretches up while left foot lifts a little), stretch diagonally left (left arm stretches up while right foot lifts a little), turn around. Result: "Up, down, right side (clap on word 'side'), left side, diagonal, diagonal, and turn around."
** If a child raises the wrong arm, I individually take his right arm and, with friendly violence, shake it vigorously. "*This* is your right arm." The vigor is more than good natured fun. There must be a sensory memory *in* the arm and a little tingle never hurts.

"Shake your right arm...Swing your right arm...Contract and stretch your right arm... Strike, circle, wave, bend and straighten, twist, and reach for the sky with your right arm." The arm should be tired; this is important for the muscular memory.

"OK, shake everything out and spin around...Now face front and lift your right arm... Fantastic! Shake everything out and spin around again...Let's see how fast you can raise your right arm...Great!"

We do this entire procedure, on different days, *only with the right*. After several reviews I ask the children to show me their right arm in more difficult ways: "Face the back of the room and raise your right arm...Go on the stage...Where is your right?...Lie down on your stomachs, facing front, and raise your right arm...Twirl around and, while spinning, raise your right arm."

Once the children know their right, I do *not* do the same with the left. Rather I start alternating movements: "Raise your right arm; raise your left...Shake your right arm; shake your left arm...Shake your right leg; left...Thrust your right hip; thrust your left...With your right hand touch your left foot; with your left hand touch your right shoulder." And so on. We then repeat, Walk Down Your Front and some direction exercises using the terms "right" and "left."

RIGHT AND LEFT BUG
 Good for: 1) Clarifying right and left sides.
            2) Teaching parts of the body.

Once the terms "right" and "left" are introduced I work on sensing the entire side by using Right and Left Bug. Right and Left Bug is a great deal of fun for preschoolers to 3rd grade. Older children actually like it too, but I introduce it by asking them if they want to pretend they are young children.

The children stand in Perfect Spots. Raising my arm and wiggling my fingers, I say, "This is the right bug. The bug is flying around." The children wiggle their right hands insect fashion while their right arms wave about. Left arms are relaxed at the side. We add a buzzing sound to the bug movement. This is the time I double check to make sure all the children are using the correct arm.

"And the right bug, flying around, lands on your head." (Right hand lands on head.) "It travels down your right side...Hello right ear." (Wiggle right ear with right hand. Children say the "hello's" with me.) "Hello right shoulder." (Right hand on right shoulder, shoulder wiggles.) "Hello right armpit!" (Right hand tickles right armpit. My face hams exaggerated surprise and the children usually jump and scream.) "Hello right side of my waist." (Right hand tickles right waist.) "Hello right hip." (Right hand on right hip, hips wiggle.) "Hello right knee." (Right hand wiggles right knee.) "Hello right foot." (Right hand tickles right foot.)

"Now shake that right bug off your right side." (The left arm and leg work to remain still while the right arm and leg shake vigorously.)

The process is repeated on the left side. At the end of the left side, I say, "Shake the left side...Shake the right...(faster)...Right...Left..." (We go faster and faster until everything is shaking.)

Right and Left Bug is much requested, with the armpit being a definite high point.

COPS AND ROBBERS
Good for: 1) Preparing for sideways locomotor movements.
           2) Teaching side-slide.

After the children are at ease using front, back, right and left sides with nonlocomotor movements, we go on to directions with locomotor movements. Moving sideways with locomotor movements is much more difficult than forward, backward, or turning. Therefore I like to prepare for this difficulty with a preliminary exercise: Cops and Robbers. The goal of this exercise is to help children move straight side rather than diagonally forward. Eric Berne notwithstanding, Cops and Robbers is one of the most requested exercises.

The children start standing in Perfect Spots. (This exercise works best if you ham it up with exaggerated facial gestures.) "You know those old time movies where the robbers crack open the safe and take the money?" (Pretend to crack a safe, take the money, and stuff it into a bag.) "Then the cops come and there is nowhere to go but out the window." (Pretend to gingerly step out a window.) "The ledge outside this window is a thousand feet up." (Pretend to be scared, high in the air.)

"Well, the cops are coming, we'd better step slowly along the ledge. Keep your back flat against the building. Step right, together (Right foot steps right, left foot slides to meet it, that is, a slow side-slide.)...Right, together, right, together...Uh oh, the cops are coming this way. We'd better go to our left. (A little faster to the left: left, together 4 times.)...Uh oh, here they come. Go right! (Right, faster, 4 times.) Uh oh, left! (Left, 3 times, fast.)...Uh oh, right! (Right, 3 times, fast.)...Uh oh, (Extremely fast, left twice, right twice, left twice, right twice.)...Uh oh, jump!"

This exercise teaches or reinforces the locomotor movement side-slide. After introducing Cops and Robbers I often say, "The movement you were doing along the ledge is called a side-slide. Can you show me that locomotor movement? Straight sides now."

LOCOMOTOR MOVEMENTS USING DIRECTIONS
Now we are ready for more general work with locomotor movements using directions. The children sit on the floor.

"If your front is leading you (I pull myself by the front of my shirt) you are going forward. If your back is leading you (I pretend to be pulled by my back) you are going backwards. If either side leads you (I pretend to be pulled by one side, then the other) you are going sideways. If your whole body is leading then you are going in the turning direction. So we have 4 directions: forward direction, backward direction, sideward direction, and turning direction."

Just for fun (and memory) ask the children to rattle off the 4 directions as fast as they can: forwardbackwardsidewaysturning. A definite tongue twister.

The children try out locomotor movements in these 4 directions. Usually I use the Free Traveling Structure. The times I do not use the Free Traveling Structure are 1) if the room is too crowded, or 2) if the children are too rambunctious and I am fearful of the backward movements. In these cases the children go from one side of the room to the other or use the Diagonal Structure.

It is important that the locomotor movements picked for this introduction be simple (a skip sideways is too hard for now) and feasible (no backward leaps). Here are some good locomotor movements for beginning direction work:

1) Walk: forward, backward, sideways, turning. The side walk can be either a slow step-together or a grape-vine (step, cross front, step, cross back).

2) Jump: forward, backward, sideways, turning. Try the turning jumps full turns.

3) Run: forward, backward, sideways, turning. Watch that the sideways run does not turn into a side-slide. It is most easily kept a run if the knees are high.

4) Crawl: forward, backward, sideways, turning.

5) With mats, roll forward (somersault), backward, sideways (log or cat roll).

WORKING ON SIDEWAYS LOCOMOTOR MOVEMENTS
"Help! My children move forward, backward, and turning OK but I can't get them to go straight sideways. It always looks frontish."

Yes, I certainly know what you mean. Sideways locomotor movements are hard. Here are 3 techniques for working on straight side movements:

1) Have the children keep their toes on the lines created by the floor tiles or floor boards. Whatever locomotor movement they are doing, tell them to move slowly until they have the idea of going straight side and then to speed it up. This approach is good for mature, motivated classes. They want to go sideways and they are willing to work on their own to do it.

2) For classes that do not really care if they ever move sideways or not, I work from Perfect Spots. In addition to Cops and Robbers, we jump, hop, walk, run, and crawl sideways doing the movement an equal number of times to the right and left side. I use this Perfect Spot base because the children are facing front. As long as they remain facing front the locomotor movement will be straight side.

As soon as a few children have the idea, I use peer pressure. "Ron, Janice, Eileen, and Javan, your sideward locomotor movements are getting so good I want to see if you can do them going anywhere in the room." Then to the class: "We'll keep practicing from our Perfect Spots here in the front of the room and let those 4 children try the movements in the back of the room...Greg, you want to join the kids back there? Well, let me see you jump straight side...Great, OK, go ahead...Shana, you want to join them? Well let me see you move straight side first..." When about half of the class is working on their own I have everyone try it.

Moving sideways takes quite a bit of concentration. Once the children want to, they generally can.

3) Another technique uses one cleared wall. Have the class begin by literally walking against the wall, heels touching the baseboard.

"You are walking straight side. Do you think you could take a step or 2 away from the wall and keep that straight side feeling? Fantastic! (If not fantastic, "Nope, the straight side is gone. Let's go back to the wall.")...OK let's try a jump. Put your back as close to the wall as possible as you jump sideways. Now take a few steps away. Can you jump just as straight? Great."

After doing several different locomotor movements this way, I ask the class to *pretend* their backs are against a *different* wall and we do several locomotor movements. If the children can move straight side pretending their backs are against each of the 4 walls, they are ready to do sideward movements anywhere in the room.

CHECKING DIRECTION WORK

Once the class has some experience moving freely in 4 directions, I use the Diagonal Structure to check each child carefully. I check run, walk, jump, and crawl in the forward, backward, sideways, and turning directions. Here I can see if we need to review or can go on to: a) more difficult locomotor movements, b) beginning directional studies, c) mixing directions with other concepts, d) direction problems, and e) full scale direction studies.

MORE DIFFICULT LOCOMOTOR MOVEMENTS USING DIRECTIONS

If the simple locomotor movements are clear, we go on to directions with more difficult locomotor movements. I introduce these more difficult movements using the Diagonal Structure and then use them as warm-ups in the Free Traveling Structure.

1) Skip: forward, backward, sideways (feasible by crossing skipping leg) and turning.

2) Gallop: forward, backward, and turning. Sideways gallop is a side-slide. Side-slide changing sides.

3) Hop: forward, backward, sideways, turning. Change legs.

4) Slide: slide forward on stomach, backward on back, sideways on side, and spin either on stomach or back. Use markers to cut the diagonal in 4th's and do the 4 slides on one diagonal. If you attempted to do one full diagonal for each of these 4 movements, it would take hours.

5) One-legged skip: forward, backward, sideways, turning.

6) Leap: forward, sideways. Just for fun you can attempt it backwards. For turning direction, run forward and turn in the middle of the leap.

7) Jazz walk: forward, backward, sideways, turning.

8) Whatever you want: forward, backward, sideways, turning.

BEGINNING DIRECTION STUDIES

The children are now ready for an initial direction study. Keep these first studies simple:

1) Run forward to the middle of the diagonal; stop; fall down and slide on your back backwards to the end.

2) Jazz walk turning to the middle of the diagonal; leap forward to the end.

3) In Perfect Spots, 4 hops forward on right foot; 4 hops backward on left foot; 4 jumps sideways; 4 jumps turning. No extra time to change directions.

4) Starting at one side of the room, do 4 gallops forward; 2 side-slides right and 2 side-slides left; 4 jumps backwards; run forward 3 steps and leap turning in the air. It forms a rectangle. (See diagram at right.)

5) In Perfect Spots, 5 steps forward, 4 steps to the right side, 3 steps to the left side, 2 jumps backward, spin around once ready to start again.

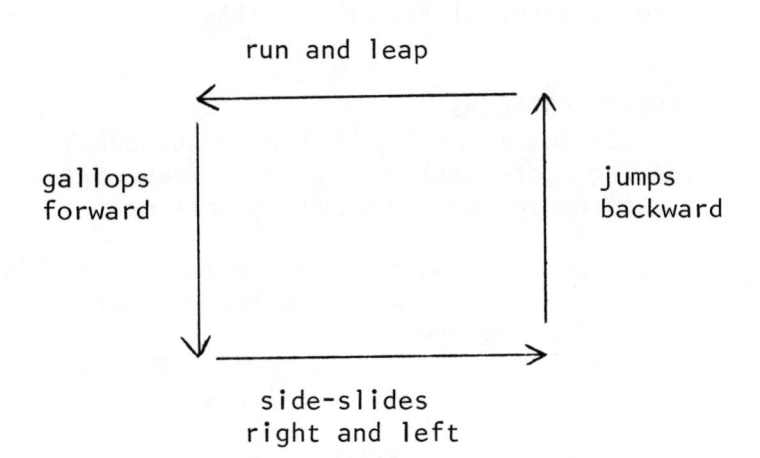

MIXING DIRECTIONS WITH OTHER CONCEPTS
The concept "directions" is now clear and solid; we can start mixing it with other concepts. I use the Free Traveling Structure and give instructions that to the untrained ear sound like an alien language.

1) "Do a locomotor movement, air level, in the backward direction; do a nonlocomotor movement that continuously changes levels; then repeat the locomotor movement but do it in the forward direction."

2) "Do a locomotor movement, knee level, sideways direction. Keep going sideways but change levels. Keep your new level but change directions."

3) "Do a locomotor movement, standing level, forward direction; when I call 'change,' change directions. Change...Change...Change."

4) "Start standing level, do a locomotor movement forward direction; when I call 'change,' change direction *and* level. Change...Change...Change."

5) "When you hear the piano, do a locomotor movement, turning direction, lowest level; when you hear the drum, do a locomotor movement, backward direction, knee level." (Alternate sounds.) For more of these sound-change problems, see Brain Catcher in Part 7.

6) Just for fun, sometimes add a partner or group to the confusion: "Get a partner. Have one of you on standing level and one on sitting level; have one of you going forward while the other one moves backwards. You have to keep touching as you move!"

7) "With a partner, pick 2 levels and 2 directions. When I say 'change' change levels but keep your directions. Remember you have to keep holding on. Change...Change..."

8) "Again with a partner get on 2 levels going in 2 directions. Now keep the levels the same but, when I call 'change,' change directions. Change...Change...Change."

9) "Get into groups of 3, each of you on a different level and each going in a different direction. You have to hold on to each other. Can you move?"

These concept mixers are great warm-up activities.* Within 10 minutes, the children's bodies are warmed-up, they have reviewed a great deal of information, their energy, if not released, is at least channeled, their brains are working, and they are focused into movement class. Plus, it's fun.

DIRECTION PROBLEMS

In addition to mixing with other concepts, directions can be used to create some challenging coordination problems. These direction problems are similar to the concept mixers except they are more specific.

Direction problems are given totally verbally (sometimes it takes great restraint to keep from moving) so the children figure them out by themselves. I almost always use Diagonal Structure.

1) Locomotor movement one-legged skip with the leg in front, forward direction.

2) Locomotor movement one-legged skip with the leg in back, forward direction.

3) One-legged skip with the leg to the side, sideways direction.

4) One-legged skip with the leg in front, backward direction.

5) One-legged skip alternating leg from front to back, turning direction.

6) Kick in back, move forward direction. (See illustration at right.)

7) Kick in front, move backward direction.

8) Kick to the side, move sideways direction.

9) Kick 2 times to the front and 2 times to the back, move turning direction.

10) Shake hands in front of you while side-sliding sideways; shake hands in back while side-sliding. Side-slide changing sides alternate shaking hands in front and in back.

11) Skip backwards while looking from side to side.

12) Skip turning around and contract and stretch at the same time.

13) Kung fu kick to the side as you move in the forward direction.

14) Kung fu kick to the front as you move in the backwards direction.

15) Run turning while your partner hops backwards and stay together. Switch.

16) Roll sideways (log or cat roll) while your partner spider crawls forward over you. Switch in the middle of the diagonal.

---

* If the children know what you are saying but cannot seem to do it, you are probably saying the instructions too quickly. Pause at the end of each phrase so that the children can visualize each section.

FULL SCALE DIRECTION STUDIES
The final component in this section on directions is a full scale study:

1) Run forward to the middle of the diagonal; jazz walk backwards from the middle to the end of the diagonal. Across the 2nd diagonal hop sideways to the middle; skip turning from the middle to the end. Keep both diagonals moving at the same time with no disasters.

2) Lowest level, slide on stomach in the backward direction; knee and sitting level, move in the turning direction; standing level, move in the sideways direction doing a grapevine; air level, run and leap in the forward direction. Each direction gets a specific number of beats, 4's or 7's perhaps, with no additional time to change.

3) One one-legged skip with the leg in back, forward direction; one one-legged skip with the leg to the side, sideways direction; one one-legged skip with the leg in front, backward direction; one waltz-walk, turning direction. Repeat. Very hard.

4) Four kicks to the back, moving forward; 4 kicks to the front, moving backward, 4 kicks to the side moving sideways; one small preparation jump and then a large jump that turns completely around.

5) "Row, Row, Row Your Boat" is one of my favorite direction studies. We begin standing in Perfect Spots. The children learn this pattern: 3 jumps forward; 5 steps backwards; 4 side-slides to the right; 4 side-slides to the left. Done in Perfect Spots, the pattern forms an "L" shaped floor pattern. (See diagram at right.)

The pattern is practiced until it is easy.

I then ask the children to get into groups, ready to do locomotor movements on the diagonal. With a grin I present this problem:

"The pattern that you have just done (3 jumps forward, 5 steps backward, 4 slides to the right, and 4 slides to the left) can be done so that it takes you completely across the diagonal--all the way to the other corner. How can it be done?"

It is still amazing to me to find so many children so stumped. Most children think it is the size of movement and proceed to take enormous jumps forward and tiny steps backward, but it will not work. Inevitably one child will get the idea of turning his body around, although it often takes 2 or 3 children to figure out that they must turn their bodies on the backward steps and both of the side-slides. The resulting pattern is diagramed at right.

Once the children understand the pattern, do it to the song, "Row, Row, Row Your Boat." The song consists of 2 phrases of 8 beats; within each phrase the division is in 4:

```
1      2      3      4      1      2      3  4
Row,  row,   row    your   boat, gently down the stream;

   1         2          3         4      1       2       3  4
Merrily, merrily, merrily, merrily, life is but a dream.
```

The movement pattern fits the large phrasing with a slightly off phrase break up of 3 + 5 and 4 + 4. I find this more exciting than a straight phrase match up. If you find it too difficult for your children, change the pattern to 4 jumps forward and 4 steps backward (the slides are the same) and this will fit the phrasing exactly.

As you know, "Row, Row, Row Your Boat" is a round with the 2nd part coming in 8 beats after the first. It is nice to do the movement pattern in a round also. The round can be done using the diagonal or a floor pattern like the one diagramed at right.

In this floor pattern the children are lined up so that they meet their partner in the middle of one side of the room. They do the 3 jumps forward and the 5 steps backward in a straight line, moving together. For the side-slides, they separate and curve around to their respective starting places while the next 2 children start the jumps. Therefore in the above diagram, children labeled "y" start their jumps while children labeled "x" are sliding.

This is a culmination study requiring attention, precision, and concentration. It will take patience to set up. But after the first few disastrous tries, the children will suddenly get the idea and the whole thing will miraculously fall into place.

MIDDLE

INTRODUCING THE CONCEPT
At this point the children are relatively at ease moving in space. They know where their front, back, right, and left sides are, and they can move in the forward, backward, sideways, and turning directions. Before we go on to patterns in space we find one point in space, middle.

The concept "middle" is not hard in itself. The trick is to make clear what it is we are finding the middle of.

I hold a piece of yarn about a yard long: "The middle is where it is the same length on either side. (For older classes I say it is halfway between one end and the other.) Let's guess where the middle of this piece of yarn is. (One child picks.) We can check to see how close Yolanda is by folding the yarn and seeing if both sides are the same." (The child that picked the middle holds that point tightly while I match the 2 sides.)

Usually the children are surprisingly accurate. If they are not close, the match up of sides will show it and I'll say, "See if you can find a point that makes the sides more the same." We do this several times with different children picking the middle.

We then pick other lines in the room and find their middles. The lines have to be clearly defined. Do not ask for the middle of a wall yet because that is too large a plane. We find the middle of one side of a door, one side of a window, the floorboard on one wall, one side of the chalkboard, the edge of the piano, one side of a poster. This is similar to finding diagonals throughout the room.

MEASURING
The children judge the middle simply by sight. With a clearly defined line, they are usually quite accurate. If they are off by too much or if you want to do a more comprehensive lesson, this is a wonderful time for work on measuring.

"Michelle picked this point as the middle of the edge of the stage. How could we measure each side, from that end to the middle and from this end to the middle, and make sure they are the same?"

"Get a ruler," is the most common reply.

"Yes, that is one good way. What are some other ways we could measure?"

I wait them out. With a hint, they will come up with different ways of measuring: hand spans, foot spans, paces, children lying down lengthwise, arm spans, pieces of yarn, book lengths, and so on. We pick one method to follow. Sometimes I will pick 2 different methods and check to see if the middle is the same. On a good day, the creative thinking and problem solving stimulated by this lesson makes me glow for the rest of the day.

MIDDLE OF PARTS OF THE BODY
Once the children understand what the middle of a line is, I go on to the middle of parts of their bodies. This is a good step between finding the middle of lines and finding the middle of large planes.

"Where is the middle of your arm?...Your leg?...Your whole body?...Your face?...Bend your arms in the middle...Bend your legs in the middle...Bend your body in the middle... Can you go somewhere like that?"

MIDDLE OF PLANES
For the middle of planes, walls, floor, and rooms in general, the children need to realize that they are finding the middle of 2 lines. For example, they can find the middle of the floor by intersecting the 2 diagonals or by intersecting the line that connects the middle of the width with the line connecting the middle of the length of the room. For young children I stick to the middle of an area being the middle of both diagonals.* For older children I mention both ways of looking at it. When finding the middle using widths and lengths, it is clearest if one child stands in the middle of the width of the room and another stands in the middle of the length and they walk and meet. This is an excellent preparation for graph work.

----

* I think it is a mistake, however, to simply say the middle of the floor is where the diagonals cross. Although it is clear to us, most children will not include the intermediate step of recognizing that the 2 diagonals cross at their middles. To them it will be another theoretical formula that works but they are not sure why. It is better to say the middle of the floor is the middle of both diagonals and let them light up with the discovery that that is where the diagonals cross.

REMOVING THE MIDDLE MARKER

The children have actually worked with middle before this lesson. When using the Diagonal Structure, one group starts their locomotor movement when the group ahead reaches the middle. The children have also used middle in numerous studies. In these cases the middle has been clearly marked with a taped "X."

Now that the concept middle is formally introduced, I take the mark away and see what happens. If the children can use the middle without the marker, I congratulate them and consider middle in the bag of known, useable, concepts.

FLOOR PATTERNS

DEFINITION
Good for: 1) Spatial awareness.
               2) Memory skills.
               3) Innumerable academic skills.

How wonderful that we are ready for floor patterns. It is one of my favorite topics.

Floor patterns are the spatial designs made by locomotor movements. This unit is one of the largest and most important in my movement program. Floor patterns cover such a broad area that I break it up into 3 parts: 1) maps, 2) line shapes, and 3) additional work.

SKILLS
To be able to create and read a floor pattern requires a number of skills:

1) The child can visualize the line a locomotor movement creates in space, that is, if I run a circle, the child can "see" the circle even though there is nothing there.

2) The child can create and follow a movement map (explained shortly). This particular skill requires: a) transferring pictorial images to space, that is, understanding from the 2-dimensional paper where to move in the 3-dimensional room; b) memorizing lines and movements; c) conceptualizing the entire design, that is, seeing that one line fits with another, seeing the picture as a whole; and d) augmenting a line representation to room size.

3) The child can recognize and create different lines in space: straight, curved, wiggly, spiral, zigzag, looped.

4) The child can identify the front, back, right and left sides of a given room.

FLOOR PATTERNS: MAPS

ORGANIZING THE CLASS TO SEE THE MAP
My introduction of maps often does not ever get to the map itself. I begin with a spatial problem. Putting a large piece of paper (approximately 18" x 18") on the floor, I say to the class, "Get so that you and everyone else can see this paper."

I wait. As usual this is the hardest part. If the children are having a lot of trouble, I will nudge them by complimenting the people in front that are sitting far enough from the paper so that those in back of them can see. Eventually they get the idea, but the real test is to hold out and let them do it.

Why bother? It would be so much more efficient, not to mention less noisy, to get them organized yourself, a nice circle of children sitting a few feet from the paper, a row of children behind them, standing or kneeling. I bother because this is an extremely important lesson in cooperation, spatial awareness, and peer group organization. To do otherwise would be to forsake the real moment to moment lesson for the grand concept. Moreover, if I seat them now I will have to seat them in the future and in the long run that is much more time consuming. Enough. On with maps.

DRAWING THE ROOM REPRESENTATION

I begin a map by drawing a stylized representation of what is in the room. At this beginning stage, I include some identifying marks to show each corner and most walls.

This room representation (starting at the top and going clockwise in diagram #1) shows the stage, piano, chairs, my desk, a cabinet, 2 tables, a double door, more chairs, and a side door. Although the drawings are abstract, the children know what the symbols stand for because each has been identified when drawn. (Technical note: use *one* dark color to draw the objects in the room because, if the room representation has a lot of different colors, the floor pattern will get confused.)

Children like this room representation and will often ask you to include all sorts of details like the tiles on the floor, the clock, the flag, the windows, their shoes. I go along with this for a short while because for most children the idea of representing a space is brand new and very exciting. However, I do not draw anything in the middle of the room. At some appropriate time I go on to the floor pattern within the room.

"CINCH" APPROACH

I keep this first floor pattern as simple as possible. I want the children to say, "This is a cinch."

"Great. That's because you're so smart," I say to them. "Wait until you see where this 'cinch' will lead," I think to myself. For older and brighter classes I go faster rather than exclude steps at this stage.

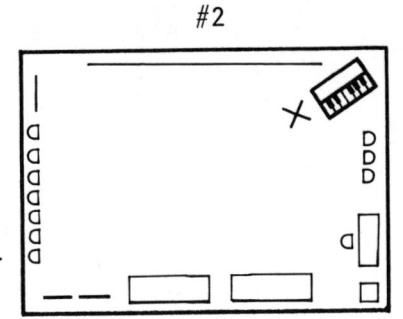

I place a red "X" in one corner of the room representation (near the piano). I ask, "If I were standing here in the room, where would I be?" (See diagram #2.)

In this example the children would have to conclude, "By the piano." One or several children stand at the appropriate spot and then rejoin the group.

If the children have any difficulty transferring the "X" from the paper to the room, check to see that the room representation is complete and that they understand it. If there is any doubt, start over, go slower, and draw another map showing even more detail.

FIRST LINE
   Now comes the first line of the floor pattern. Keep it straight and simple. Curved, wiggly, and angled lines require specific attention. Also there is more chance of success if the line goes to a clearly marked spot in the room rather than an undefined area. Even if the concept middle has been taught I do not use it unless there is an identifying mark. So, keeping it straight and ending at an identified spot, I draw the first line. It is drawn with the same color magic marker as the starting "X" and the locomotor movement (in this case "run") is written in the same color on the line. (See diagram #3.)

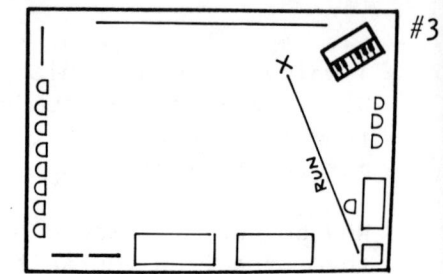

"Where does the line go?"

"To the cabinet."

"Anthony, start at the beginning 'X' and run the red line."

With a young class, several children try out the red line. With older classes, I move immediately to the next line.

SECOND LINE
   The second line starts where the first ended and is a different color. (See diagram #4.)

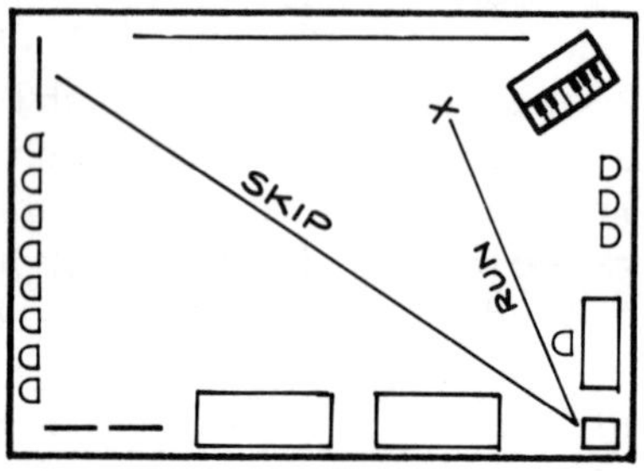

"Where does the green line end?"

"At the door."

"The double doors?"

"No, the door by the stage."

"Right. Alice, start at the beginning 'X,' run the red line, then skip the green line."

THIRD LINE
   Staying faithful to the "cinch" approach, the 3rd line might be the last. It is drawn in a different color. I am fond of having the last line end where the first began in order to repeat easily. Another child shows us the movement in the room. (See diagram #5.)

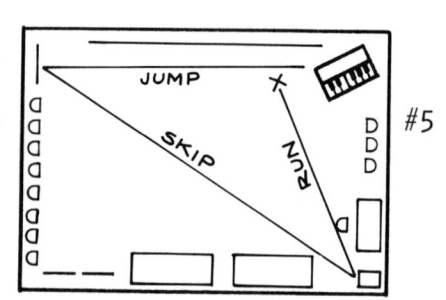

OTHER BEGINNING FLOOR PATTERNS
   See diagrams #6a and #6b below and #6c and #6d at the top of page 97.

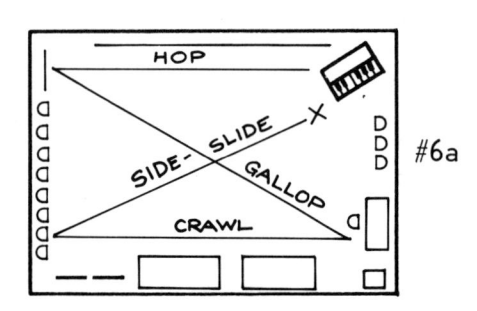

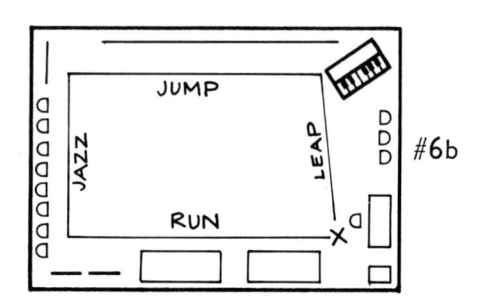

96

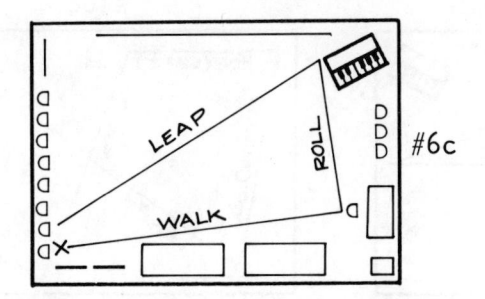

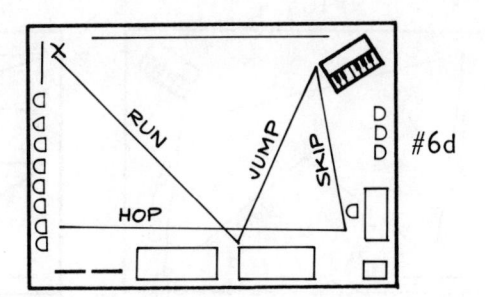

GROUPINGS

When this first map is completed, the children form groups so that everyone does the pattern. In the original example the groups stand ready to begin at the piano. (See diagram #7.)

I watch each group complete the entire pattern once and then have them continuously feeding in: "When the group ahead finishes the red line, the run line, you start."

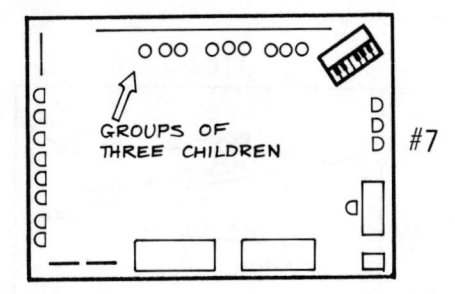

In a different initial map the children line up at the appropriate side. (See diagram #8.)

SUBSEQUENT CHANGES IN FLOOR PATTERNS

That is our first map. Does it seem terribly mundane, plodding, and simple? Just wait....

In subsequent maps 2 changes occur: the room representation gets less detailed and the floor patterns get harder and longer.

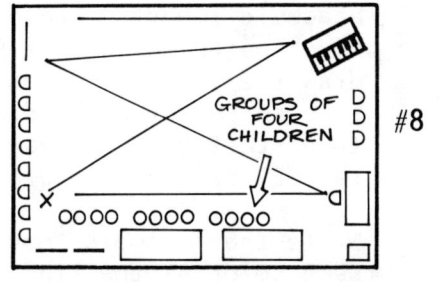

Diagrams #9a, #9b, and #9c below show the room representation getting less and less detailed.

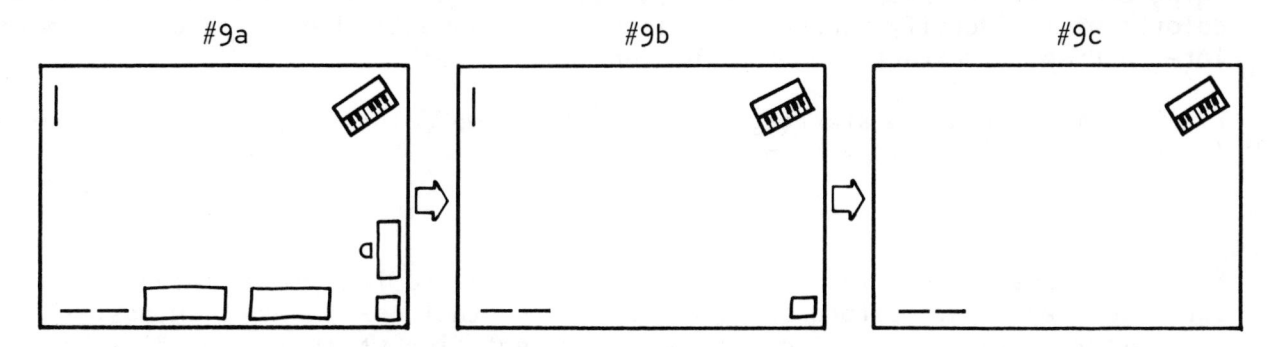

The children will want to know why you are drawing less. I tell them because they do not need it: "James, would you know where to go if I asked you to stand in this corner? (I point to a corner of the paper that has *no* identifying mark.) See, you know where everything is just from one or 2 things drawn."

Until I introduce specific line shapes, I keep the lines straight. Subsequent floor patterns are shown by diagrams #10a, #10b, #10c, #10d, #10e, and #10f at the top of page 98.

#10a, #10b, #10c, #10d, #10e (THIS IS A FAVORITE), #10f

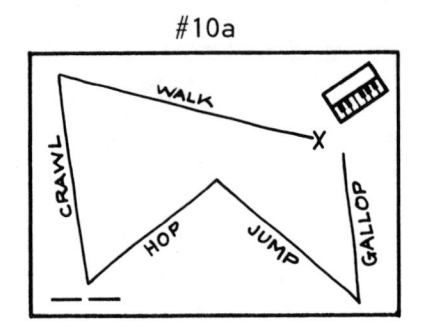

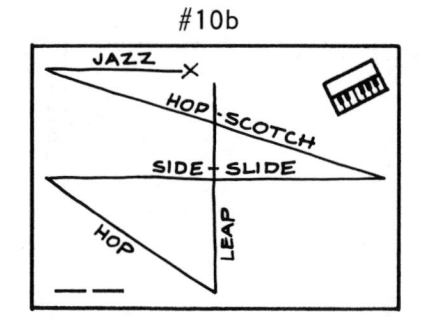

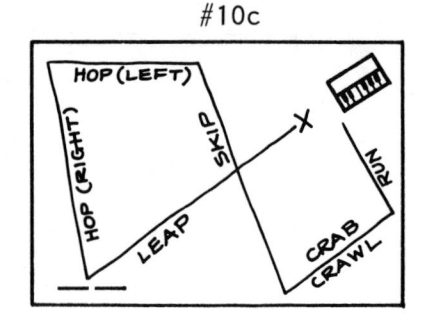

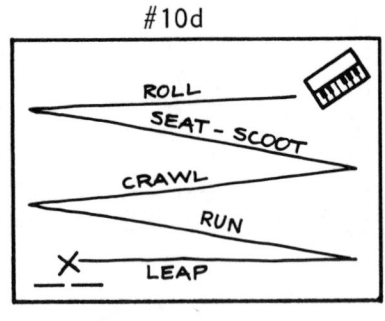

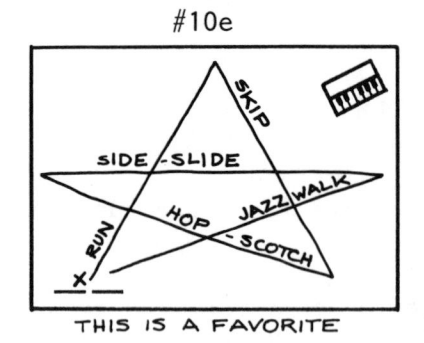

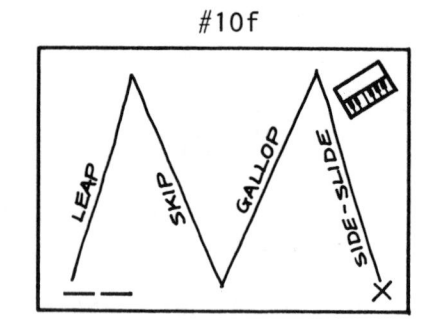

SOME MISCELLANEOUS NOTES

Straight lined letters and numbers are fine at this point; I de-emphasize their academic importance and just treat them as shapes. (More on number and letter floor patterns in Part 9.) If you are doing a shape that requires backtracking, draw the line twice and mark the beginning and end of the line so that the children backtrack to the place where they started. For example, the middle line of the letter "E" as shown in diagram #11.

Write the locomotor movements on their lines in the same color as the line, for example, "skip" written in green on the green line. This might be more for you than the children, but it does help keep everything orderly. However, do *not* always use the same color line to identify a particular locomotor movement; that would cause problems later and would detract from the inherent memory work.

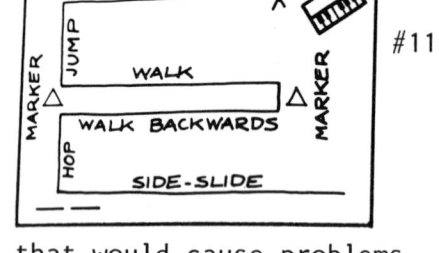

Finally, make sure the starting "X" is in the same color as the first line so you can tell which way the pattern goes.

OWN PATTERNS

Even at this straight line stage it is a good idea to let the children create their own floor patterns. Before setting them out on their own, I do 2 things: 1) I have the children practice putting the room representation straight, and 2) we do a "helping" floor pattern, that is, a floor pattern done with the children drawing the lines.

Putting The Room Representation Straight

In preparation for their own patterns, I mimeograph a number of moderately detailed room representations on regular 8½ x 11 inch paper. This mimeographed room representation presents the first difficulty. In the initial floor patterns, I drew the room while the class watched. Now the children are presented with an already drawn room representation and they have to figure out how it fits within the room. In addition, the paper is much smaller.

The class gathers around me on the floor and I show one of the mimeographed room representations:

"This is a picture of our room. Here is the piano, the door, my desk, the stage. If I placed the paper like this (turned upside down) the room would be upside down, the piano would be way over in that corner. Alex, can you turn the paper straight the way things are in the room?...Yes, very good." (Or, "No, the piano goes in this corner.")..."Omar, you try it." (I shake the paper and turn it several times so it will be "mixed up" and then hand it to a child to lay straight "the way things are in the room.")

Ideally I have every child practice putting the room representation straight. This is usually not possible so I pick the ones that I think might have trouble later.

Making A "Helping" Floor Pattern
"Now we are ready to make our floor pattern. Rachel, pick a color...(she picks a crayon) put an 'X' where you want the floor pattern to start. It can start anywhere...(She puts an "X" on the paper). Now draw your first line. It can go anywhere...(She draws a line). Now write what locomotor movement you want in the same color on the line; I'll help you spell if you need it..." (She writes the movement.)

"OK, Mark, you are going to draw the 2nd line. Pick a different color...(He picks). WHERE DOES YOUR LINE *HAVE* TO START?" (Stop and steel yourself! It is *not* obvious to the children that the lines have to connect. Teaching them to connect the lines is the main reason why it is necessary to do this helping floor pattern before they make their own.) "Nope, line number 2 *has* to start where line number one stopped. Now draw your line...(He draws) and write the locomotor movement you want...(He writes the movement in the same color on the line).

"OK, Anthony, you do line number 3. (He picks a different color). Where does line number 3 *HAVE* to start? No...No...No...Line 3 has to start where line 2 stopped."

Drawing Their Own Floor Patterns
We do this painstaking procedure for 4 lines. "Do you think you can make your own floor pattern?" If they answer "No," I recommend not to do it that day. If they answer "Yes," I ask them to divide into groups of 4. Each group gets one mimeographed room representation and one container of crayons.

"Make a floor pattern that has 4 straight lines, each a different color, each a different locomotor movement." I almost always start with groups of 4 making a 4 line floor pattern because 1) every child makes one line and that simplifies the social arrangements, and 2) the floor pattern is long enough to be challenging but short enough to be feasible. Of course, the assignment can be made longer or shorter to fit your class.

I found it works best if the helping floor pattern immediately precedes the children's own patterns. Therefore, if we made a helping pattern at the end of one class I would quickly do another helping pattern at the beginning of the next class and then let the children make their own.

Practicing Their Patterns

When the group floor patterns are drawn and checked, the children practice them. Yes, all the groups end up practicing their patterns at the same time. Yes, it is confusing and noisy, but a group that can practice and perfect its pattern despite all that distraction certainly has had a study in concentration. (Plus that, I do not know a way around it.) I ask the children to know their patterns well enough to do it without the map.

After this practice time the groups watch each other perform. When performing I hold the map and play appropriate music on the piano or drum. If a group does not move like the pattern they have drawn, I emphasize the difference rather than say one is right and one wrong. They can change either the map or their movements as long as the 2 correspond.

MORE DIFFICULT ASSIGNMENTS

As the children become more at ease with floor patterns, 2 more changes occur simultaneously: I introduce line shapes, which I will introduce to you shortly, and the assignments get harder. Examples of assignments:

1) Draw a floor pattern using 5 lines (the line shapes allowed here and in the following assignments depend on what has been introduced), each in a different locomotor movement on a different level.

2) Draw a floor pattern using 4 lines, each a different locomotor movement in a different direction.

I like to save this study until the children know 4 different line shapes. The assignment then becomes: "Draw a floor pattern using 4 different line shapes, each in a different locomotor movement, each using a different direction." This study by necessity clarifies the difference between direction and floor pattern. It is an enormous undertaking.

I break up the assignment into 2 stages. First, the children draw their floor patterns using 4 different line shapes, each using a different locomotor movement. (See diagram #12.)

#12

They practice the pattern and I check it. Second, the children assign a different direction to each of the lines. This makes it very difficult. (See diagram #13.)

#13

When the children are ready to add the directions, I take a few minutes to clarify the problem:

"Each time you move in space (I walk an ordinary walk across the room.) you do 3 things *at one time:* One, you make a line shape. What line shape did I just do?"

"Straight line."

"Two, you use a locomotor movement. What locomotor movement did I just use?"

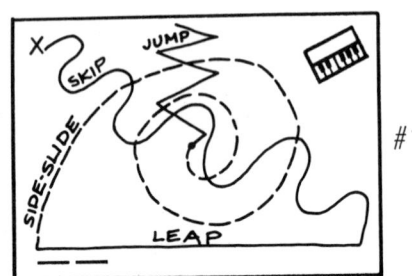

"Walking."

"And three, you go in a direction. What direction did I go in?"

"Forward."

"I can do almost any line shape, in almost any locomotor movement, in almost any direction. For example, what am I doing now?" (I do a wiggly line by jumping backwards.)

"A wiggly line...jumping...backwards."

"OK you solve these problems. Do a wiggly line, hopping, sideways direction." (One or several children attempt it. I correct them if necessary.)..."Do a spiral line, skipping, turning direction."..."Do a zigzag line, walking, backwards direction."

"Great. Now let's go back to the floor patterns you made. So far the patterns have different line shapes and different locomotor movements. Now each line will also include a different direction. Decide which line you want to be forward, which backward, which sideways, and which turning. It is a good idea to make the most difficult line move in the forward direction."

Generally only half the class will understand and I scurry around helping others. It is worth the trouble. Once a child understands this problem and can perform the resulting pattern, he has an enormous grasp of both direction and floor pattern.

Continuing floor pattern assignments:

3) Draw a floor pattern using 4 lines, each a different locomotor movement on a different level, going in a different direction.

4) Use 4 to 7 lines. Each line must combine a different locomotor movement plus a nonlocomotor movement, for example, skip plus contract and stretch, jump plus shake in the hands.

5) Use 4 to 7 lines, each a different locomotor movement. Include a 10 second nonlocomotor movement between each line.

6) Pick 6 locomotor movement cards at random. Make a floor pattern that uses those 6 movements.

7) Draw a floor pattern of 4 lines. Each line must combine 2 or more locomotor movements, for example, 2 jumps and 2 hops for one line; run, leap, fall, and roll for another line. No locomotor movement can be used twice!

8) A Christmas Tree floor pattern: (See diagram #14.)

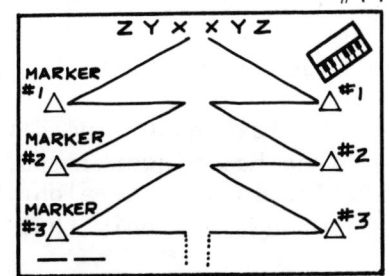

Two children start together ("X" and "X"). Other partner groups start on either side of the beginning 2 children, that is, "Y" and "Y," and "Z" and "Z." The children skip 4 beats to the first markers and then side-slide 4 beats to join each other; they skip 4 beats to the 2nd markers and side-slide 4 beats to join; they skip 4 beats to the 3rd markers and side-slide 4 beats to join. Finally they jump 4 beats for the "stem" and run on the outside of the tree to take their place at the end of their line.

Have each partner group perform the entire Christmas tree. Then ask groups to begin 8 beats apart, that is, group 2 starts when group one begins skipping to marker #2. This is a wonderful demonstration for the annual Christmas assembly.

FLOOR PATTERNS: LINES

USING NEW LINES IN FLOOR PATTERNS

Curved, wiggly, spiral, zigzag, and looped, are the specific line shapes we work on. If the children can do these they can do just about any. (See diagrams #15a, #15b, #15c, #15d, and #15e.)

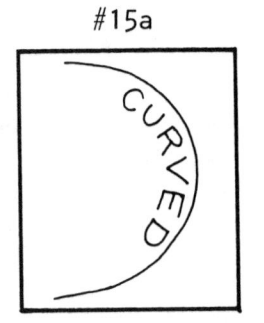

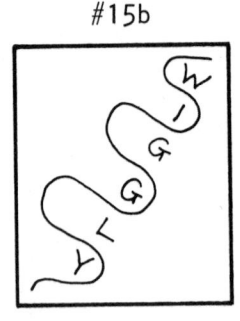

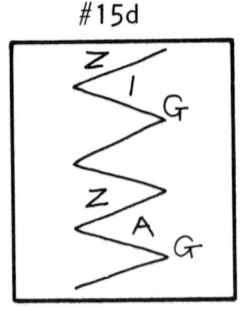

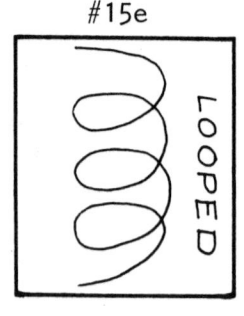

#15a #15b #15c #15d #15e

I introduce one line at a time, usually in the above order. This line sequence progresses in difficulty, but it is not crucial to teach them in sequence.

After we work on various ways of doing the line, we use the new line in a floor pattern with any previously learned lines. Therefore, after curved lines are introduced we do a floor pattern combining straight and curved lines; after looped lines are introduced we combine straight, wiggly, spiral, zigzag, and looped.

THE CONCEPTUAL METHOD OF TEACHING THE WIGGLY LINE

Since I teach each new line in about the same way I will describe fully how I teach one of them: the wiggly line.

The children stand ready to move on the diagonal. If possible, each child moves individually; if the class is too large or the time too short they move in small groups.

First we examine the picture of a wiggly line. Then, without any further instructions, the children run the line. I mutely watch the results, allowing all interpretations. Usually there is a pattern to the "mistakes," namely, the curves are more shallow than the curves in the picture. Showing the picture of the wiggly line, I say, "This red line is the line I asked you to do. Most of you did a line that looks like this yellow one." As I say this I draw the yellow line. (See diagram #16.)

#16

We talk about the differences between the 2 lines: "The red has bigger loops." "The red is more hilly." "The yellow is more straight." The emphasis here is not to say that one is right and one wrong, but only that they are different.

I ask them to run the red line again. We repeat this process of comparing the line they run to the visual representation until the children can do approximately the kind of line they see.

Once this happens we can play with the whole idea of wiggly lines. First, we use more difficult locomotor movements: hopscotch, skip, skip backwards, skip turning, side-slide changing sides. Second, I make the same line shape go to different places. (See diagrams #17a, #17b, and #17c.)

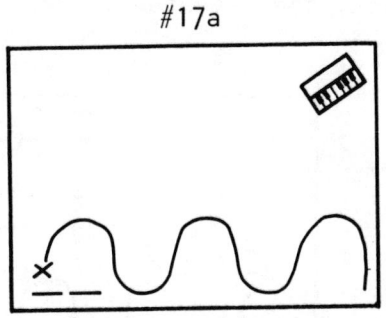

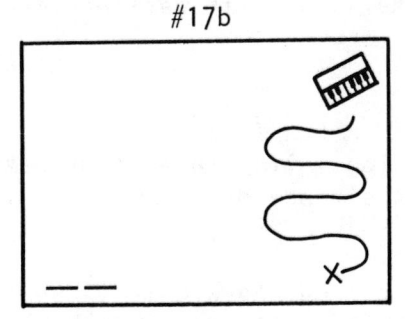

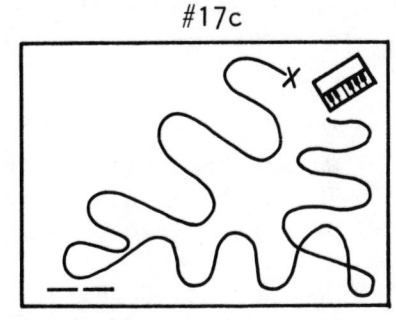

#17a #17b #17c

Because the children did the first line from sight they usually have no trouble with this place transference. If they do, I simply repeat the process of drawing what they did in relation to what they saw. Third, in some classes, we move in different types of wiggly lines, for example, the wiggles getting larger or smaller. The possibilities are endless.

I prefer this conceptual method of teaching line shape. Even though it is quite abstract most young children do surprisingly well. Because the children learn the shape without demonstrations or physical markers, the idea is immediately internalized and applicable.

THE MARKER METHOD OF TEACHING THE WIGGLY LINE
However, if you have an immature class or if this method is not working, there is nothing wrong with using markers. This is the progression I use for teaching the wiggly line with markers:

#18

1) I put tape numbers* on the floor. The children run around them to achieve the wiggly line. (See diagram #18 .)

   It is better to have them run around the outside of the marker than on it because, if they just run to each number, the line ends up angled.

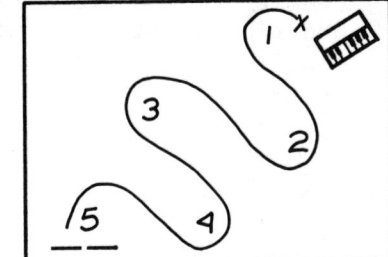

2) In a following lesson I substitute taped "X's" on the floor instead of the numbers. Again the children move around the markers to achieve the wiggly line. We do it with many locomotor movements. This step is not essential. If the class moved smoothly and easily with the numbered line, I skip this step.

3) The taped "X's" are replaced by moveable markers. Those bright orange traffic cones (game cones) are perfect, but anything, shoes, boxes, chairs, will do. The children run the wiggly line again. "Can you run the exact same wiggly line if I take away a marker?" I proceed to take away one marker at a time.

---

* It is better to form the numbers out of tape than to put a piece of paper with numbers on the floor. Paper on the floor, no matter how firmly attached, will be demolished quickly.

The children run the line each time another marker is removed. Take the markers away in a random pattern, but leave the first marker until last. It is strange but true, that if they start the line correctly they will go on doing so.

The problem with the marker method is that the lines are set. It is difficult to transfer the idea of a wiggly line to the other diagonal or across the middle of the room. Often it is necessary to go back to the moveable marker stage for a newly placed line. But with patient repetition, they eventually get the idea.

#19

COMBINING A WIGGLY LINE WITH OTHER LINES

We are ready to use the wiggly line in a floor pattern. The children have perhaps already done a wiggly line pattern. (See diagram #19.)

Now we include straight, curved and wiggly lines together. I draw the first few patterns. Later the children do their own. (See diagrams #20a, #20b, #20c, #20d, and #20e.)

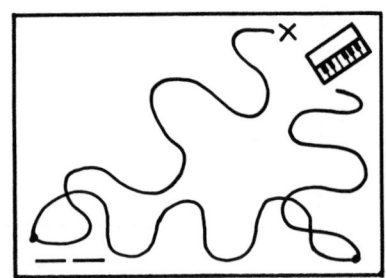

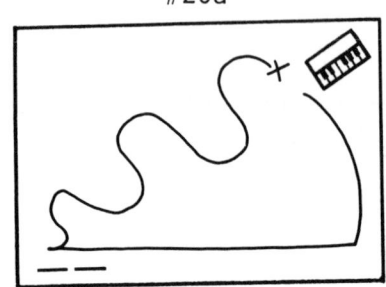

#20a #20b #20c

#20d #20e

The techniques I use to teach the wiggly line are basic to all line shapes. However, below are a few additional notes on some peculiarities of the other shapes.

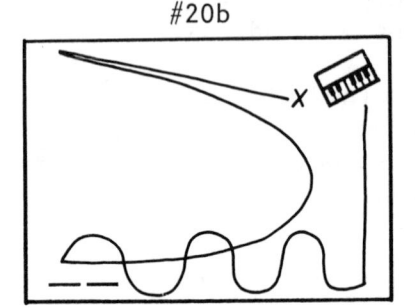

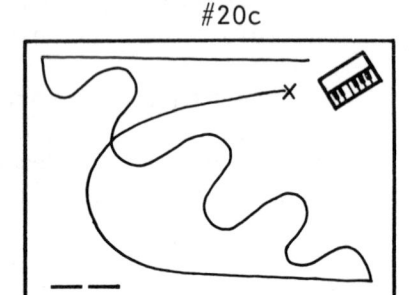

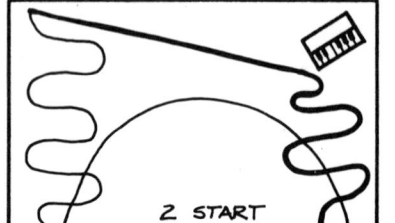

CURVED LINES

The difficulty with the curved line is that the children are not sure how deep to make it. It works best if the curve comes near one side of the room. (See diagrams #21a and #21b.)

The children know they have to go very close to that side of the room.. In diagrams #21a and #21b I mark the point at which the first curve ends and the 2nd begins.

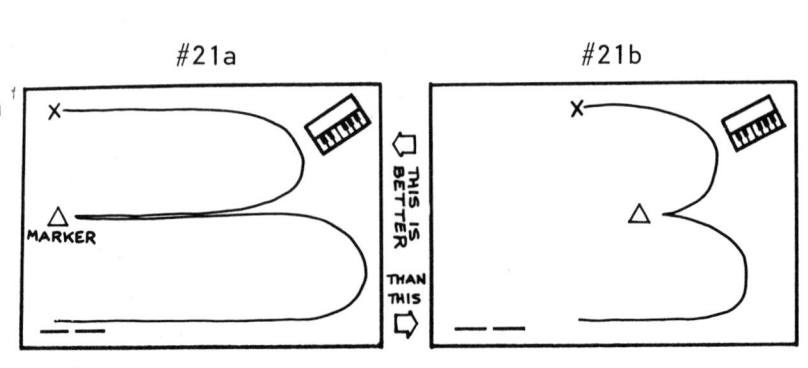

#21a #21b

THIS IS BETTER THAN THIS

104

For a shallow curve, have the children go around markers. (See diagram #22.)

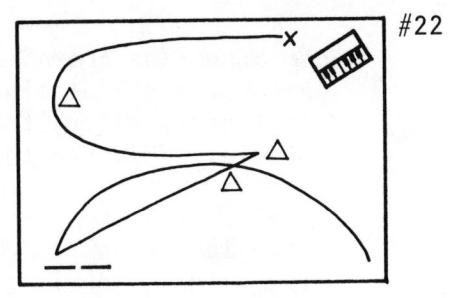

Once the curved line is introduced and the children have combined curved and straight lines, all letters and numbers become feasible floor patterns. Children love to do their own names in floor patterns. At this stage each letter becomes a separate map. Therefore, the name Mary takes 4 floor patterns as shown in diagrams #23a, #23b, #23c, and #23d.

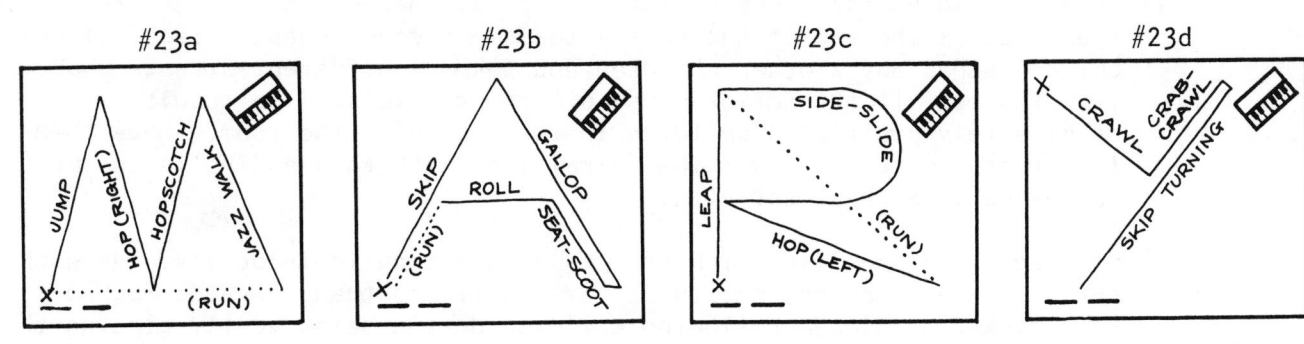

If she wanted to include her age, 12, that would take 2 more floor patterns. (See diagrams #24a and #24b.)

Mary does these 6 patterns, in sequence, remembering all the line shapes and all the different locomotor movements. Quite an accomplishment.

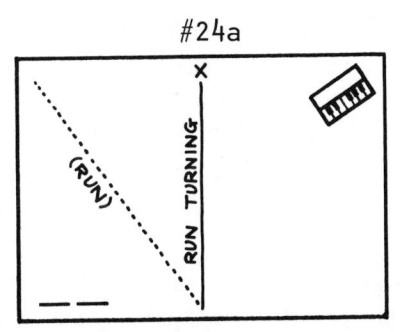

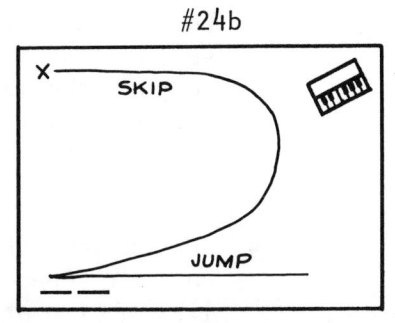

If you want the children to work in groups, use common words or phrases: $6,000,000 Man, Merry Christmas, Welcome Back (Kotter), The Hustle, and The Bump, are favorites as of this writing. Obviously, almost anything will do.

SPIRAL LINES

Most children prefer the spiral line over any other. I think it looks more difficult to us than it does to them. If you want your class to follow the floor pattern exactly, a simple spiral works better than a many layered one. (See diagrams #25a and #25b.)

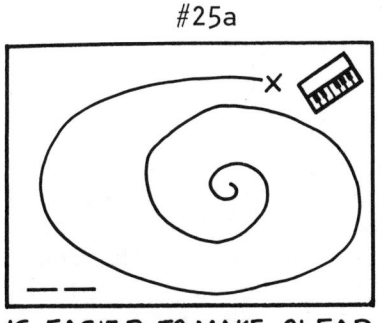

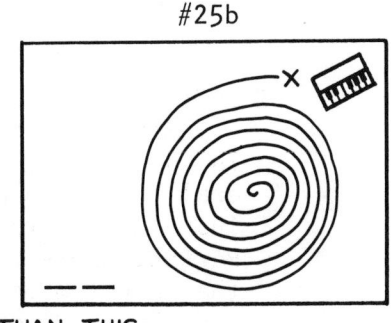

IS EASIER TO MAKE CLEAR THAN THIS

In the first spiral, as shown in diagram #25a, the child knows that the first circle goes near the sides of the room, then there is a medium sized circle, then a tiny circle in the center of the room. It is clearly defined. I usually use this simple spiral; sometimes just for fun I use a many circled one. When I do, I am not terribly fussy about the number of circles as long as the circles keep getting smaller and smaller as in diagram #25b.

Body Size Plus Spiral Line
Because a spiral line gets smaller and smaller, it is natural to make the movement get smaller, that is, use lower levels, as the children get closer to the middle. This can then be reversed, the child getting bigger as he spirals out.

Ending The Spiral
The spiral line is great for grand finales because the entire class or group ends in the center of the room. Some possible climaxes are:

1) Do a fast locomotor movement for the spiral shaped line. The first child that reaches the end of the spiral takes a strange shape. Each following child touches any 2 other children and takes a different strange shape. It works best if the children use different levels. The result is a maze of bizarrely positioned children in the middle of the room. Have them stay like that and take a bow. The spiral line with this ending is the most requested line shape activity.

2) Do a spiral shaped line with the children moving individually. As each child reaches the end, he stands very stiff and then proceeds to "boil down to a cooked noodle." Following children do the same, gently placing themselves over other children to form a giant plate of Spaghetti (see Part 7).

3) Place a mat in the middle of the room. Divide into groups of 6 to 10, each group doing a spiral line individually. As each child reaches the mat, he assumes his prepared place until the entire group has formed a simple gymnastic pyramid. (See diagram #26.)

4) Do you know the theater game "machine"? One child starts a machine-like motion which is simple and repetitive. One by one, new children join the first, adding their own related movement until the group forms one united mechanism. It is especially effective if each child adds his own machine noise along with his own movement. Move in a spiral shaped line and create a machine at the end.

ZIGZAG LINES
I demonstrate this line probably more than any other. The difficulty is in getting the angles sharp. Several things help: 1) Have the entire class practice just the "sharp corners." They can start either in Perfect Spots or on one side of the room. "Face the corner where the piano is, when I say 'switch' *quickly* turn your whole body to face the corner where the mats are. Switch...Switch..." (This is good preparation for focus, Part 10.) 2) Make the line segments of equal length and play marching music so that the effect is militaristic: step-2-3-4-change, step-2-3-4-change.

Once the children catch on to the whole body, military turn, they can apply it to other locomotor movements. Keeping in this military vein, have 2 children start simultaneously from different points in the zigzag. For example in diagram #27, "A" starts as "B" begins.

106

COMBINING 4 LINE SHAPES

If the children know straight, curved, spiral, and zigzag lines they can do one of my favorite floor patterns. (See diagrams #28a, #28b, #28c, #28d, and #28e.)

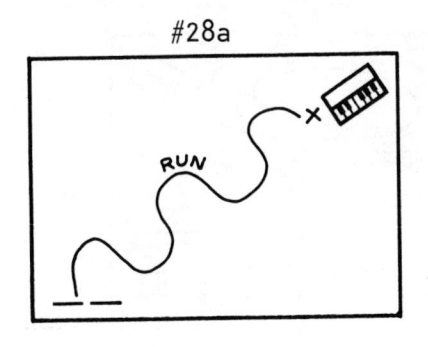

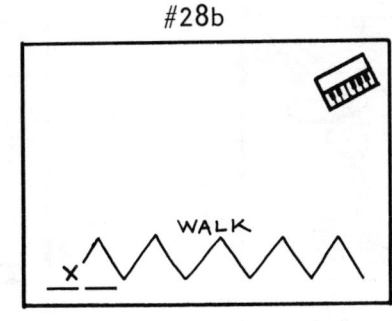

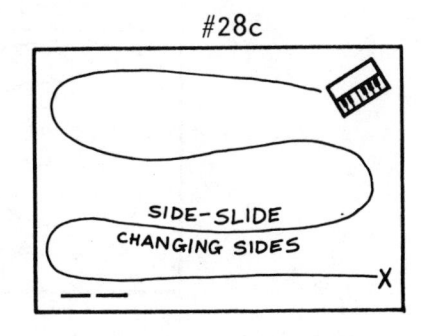

#28a — RUN

#28b — WALK

#28c — SIDE-SLIDE CHANGING SIDES

The children move individually, one wiggle apart. (Ideally everyone should have at least started the wiggly line before the first child starts the curved line.) At the end the children hook

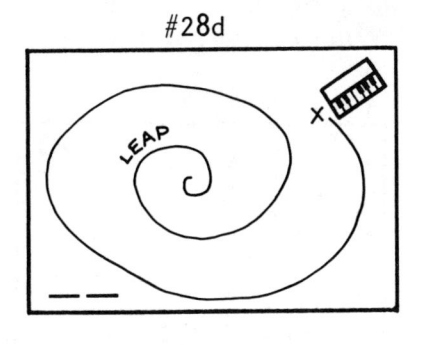

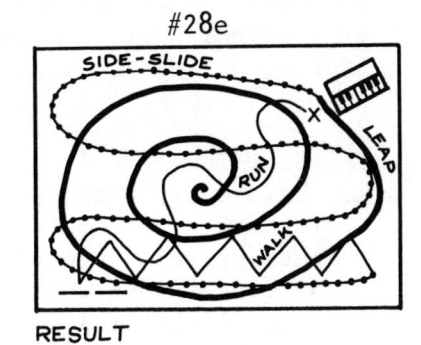

#28d — LEAP

#28e — RESULT (SIDE-SLIDE, LEAP, RUN, WALK)

on to each other in strange shapes and hold these positions as they bow. For a little extra added spice, let each child have a scarf to hold or to wear.

LOOPED LINES

Looped lines are hard. I do not introduce this line to children under 2nd grade unless there is a lot of time. The difficulty with the looped line is that the children will want to make them wiggly. That is, they will not cross their own line. (See diagrams #29a and #29b.)

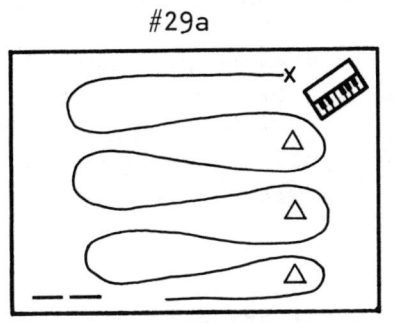

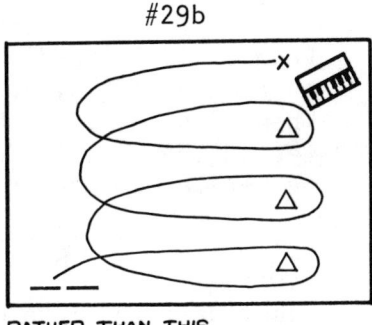

#29a — CHILDREN WILL TEND TO DO THIS...

#29b — RATHER THAN THIS.

If this happens it is a good time to use the technique of comparing their actual line with the representation. Then do a floor pattern that uses both types of lines. (See diagrams #30a, #30b, and #30c.)

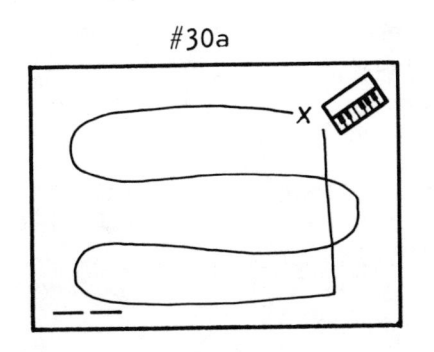

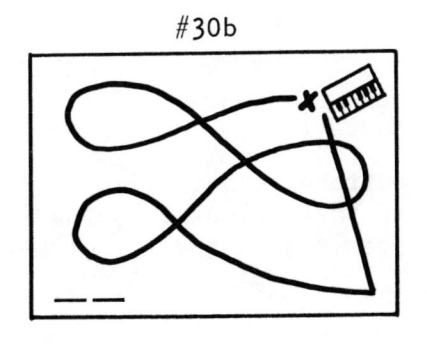

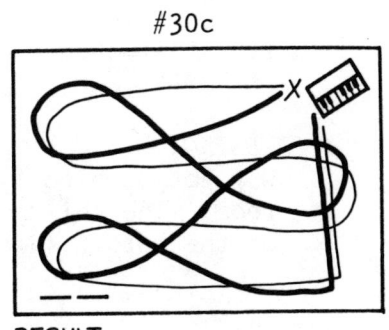

#30a

#30b

#30c — RESULT

107

With the looped line under our belts we can use any line combination to form varied and wonderous patterns. (See diagrams #31a and #31b.)

#31a   #31b

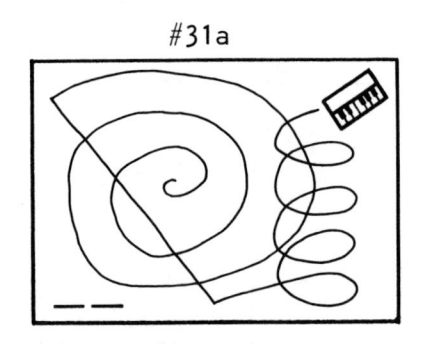

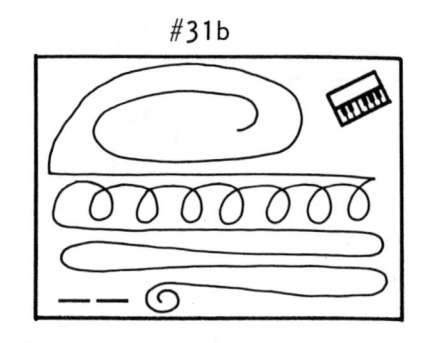

FLOOR PATTERNS: ADDITIONAL ACTIVITIES

Floor patterns are an enormous well of movement ideas. Here are a few additional activities they have spawned: individual maps, art works, tumbling patterns, voice box patterns, and designs.

#32a   #32b

INDIVIDUAL MAPS

I have drawn about 40 different floor patterns. These patterns use all the line shapes and are quite difficult. To make them even a little harder, I do not write the locomotor movement on the line but color code it on the back. (See diagrams #32a and #32b.)

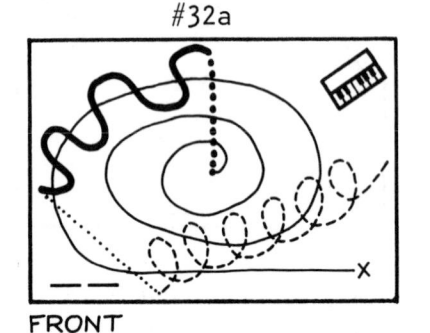

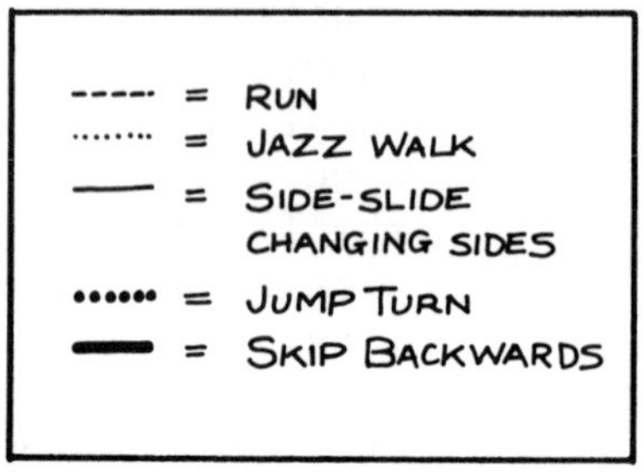

- - - - = RUN
.... = JAZZ WALK
———— = SIDE-SLIDE CHANGING SIDES
•••••• = JUMP TURN
━━━━ = SKIP BACKWARDS

Each child is handed a floor pattern. Soon there are 34 different patterns going on at the same time. (For a little less chaos give groups of 3's or 4's a map.) When a child learns his map, either I or another child checks him. If it is "perfect," that is, the child does exactly what is on the paper without looking at it, he gets a new map or trades with someone else. Chaotic? Yes. Worth it? Definitely.

ARTWORKS

Floor patterns make wonderful art projects. Sometime when you have time let the children draw their own room representations in as much detail as they want. As long as they keep the picture aligned I allow anything and everything drawn, in as many colors as they want.

When the children are ready to add their floor patterns, I ask them to draw their conception of the movement: "How would a run look on paper? A jump? A skip?" There are amazing results when a child attempts to draw a skipping line going in a looped shape. This is obviously more art than movement. Since the goal is beauty rather than clarity, I am not my usual strict self.

TUMBLING

Why not combine floor patterns and tumbling? I place a long line of mats in the room. The children make their floor patterns incorporating various gymnastic moves on the mats. (See diagram #33 at the top of page 109.)

Safety warning: Have all the children start their tumbling at the same end of the mats. This way when they are practicing their patterns, there will be no disasters.

#33

VOICE BOX

I have decorated a box, large enough for a child to fit in, and labeled it the Voice Box. On one side is a hole large enough for a small face. With this box we play a language game. One child leaves the room. The rest of the class and I make up a difficult floor pattern. We go through it a few times so that everyone knows it. One person is picked to go into the Voice Box with the floor pattern; the rest of the class sits down. The outside child is retrieved and the game begins. The child in the box, obviously using no other aid than his voice, must command the other child to do the floor pattern:

"Start at the door."

"Which door?"

"That door."

"Which one?"

"Over there by the side of the stage...OK now run a wiggly line...No not to there, to the other side..."

I diabolically enjoy putting a timid child in the voice box with a bossy child as the mover.

The problem, as you have probably noticed, is that only 2 children can play at one time. The other children enjoy watching but I dislike having them sit for so long. I have not figured a way around that. Using more than one child as the mover has not worked for me. So I use the game only rarely.

DESIGNS

Doing abstract designs spatially is the most advanced stage of floor patterns. I do not do it with all classes and I would not do it below 2nd grade. Actually, it is good to use designs for the more advanced students within a class, so that perhaps half the class is doing floor patterns with maps and half are doing floor patterns with abstract designs.

What these designs entail are simply designs. I draw some and the children draw their own; sometimes I find interesting designs in magazines and art books. (See diagrams #34a, #34b, #34c, #34d, and #34e.)

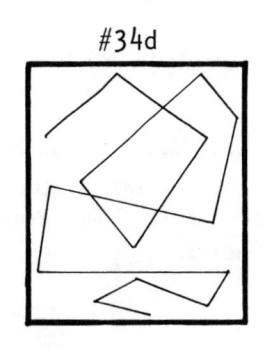

#34a   #34b   #34c   #34d   #34e

The children do them in any way that fulfills the design. The difficulty comes from the absence of a room representation. The design can be fitted any way into the room. The children must keep the invisible room representation in mind at all times.

ROOM DIRECTIONS

FRONT, BACK, RIGHT AND LEFT SIDES OF A ROOM
   When the children are at ease with floor patterns, it is time to clarify the idea of room directions, the front, back, right, and left sides of a room. If the children are clear with directions in their bodies they will have no trouble with this.

The children are already perfectly at ease with facing front from Perfect Spot. "The front of any room is simply the wall we pick to be front. We already have the chalkboard wall as our front. Face front; the wall that is in back of you is the back wall; the wall that is to your right is the right side of the room, and the wall that is to your left is the left side of the room."

With a sophisticated class you might want to take a few minutes and work with a variable front. "OK *whatever* wall I stand next to is front. (I choose a wall.) Face front; face back; point right; point left. (We do this with several walls as front.) Great."*

BODY DIRECTIONS COMBINED WITH ROOM DIRECTIONS
   "Now let's face the front that we usually use. I have some tricky questions for you." These instructions combine the children's body directions with room directions.

   1) Face front; point front with your right arm. Face back; point to the front of the room with your right arm.

   2) Point right with your right arm; point right with your left arm; point right with your left arm and hop to the right side of the room on your left foot.

   3) Face back and move toward the front of the room. What direction are *you* traveling in?

   4) Move toward the back of the room going in the forward direction.

   5) Move toward the front of the room going in the sideways direction.

   6) Move toward the right side of the room going in the backward direction.

   7) Move toward the left side of the room going sideways, right side leading.

----
* If it is not great, I would be willing to bet the children need a review of directions on their bodies. Walk Down Your Front, Right and Left Bug, and exercises using directions all help here.

8) Make your feet point right; make your arms point left; move backward toward the front of the room.

SYMMETRY AND ASYMMETRY

WHY INCLUDE IT WITH FLOOR PATTERNS?
The ideas of symmetry and asymmetry are certainly not limited to floor patterns but they inspire such marvelous ones that I include them in this section.

INTRODUCING THE WORDS
I begin by teaching the words "symmetry" and "asymmetry" without saying what they mean: "Here are 2 new words: 'symmetry' and 'asymmetry.' (We practice saying them.) I'm not going to tell you what they mean; you are going to figure that out." I get my body into a symmetrical position, both sides exactly the same, and state, "Symmetry." Taking an asymmetrical position, I state, "Asymmetry." After several examples I ask the children if they can tell the difference. Very often they will throw in other elements: "Symmetry is straight and asymmetry is contract." Rather than just say "no" I will show a contracted symmetrical position and a straight asymmetrical position. Most children eventually conclude that symmetry means the same on both sides while asymmetry has different sides. If they give up or I get exhausted, I go ahead and tell them. Even if I have to tell the definition, children like this guessing game and are more receptive to the information.

SHAPES
I ask the children to make their bodies into symmetrical and asymmetrical shapes. (In order to avoid the adjective form of the words, I say, "Put your body in a shape that has symmetry.") To get a greater variety of shapes I ask for different levels. Occasionally I ask the children to stay in their shapes, pick a locomotor movement, and travel.

Next I ask the children to make a symmetrical shape with a partner. They can either face each other and take identical shapes or they can position themselves side by side and make one symmetrical shape between the 2 of them. (See illustration #35.)

FLOOR PATTERNS USING SYMMETRY AND ASYMMETRY
When the concepts of symmetry and asymmetry are understood I use them in floor patterns. (See diagram #36 for an initial symmetrical floor pattern.)

The class divides into partners; one child starts at one "X" while the other child starts *at the same time* at the other "X."

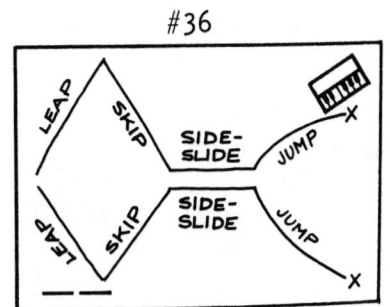

More examples of symmetrical floor patterns shown in diagrams #37a, 37b, and 37c.

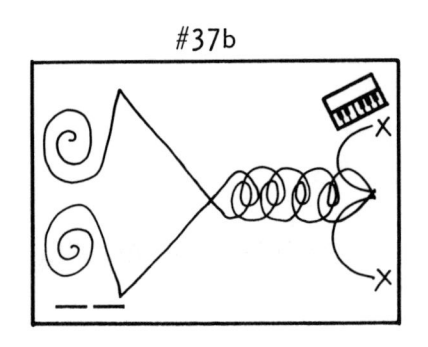

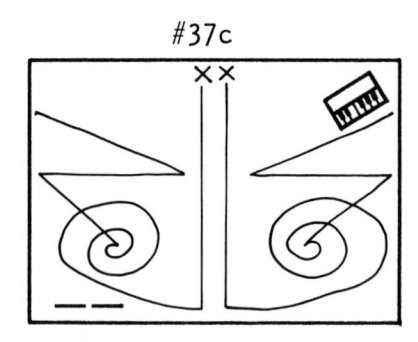

#37a #37b #37c

THEIR OWN PARTNER PATTERNS

After doing symmetrical patterns with the whole class, children divide into partners and make their own patterns. The patterns work best if the children decide how many beats each line is to have so that they complete their respective lines at the same time.

Asymmetrical partner patterns are simply 2 children doing different lines. (See diagram #38.) An interesting study on asymmetry is to ask both children to complete their respective patterns within the same number of beats.

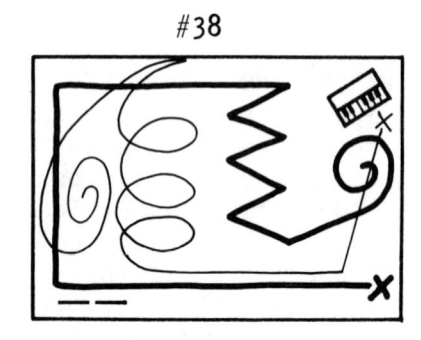

#38

If your children have just completed a symmetrical floor pattern, you might sit down and appreciate how many concepts they have incorporated in their activity: spatial design, memory, muscular control, cooperation to name a few. They have come a long way from that first floor pattern when they were saying, "This is a cinch."

PART 7
GIMMICKS

WHERE WE ARE

Parts one through 6 form the foundation of a movement curriculum: Perfect Spots, locomotor movements, Free Traveling and Diagonal Structures, nonlocomotor movements, direction, and floor patterns. Now we will build on this foundation: we will add props, we will use movement in an academic context, and we will look at some advanced work. Before we do, however, I offer a few gimmicks.

TRICKS OF THE TRADE

Every subject has problems and solutions that are unique. Part 7 presents a collection of miscellaneous tricks of the trade, those little discoveries that make teaching a little easier. These gimmicks range from the crying child, to aligning posture, to heaping children on top of one another. They are not crucial, but one or 2 might hit the spot.

ARE YOU ALIVE?
   Good for: 1) Calming a scared child.
                 2) Class tone.

Moving children are bound to fall down, bump into someone, or run into something. With young children this will happen with regularity. If a child is seriously hurt, he of course needs care and sympathy. But often a young child will start crying when startled to find himself suddenly on the floor. When this happens it is time for Are You Alive?

Are You Alive? works only with young children, those small enough to pick up. Pick up the crying child and sit him on a high place; a piano top is perfect, a table or chair will do. "Let's see if Cynthia is going to live." I gently shake one arm: "Is this arm alive?...Nope." Taking the other arm, "Is this arm alive?...No." Gently shaking one leg, "Is this leg alive?...No." "Is this (the other leg) alive?...Not a chance." Gently touching the child's head, "Is Cynthia's head alive?...Uh, oh, no!" Tickling the torso, "Is your torso alive?...Nope!" I pick the child up, holding him upside down by the knees, "I guess we'll have to take you to the dump." (See illustration at right.) I walk around the room, find a "dump" place, and gently lower the child.

Other children love to watch Are You Alive? (it only takes about 30 seconds). The only trouble is that you will have a lot of requests for it without the need.

THE FOAM
Good for: 1) Large muscle coordination.
           2) Practice with locomotor movements.
           3) Risk taking.

This movement idea is so simple I am a little embarrassed to write about it, but it is too dearly loved and too useful to keep to myself. Bring out a big piece of foam rubber (I use one about 2 feet by 2 feet) and let the children jump over it. I told you it was simple.

I use the Diagonal Structure when working with the foam and usually include it at the end of other locomotor movement work. The children move individually on the diagonal. First the foam is laid flat. The children 1) leap or gallop over it, 2) jump over it, 3) hop over it (be sure to do the other foot), 4) fall on it and roll off, 5) run and turn in the air over the foam.

Secondly, I fold the foam in half. The children 1) leap or gallop over it, and 2) jump or hop over it.

Finally, I unfold the foam vertically to its full height and let the children go over it any way they can.* (The foam will not stand by itself so I have to hold it.) Young children are often over-awed. I let them decide if they want the foam folded in half or extended straight. Older children are allowed to jump the foam at any height they say; they motion for me to either raise the foam off the ground or lower it. Then they jump, gallop, leap, or stumble over it. I use mats to soften their landings.

The foam jump is great for a number of reasons: 1) It is one of the few times the children have control over the teacher; I lift or lower the foam at their request. 2) They have to judge their own level of success. 3) There is something (it would be great to have a real psychological study done) about running and taking a flying risk that says a lot about a child. The child that runs and then slows down right before jumping is usually timid in other areas of life, on the playground, academically, and with friends. Mastering this risk is a small but significant part of the program to build the child's confidence. 4) A high foam jumper gains a lot of respect from the other children. Often this honor is bestowed on a child who really needs it, namely the one who is having academic or social problems. It is beautiful to see the glow of pride on their faces. 5) The children love it. In especially rambunctious classes I sometimes use the foam jump as a reward for finishing other work.

So far I have been talking about one piece of foam, which is all that is needed. However, if you can get several pieces of foam that is even better. Recently I acquired 10 foam squares, all about 2 feet by 2 feet. Now I do not have to hold the foam up, I stack them up. For younger grades I use this stack for mathematical computations (see Part 9). I also use the foam pieces for the In and Out Game (see Part 9). Jumping the foam is an amazingly simple idea, but its possibilities are endless.

---

* Children will want to jump the foam's full height immediately. Despite the protests it is important to do one or 2 jumps with the foam low so that the feet and ankles get fully warmed-up.

THE STAGE
  Good for: 1) Precision work.
             2) Performance experience.

If you are teaching movement classes in your school's auditorium and if that room has a stage, you have an invaluable tool at hand. If you do not have a stage, you can use the idea of a stage with almost as much ease.

I use the stage as a motivation for precision work: "When this pattern is perfect we will do it on the stage."* The only way the stage becomes a source of enjoyment is if the children are not allowed on it unless they are performing a finished piece. What is perfected and what is not is, of course, a matter of personal judgment. If a kindergarten class remembers the movements and gets the basic rhythmic framework, I consider that "perfect." For a 6th grade class, "perfect" means exact counts and appropriate dynamic qualities in the movements.

The idea of designating the stage as a reward for completion came from a mundane problem. Children are fascinated by the stage; their first impulse upon entering the auditorium is to play on the stage. This is not workable. A wild stage party would create havoc with the idea of an orderly class and there are curtains, stored stage sets, lights and other things that can be destroyed. It was clear to me that use of the stage had to be limited and clearly defined. Why not use the stage for its original intention? A stage is the end result of finished productions and, on a small scale, that is exactly what it is used for in my class.

I have known of no child that has not liked the stage. Some may be timid, but they are still fascinated. It is a sought after reward.

However, I do not use the stage competitively in the sense of child against child. (Very rarely do I pick some children to go on the stage and not everyone. This happens maybe once a year when one or a few children have done something extraordinary.) An entire class works to complete a pattern; if 90% of the class perfects the study, then everyone performs. A fourth to a half of the class performs on stage while the rest watch. (The number depends on how large the movement pattern is in relation to the stage size.) We alternate until all the children have had a turn.

With performers there is also an audience. Most children do not know what it means to be an audience. So I tell them: 1) An audience is absolutely quiet. 2) They give their full attention to the performers. 3) They *never* "boo." (The performers, meanwhile, are taught to take a gracious bow.)

This sounds very formal. It is. If we are going to perform we might as well go all the way, and despite, or perhaps because of, the formality, the children love it. They love to scramble on stage, to stand expectantly in their starting positions, to perform, and to receive the clapping adulation of the crowd.

ALIGNMENT
  Good for: 1) Correct centering of the body.
             2) Balance.
             3) Ease and grace of movement.

---

* In situations where there is no physical stage I simply divide the class into audience and performers, each taking turns. Therefore I say, "When this pattern is perfect we will perform it." I ham up the performance with a grandiose introduction.

"Forget everything your Mom or Dad ever said about standing up straight, anything you ever heard about sticking your chest out and your shoulders back." That is the introduction to my method of teaching alignment. I call it "alignment," rather than posture or standing up straight, because the associations with what is supposed to be straight are usually wrong. When children try to stand straight they stick their chests out, curve their spines into terrible sway-backs, and give themselves double chins. That is why I ask them to forget all that.

Instead, I ask children to feel, with their fingers, the lowest part of the spine. With closed eyes (the better to feel with) they go up the center back, touching each vertebra, until they reach the back of the head. I ask them to pretend to hold the very top of their spine, *at the back of the head*, and pull up. They pull their spine *taller* so that the whole body is lifted. This is essentially the entire process of alignment: feeling the spine, pulling the body taller, and suspending the body weight from the back of the head.* To emphasize this feeling I ask the children to pull their spines even further up, lifting their bodies to half-toe (the ball of the foot). The children are asked to stay there, that is, weight up and forward toward the toes, while they lower their heels to the floor. The result should feel tall, light, ready to spring into action.

In general, this process of pulling the spine taller fixes most postures. Later, extreme cases of sway-back (arched spine) or stuck out ribs can be corrected individually.

My process of pulling *up* from the *back* of the head is different than what is often taught. In magazines and gym classes, we are told to imagine a plumb line from the top *center* of our heads *down*, putting shoulders on top of hips, on top of center feet. The dual instructions, center and down, simply do not work. If one pulls from the center of the head, rather than from the back of the head, the chin will automatically stick forward and out, the neck will compensate by curving forward and up, the back will arch, the ribs will stick out and the seat will pull back for balance. Perhaps it is fortunate that nobody can hold this position very long. In addition, this traditional approach pulls the energy weight down: head to shoulders to hips to feet. It is very important to pull that energy up. Almost anyone who is reaching up, extending, pulling his weight taller is going to have good posture. Consider an outfielder stretching to make a catch, a basketball player shooting, a dancer leaping; all pull up, all look wonderful. Consider when the weight is pulled down: the losing team walking off the field, a dancer tired at the end of a rehearsal; all pull down and all look terrible. A spine pulled down is more than an awkward posture; it just does not help when shooting for stars.

TURN OUT
   Good for: 1) Correct body positioning.
                  2) Hip joint flexibility.

"Turn out" is a dance term that means to turn the legs, from hip joint to toes, toward the outside of the body. Turn out is an integral part of ballet and modern dance, though modern dance frequently uses other rotations of the leg.

---

* At first, pulling the weight up from the back of the head makes people feel like they cannot pivot their heads. They walk around like stiffnecked robots. The robot-like appearance is OK and will disappear as soon as the alignment begins to be internalized. The stiff neck is simply illusion. When this happens gently take the head and move it from one side to the other (like saying "no") demonstrating that the head can move while the body remains lifted.

In dance classes a great deal of time is devoted to turn out and its development. Exercises are done specifically to increase turn out and extra care is given to see that it is used unless otherwise specified. In a general movement class, however, I emphasize turn out in only 2 areas: wide stride stretches and plies.

Turn out is necessary in wide stride stretches in order to have a careful, correct stretch that does not hurt the leg, and in order to stretch the inner thigh. In plies, turn out is necessary for safety of the knees and proper use of the muscles.

When the children are sitting in wide stride I explain and demonstrate (with the children imitating) that when the knees and toes are turned to face one another it is called "turned in," when they face out it is called "turned out." "Turn in, turn out... (faster). Turn in, turn out; (faster and faster)...in, out, in, out..." Legs end up just shaking back and forth at this speed. This is good to loosen the hip joint as well as learning the positions of the leg.

I then ask the children to get their legs (both of them) to turn out and keep them there. Most often this is done before stage 3 of Blast Off where the back rounds down with the legs in wide stride. Lowering the back while the legs are kept wide and turned out is difficult; almost all legs want to turn in. I ask the children to become their own teachers: "You be your own teacher and make your legs mind you. (I point threateningly at my own legs and the children follow suit with their legs.) You make your legs turn out even if they don't want to. If you can't round your back as low keeping your legs turned out, keep them turned out and don't go as low." As we start to lower the backs, if a child's leg starts to turn in *I do not correct the leg*. I say, "Henry, your leg is not *minding you*."

Having the children make their own legs mind them is more important than might seem. This is truly a case of self-discipline and self-responsibility. When the child becomes the boss of his own legs it is a step toward the beauty of a body with inner force and control. The child must decide if he is going to do it and then take charge of the process himself. Later, when turn out becomes a habit, it can be relegated to the domain of muscular memory. This process of decision, self-discipline, and internalization, applies to many areas, from alignment to reading. If a child does not align his own body, or if a child decides not to read, no outpouring of instructions or reminders from you will do it.

In plies, turn out means keeping the knees back as the body lowers. Easier said than done.

A first position plie begins with the back perfectly aligned, legs straight and turned out, heels touching.* The knees bend only as far as the heels can remain on the floor; turn out is maintained throughout with the knees lowering *behind* the big toes. The feeling is one of pushing one's pelvis forward while pushing the knees back, meanwhile keeping the torso ramrod straight. The grimace will come off later.

In 2nd position everything is done exactly the same way but with the heels one to 2 feet apart.

A plie done correctly, with energy, is a magnificent exercise. Five or 6 perfectly done plies will knock you out.

---
* To get one's own true turn out, start with feet parallel, that is, toes facing straight front. Tighten the seat, "as if a bee stung you in your seat," rock back slightly on the heels and turn toes out, then come down evenly on both feet. Wherever they land is your own true turn out; do not maneuver the feet to turn out more.

Wide stride stretches and plies are 2 of the areas in which I pay special attention to turn out. In more advanced classes, turn out becomes an integral part of the movement vocabulary and is incorporated into leaps, one-legged skips, extensions, and jumps.

TWIRLS
  Good for: 1) Tone of class.
            2) Children's feelings of self esteem.
            3) Vocabulary review.

There are many good reasons for picking a child up and twirling him around. 1) It is fun. 2) It is a moment of closeness with the teacher as a real person. 3) It is a special moment of individual attention, a moment in which the child is told, "I like you."

If a child is young, little, and scared, I pick him up in standard "baby style." As the child gets braver, I let go of the head and torso while holding firmly to the knees; thus the child twirls upside down.

Medium-sized children can get "airplane twirls": hold a wrist (not the hand because it can dislocate) and an ankle and spin the child. (See illustration #1.) Make sure you have enough room for this twirl.

As the children get too big to lift, I use a special twirl I developed. The child sits on the floor, knees bent, and holds his hands firmly *under* his knees. The child needs to be quite tightly contracted. I pick him up by the ankles and use the momentum of the body weight swinging around to twirl the child in the air. (See illustration #2.)

In this way I have twirled 115 pound youngsters, which covers most kindergarten to 6th grade children.

Ideally, I would like the time, energy, and back strength to twirl every child just about every class, either as a grand "hello" or as a happy "goodbye." Obviously impossible. So I sometimes use twirls for a dual purpose. As the children finish taking off their socks and shoes and find their Perfect Spot, I ask, "What does 'locomotor' mean?" I only entertain answers from children sitting in their Perfect Spots. (This has the effect of getting the children barefoot and in their spots *quickly*.) If the child answers the question right, he gets a twirl. I ask for definitions of all concept words known so far; each correct answer gets a twirl. Sometimes it is nice to switch: say the definition and ask for the concept word, for example, "What word means 'going somewhere'?" It is as simple as that. I keep a vague mental record of who I have twirled and try to give twirls to everyone by about every 4th class. In this way the children get a verbal review, and the beginning procedure of removing socks and shoes and finding Perfect Spots is speeded up.

Of course, special occasions like birthdays and last days of school get special twirls. And then there was the time a group of children decided it was not fair that I did not get twirled.....

BRAIN CATCHER GAME
  Good for: 1) Memory.
            2) Review of movement concepts.
            3) Visualization and problem solving.

"Usually when someone, especially a teacher, says something to you it goes in one ear and out the other. Now we are going to play a game where your brain has to catch the instructions as they come in one ear, before they leave through the other. The game is called the Brain Catcher." This is my introduction to a "game" that is simply a memory exercise.

To play the game, I say a movement sequence and the children remember it. I use the Free Traveling Structure. For example, "When you hear the piano for the first time, skip; when you hear the piano the 2nd time, swing; when you hear the piano the 3rd time, run. Don't forget to freeze when the sound stops."

The above example is the most common form of Brain Catcher; it uses one (the same) sound a number of times. You can make it easier by adopting the appropriate rhythm for each movement, or harder by using the same or a non-committal rhythmic pattern for all the movements.

Another form of Brain Catcher is to have many different sounds, each representing a different movement: "When you hear the drum, run; when you hear the bell, shake; when you hear the piano, skip; when you hear the tambourine, spin on your seat." After the children have mastered the sound/movement relations in order, mix them up. In future games do *not* use the same sound/movement relationships; keep changing them.

One final approach to Brain Catcher is simply playing with memory work. For example, turn things upside down: "When you hear the *sound*, freeze; when you hear *no sound*, move. That's a switch isn't it? OK, the first no-sound, gallop; the 2nd no-sound, strike; the 3rd no-sound, leap." Another favorite mix-up: "When you hear the sound, move in silence; when the sound stops, freeze your body but start talking to someone; when the sound starts again you have to be silent. OK? The first sound, twist; 2nd sound, roll; 3rd sound, run."

I give sequences that are 3 to 7 (yes, 7) parts long. I work to push classes to remember more than they think they can remember. What if they forget? Since the entire class moves at one time, someone usually remembers and the rest pick it up. If it is truly too difficult I shorten the sequence and say it again.

In subsequent Brain Catchers, I attempt, though I doubt I fully succeed, to continuously give new sequences even if the variations are minor.

That is it; that is the entire game. Not only is this excellent work in memory and concentration, but Brain Catcher can be used to reinforce numerous concepts. With so many weighty purposes being served, I do not know why children like it so much. Here are some ways the game can be used.

To reinforce the concepts locomotor and nonlocomotor:

A) 1) locomotor gallop, 2) nonlocomotor contract and stretch, 3) locomotor jazz walk, 4) nonlocomotor swing.

B) 1) nonlocomotor strike, 2) locomotor run, 3) nonlocomotor twist, 4) locomotor run, 5) nonlocomotor shake, 6) locomotor run, 7) nonlocomotor swing.

C) 1) any fast locomotor movement, 2) any nonlocomotor movement, 3) any slow locomotor movement, 4) any nonlocomotor movement, 5) any medium tempo locomotor movement, 6) any nonlocomotor movement.

To reinforce the concept level:

A) 1) air level skip, 2) standing level swing, 3) lowest level roll.

B) 1) contract on lowest level and stretch on knee level, 2) any locomotor movement that continuously changes levels, 3) contract on knee level and stretch on lowest level.

C) 1) any locomotor movement on knee level, 2) any nonlocomotor movement on lowest level, 3) any locomotor movement on air level, 4) any nonlocomotor movement lowest level, 5) any locomotor movement knee level. I point out the symmetry of a pattern like this:
        knee   lowest   air   lowest   knee
        loco.   nonloco. loco.   nonloco. loco.

    It is important not only to ask children to remember, but to give them the tools with which to remember. Finding patterns is an important intellectual procedure in itself, as well as an excellent memory technique. (More on patterning in Part 9.)

To reinforce the concept direction:

A) 1) run forward, 2) run backwards, 3) run sideways, 4) run turning.

B) 1) jump backwards, 2) skip turning, 3) crab crawl sideways, 4) leap forward.

C) Using any locomotor movement: 1) go forward, 2) go backwards, 3) go sideways, 4) go in the direction that you did not go.

To reinforce the ideas of tempo and size and to differentiate between them:

A) 1) do a locomotor movement very big and very fast, 2) do a nonlocomotor movement very small and very slow.

B) 1) run big in slow motion, 2) run small in fast motion, 3) swing big in slow motion, 4) swing small in fast motion.

C) Pick any nonlocomotor movement and do it: 1) big and slow, 2) big and fast, 3) small and slow, 4) small and fast.

To work on combined locomotor and nonlocomotor movements: 1) jump and shake your head, 2) side-slide and swing your arms, 3) skip and contract and stretch.

For problem solving--parts of the body: 1) move with 2 parts of your body on the ground, 2) move with 5 parts of your body on the ground, 3) move with one part of your body on the ground.

ROCKING AS A RELAXER
  Good for: Calming young classes.

    Sometimes the immediate task is not to create movement but to quiet it. I like to calm a class down at the end of a lesson before sending them back to their rooms; otherwise children coming from movement class tend to explode onto the rest of the school. (This is especially true of kindergarten to 3rd grades.)

Luckily, there is the versatile Rocking Song. In Part 2, "Teaching Locomotor Movements To Very Young Children," the Rocking Song was used as the core of a lesson to teach locomotor movements and the Free Traveling Structure. (See page 29.) Here this same little song becomes a marvelous relaxer.

Generally, I ask the class to get their Perfect Spots; this is somewhat of a calmer itself. If I am in a hurry I will ask the class to sit wherever they are.

There are several ways the song can be used: rising levels, fast and slow, softer and softer.

Rising levels. The children sit and sing the Rocking Song as they sway from side to side. They repeat the song and movement on knee level and standing level. (Do not go to air level because it is too active and breaks the calm.) Finishing on standing level, with one foot off the floor, I say quietly, "Be still on the inside so you can balance like this forever."

Fast and slow. This is all done on sitting level. The children sing and rock with the song at a moderate speed. We then do it as fast as possible. Conclude by singing and rocking as slow as possible.

Softer. Sing and rock, sitting level, at normal speed and volume. Gradually get softer and softer (you can move down to lowest level, if you wish) until the song is "sung" silently.

The Rocking Song works well for kindergarten through 3rd grades; occasionally it can be used in 4th grade but certainly no older.* It is the combination of repetition and the swaying motion that soothes the young savage beast.

SPAGHETTI
Good for: Class tone.

Spaghetti is the kind of activity about which children will groan "Oh no," and secretly love. I know because they have told me so.

There are 2 ways to start Spaghetti; the end result is the same. The first way (easier to control, harder on your back), the children find their Perfect Spots and lie on their backs. They are to be "limp as cooked spaghetti."

"Now we'll make a plateful of spaghetti." I take one child by the legs and drag him gently to the middle of the room. I drag another child and place his legs over the first's stomach. I then proceed to layer children in a big heap. (See illustration at the top of page 122.)

If a class is very giggly and tickly, I ask them to rest their hands in back of their heads. I then ask the children if we can hold the Spaghetti and be completely silent for, say, 10 seconds. It might take 5 or 6 tries.

---
* Note on older children: I find that older children (5th and 6th grades) do not need a specific end of class relaxer. Perhaps because they are generally more contained ("cooler") than the younger classes. In any case, if they do need to be calmed down I use standard relaxation techniques like slow breathing or conscious relaxation of isolated body parts, that is, "Tense your fingers...Now let them go; tense your hands...Now let them go; tense your arms...Now let them go."

Since I invariably do Spaghetti at the end of class, I conclude by saying, "Turn yourself into a meatball and gently roll to your shoes."

The other way to start Spaghetti (harder to control, easier on your back), uses the Diagonal Structure. The children move across the diagonal one at a time. They walk stiffly, like "uncooked noodles." When they get to the middle, they pretend to step into a pot of boiling water, slowly melting from the bottom up. The next child melts gently on top of the first and so on until the class is in a layered heap. Warning: It is necessary to guide a class through the layering several times before allowing them to do it alone. Otherwise, they get carried away with football tackles and heaping players.

Why heap children on top of one another? It is fun and the children like it. If that is not enough, it is useful for class unity, for friendships and group work, and it gets away from "girls on this side and boys on that side" kind of situations. Further, it sets a nice friendly tone for the end of class.

Spaghetti is great for all ages, kindergarten on up. I do it with adults at teacher workshops---never can get teachers to stop giggling for 10 seconds.

PART 8
PROPS

WORKING WITH PROPS

THE BENEFITS AND DANGERS OF PROPS

Props are heaven sent. They spice up a class, bring concepts together, make great shows, embolden the timid, utilize memory and sequential skills, and build coordination. Plus, these miracles are wrought from objects easily acquired: balls, scarves, ropes, hula hoops, marbles, balloons, parachutes, costumes, whatever.

Why, then, are they so rarely used? Many teachers worry about the chaos that a prop can produce. They are right! Props are exciting and unleash enormous exuberance in children. Thirty-six balls flying about, scarves whipping every which way, 5 dozen hands grabbing the parachute: nightmarish visions! They can, but need not happen.

FORMULA FOR USING PROPS

Props need structure to be orderly and fun. Here is my basic formula:

1) Plan in advance how to distribute the prop.

2) Provide free time. Free time lasts from 2 to 10 minutes and is done in the Free Traveling Structure.

3) Introduce movement ideas. The children explore new prop movements by incorporating general concepts. For example, the children use different parts of the body, tempos, directions, levels, locomotor and nonlocomotor movements. "Move your hula hoop and change levels. Keep your balloon in the air while moving slowly, now quickly. Move your ball while doing a nonlocomotor movement." These ideas steer the children away from stereotyped movements.

In addition to general concepts, I often suggest specific movement ideas. "Bounce and catch your ball with just your right hand. Circle your scarf and gallop at the same time."

Notes: a) If a class is either extremely timid or very rambunctious I reverse steps 2 and 3, that is, I guide them with some ideas first and then give them some free time with the prop. b) If a class does not want to do guided movements, they have not had enough free time.

4) Conclude with a prop study. Ideas are put together in an ordered, remembered progression. These studies can be done with the class as a whole, with small groups, or with individual children.

The most convenient organization for studies is the Free Traveling Structure: "When you hear the piano the first time, run and bounce your ball. When you hear the piano the 2nd time, move the ball with just your feet. When you hear the piano the 3rd time, skip while throwing and catching the ball." The piano accompaniment can be different for all 3 movements, making remembering easier; or the tune can be the same, making it harder.

Other structures for prop studies, like beats or visual cues, are, of course, available. The important thing about the studies is that they are remembered and repeatable.

5) Have a plan for putting the prop away.

USES OF THE FORMULA

This formula is geared for props that are distributed one per child. Communal props like the parachute or costumes are handled differently.* If I do not have enough props, if the room is small, or if a class is particularly rough, I use the above formula but have half the class work and half watch at a time. When extra control is needed this half and half arrangement is worth the time. Surprisingly, children like to watch almost as much as they like to move. It works best if the children with short attention spans watch first.

This progression from free time to guided movements to prop studies can take one or several classes. Ideally, I take several classes. For example, I like to introduce balls for a few minutes at the end of one class. In the next class the children have additional free time with the balls and are introduced to guided movements; we also roughly sketch out a study. In the 3rd class we perfect and perform the study.

BALLS

START WITH BALLS
Good for: 1) Large muscle coordination.
2) Eye/hand and eye/foot coordination.
3) Sequencing and memory skills.
4) Partner work.

Balls are an excellent first prop. They are fun, easy to pass out and put away, good coordination tools, and cheap. For simplified storage, I use mostly 3 inch rubber balls. For kindergarten and first grades, I begin with the standard 6 inch kindergarten ball. Balls that are all rubber last much longer than air filled balls.

PASSING OUT THE BALLS
There are several ways to pass out the balls. If the class is already in groups, I ask one group at a time to pick their own out of the ball box. In gentle classes I might ask the whole class to carefully pick their own balls. My favorite way is to throw them: "I will throw you a ball. Wait until I call your name. (This is important otherwise it will turn into a free for all.) Catch it." With older children

---
* A completely different use of props is in the section on Stations, Part 11.

I sometimes add that the ball be caught with one hand or while jumping in the air. This method does take a little longer (surprisingly not much) but the children like it and it is good practice.

FREE TIME

Once each child has a ball, the class has 5 to 10 minutes free time. Of course, free time is not completely free. I do not allow the balls to be thrown 1) against painted walls (leaves marks), 2) against the ceiling (lights), or 3) at people. Children comply easily with prop rules: no one wants their ball taken.

GUIDED MOVEMENTS

The next step, after free time, is guided movements. I encourage new ideas by asking the children to use different levels and directions, and to use different parts of their bodies to move the ball: "Can you move your ball while on the lowest level?... Air level?...While changing levels?...Can you move your ball in the backward direction? ...Turning direction?...Can you move your ball with 2 hands?...One hand?...No hands?..."

In addition, I ask for some specific movement ideas:

1) Walk and bounce catch the ball; run and bounce catch.

2) Put the ball on the ground and move it using no hands or feet. (See illustration at right.)

3) Put the ball on the ground and roll it using just your feet, like soccer. Do *not* kick it in the air. Move it backwards.

4) Spin the ball, like a top, and get your body to move like it. Change levels.

5) Start the ball bouncing and then let it bounce on its own. Jump the way the ball bounced, getting smaller and smaller, then rolling.

6) Dribble your ball like fast basketball dribbling. (You can designate right or left or alternating hands.) Pretend to shoot baskets.

7) Carry your ball without using hands, for example, in arm pit, under chin, between feet.

8) With the ball under your chin, using no hands, roll.

9) Using no hands, lift your ball off the ground and bounce it. Can you catch it without using hands?

10) Put the ball between your feet, sit and spin.

11) Put the ball between your feet and roll backwards.

12) Bounce the ball while changing levels at all times: air level to standing level to knee level to sitting level to lowest level and back up, without a break in the bounce.

13) Throw the ball gently in the air and catch it. Skip at the same time. Skip and turn around and catch it. Run and leap and catch it.

14) Throw and catch the ball with only one hand (designate right or left). Move at the same time.

15) Start with the ball between your feet; jump, keeping the ball between your feet, and catch it with your hands, mid-jump.

16) With the ball between your knees, jump.

17) With the ball behind one knee, hop; change legs.

18) Bounce the ball with your hand and swing your leg over it; change legs.

STUDIES

When the children have explored a number of movement possibilities with balls, it is time for a study. The goal of these studies is sequential memory. At first we practice the study while I call out what to do. Next, I say only "Number one thing to do (accompanied by the drum or piano sound)...Number 2 thing to do (sound)..." and so forth. Finally, the sound is the only signal of movement change. Examples of studies:

A) 1) Walk and bounce catch the ball. 2) Sit and spin with the ball between your feet. 3) Move the ball with just your feet.

B) 1) Move the ball with just your feet, backward direction. 2) Run and bounce catch the ball. 3) Move the ball using *no* hands or feet.

C) 1) Dribble the ball and pretend to shoot baskets. 2) Roll with the ball held under your chin. 3) Skip and throw the ball gently in the air. 4) Do anything you want *except* what you just did. (This is a nice way to structure improvizations and it also provides an extra memory problem.)

D) 1) Bounce the ball while changing levels at all times. 2) Alternate one skip and one gallop while throwing the ball gently into the air and catching it. 3) Bounce the ball and swing your leg over it, alternating legs. 4) Put the ball between your feet, jump it into the air, and catch it. 5) Bounce the ball and follow its movements exactly with your body.

E) For individual or small group studies: Pick 3 to 7 ball/movement ideas and put them in a remembered sequence.

PARTNER WORK

An entirely different use for balls is in partner work.

1) Partner pass. Two children play catch with one ball. First they sit and roll the ball (Yes, even 6th graders like this! They suck their thumbs and carry on like babies.) then they kneel and bounce pass the ball, then they stand and bounce pass the ball. Finally, they continue to pass the ball but move at the same time. They run, skip, gallop, roll, seat-scoot, jump, or leap continuously while passing the ball back and forth. For older children I sometimes add another ball so that there are 2 balls to be passed while moving.

2) Partner carry. Without using hands, the children hold a ball between them and go somewhere. They can hold the ball back to back, front to front, foot to foot, forehead to forehead, hip to hip. Later one part of one child's body holds the ball

against a different part of the other child's body, for example, head to hip, seat to tummy, foot to hip.

I rarely use these partner activities in studies although it is possible. They are mainly for fun (and for friendship, and cooperation, and eye-hand coordination, and eye-foot coordination, and general coordination, and...).

OTHER USES
After balls have been formally introduced, they can be used as a fast warm-up activity or as an end of the class treat. I have, on occasion, dumped all 36 balls in the middle of the room: "Find a ball and move it." Just make sure the doors of your room are closed and have a ball.

SCARVES

WHAT KIND OF SCARVES?
Good for: 1) Fantasy play.
2) Large muscle coordination.
3) Sequencing and memory skills.
4) Partner work.

After balls, scarves are 2nd in all around usefulness. Any kind of scarf will do. When I have felt rich I have bought nice crepe-like material, which makes lusciously beautiful scarves, and when I have the time I search out unusual scarves at garage sales. But the basic ingredients in my scarf box are dozens of inexpensive, sheer head scarves. It is best if kindergarten and first graders use scarves no bigger than 2 feet square, and it is important that all the scarves are washable. Otherwise, almost any size, length, material, and shape works fine.

PASSING OUT THE SCARVES
There is a dilemma with passing out scarves. It would take 20 chaotic minutes for each child to pick his own scarf. On the other hand because scarves foster a personal, individual reaction, it is nice for each child to have the one he wants. Compromise: I walk around and ask what color each child wants and give him his preference when possible. After the scarves have been used once, a child might ask for "the big red one" or "the long black one"; as much as possible I give the child his choice. When each child has a scarf, I allow a few minutes of trading. Trading is fine, but if left unchecked it can supplant even playing with the scarf. At the appropriate moment I say, "This is the scarf you have for today."

A faster method of distributing scarves is the "closed eye drop." The children sit on the floor. "Close your eyes and I will drop a scarf on your head." Since I use this method when I am in a hurry I do not pay much attention to what scarf lands on what child. Generally, this turns out almost as good as individual deliberations.

FREE TIME

Scarves trigger a child's fantasy. Children use them as brides' veils, Superman capes, make believe animals, blankets, hats, toreodor capes, skate boards, and who knows what else. If this type of fantasy play is going on, I extend the initial free time. The ability to imagine is a precious part of our lives. It is difficult to make time for it during the school day and scarves offer the perfect opportunity.

GUIDED MOVEMENTS

When the children stop pretending to be matadors and start acting like bulls (which happens in about 15 minutes), we go on to guided movement ideas: "Move your scarf on air level...Move it on lowest level...Change levels...Do nonlocomotor movements with your scarf...Do locomotor movements with your scarf...How about doing locomotor movements in the backward direction?...Can you move your scarf in the turning direction?..."

In addition to general movement ideas I offer specific ideas:

1) Hold your scarf in one hand, make a circle with the scarf and gallop.

2) Twirl yourself and the scarf. Change levels.

3) Drop the scarf on the floor and pick it up with your toes (excellent for foot muscles). Holding the scarf in your toes, shake it and hop (on the other foot) at the same time. Change legs.

4) Hold the scarf by one corner; outline a circle with it while rolling at the same time.

5) Put one end of the scarf in the toes of one foot and the other end in the toes of the other foot. Make the scarf taut. Wrinkle the scarf. Balance on your seat and wrinkle and tighten the scarf.

6) Throw the scarf in the air and catch it. Catch it with your elbow, head, shoulder, tummy, seat, hip, knee, foot, anything but your hands.

7) Spin on your seat while holding the scarf in your toes.

8) Put the scarf on the ground and slide on it on your tummy, seat, back.

9) Possibly the all time favorite for kindergarten to 3rd grade is "Magic Scarf." "The scarf is going to be magic; it is going to stay on your torso without being held." I demonstrate by arching slightly and running very fast. The air pressure keeps the scarf up. When doing Magic Scarf, children need to all go the same way in a circle because they do not watch where they are going. Make sure the children stop if the scarf starts slipping down past their knees; it can be dangerously slippery.

10) Lie down and put the scarf over you: "Now children it is time to go to sleep. Pull up your blankie and take a nap."

STUDIES

After free time and guided movement, we put together a study.

A) 1) Gallop while making a circle with your scarf. 2) Spin on your seat with the scarf in your toes. 3) Do Magic Scarf.

B) 1) Throw the scarf in the air and catch it with different parts of your body. 2) Drop the scarf, pick it up with your toes, and shake it. 3) Slide on your scarf. 4) Pull up your "blankie" and take a nap.

C) 1) Do Magic Scarf. 2) Twirl yourself and the scarf, changing levels without stopping. 3) Put 2 ends of the scarf in your toes; wrinkle it and make it taut. 4) Roll and circle your scarf.

D) This is a dramatic study for older children. (I have not done this study with a full school class, only with a dance studio class.) 1) Hide your scarf (in sleeves, pant legs, pockets, etc.). Walk shyly, slowly pulling out the scarf. As the scarf appears, become more and more free and large with your movements, until the scarf is completely out and you are doing enormous leaping twirling movements. 2) Do nonlocomotor movement twirl, changing levels at all times. End in a shape and freeze. 3) Those who want, do individual dances. The scarf becomes whatever they choose: costumes, "freedom," "happiness," "a weight," "entanglement," or simply an abstract design element. The soloists leave the stage area when they are finished. The other children remain frozen while the soloists perform. 4) The children who did not solo prepare a simple unison movement pattern which moves them off the stage area.

PARTNER WORK

An entirely different use for scarves is blindfolds. One of the nicest things to do with a blindfold is "Trust Walk." The children, mature 2nd graders and older, get partners. One child is blindfolded and is *silently* led by his partner. The leaders carefully move their charges all over the room, sitting them down, getting them to the water fountain for a drink, climbing stairs, having them feel different textures, and doing all sorts of movements together. Of course, they switch. Trust Walk can be done in many different environments, in an auditorium, on a beach, even in a playground. If the children are ready to assume this care for one another, it is a wonderful activity.

PUTTING THE SCARVES AWAY

At the end of a scarf lesson even the youngest child folds and puts away his own scarf. I do not yield on this point. I refuse to clean up after children unnecessarily.

Older children, of course, know how to fold and are simply told to do so. Young children often need a folding lesson: "Put your scarf *flat* on the floor...Fold 2 corners to 2 corners, (I do it with the children.)...Turn the scarf (The scarf is turned lengthwise to the child so that the folding action is up rather than across.) and fold 2 corners to 2 corners again...Now we will make it smaller. Fold 2 corners...Turn... Fold 2 corners to 2 corners..."

I watch as the scarves are placed in the box and if they are not well folded the child does it over. This sounds rigid and yet I am certain the procedure is correct. How do I know? The children look so pleased with themselves.

ROPES

WHAT KIND OF ROPES?
Ropes are a secondary prop. That is, they are fun and useful but they do not lend themselves to as wide a range of activities as do balls or scarves. I use both "Chinese jump ropes" and regular straight ropes.

CHINESE JUMP ROPES
Good for: 1) Large muscle coordination.
2) Some concept work in geometry.
3) Sequencing and memory skills.
4) Partner work.

Chinese jump ropes are elastic circle ropes approximately 2 feet in diameter. They are great for stretching. Often a child will get so intrigued with the shapes the rope can make that he stretches much harder. This is my goal. "Make your rope into a triangle...A square...A rectangle...A circle (Impossible!)...A tangled up mess...Make your rope as long as possible...Make it as taut as possible...Make it as big as possible... Use only your legs to stretch the rope...Move your shape to standing level and go somewhere...Roll, keeping the rope taut...Change levels and move."

STUDIES

A) 1) Make your rope as big as you can and go somewhere. 2) Make your rope as small as you can, without using hands, and stay in place. 3) Make your rope as long as you can and go somewhere.

B) 1) Make a triangle with your rope. 2) On a different level make a rectangle. 3) On a different level make a square. 4) On a different level make a star.

C) 1) Stretch your rope as big as you can with just your legs; get on lowest level and go somewhere. 2) Stretch your rope as long as possible using one leg and one arm. Do a nonlocomotor swing with your stretched arm and leg. 3) Make your rope as wide as possible using both arms and legs, sitting level. Can you spin?

D) Pick 4 different shapes, on 4 different levels with your ropes. Keep the shapes and make them go somewhere. Remember your pattern.

Once a rope study is clear and remembered, I sometimes ask that the ropes be dropped and see if the study can be imitated without them. With older children I am fussy that they stretch as they did with the ropes. If they do not, I will ask the children to do the study again with the ropes and then remove the ropes once more. We will perhaps do this several times. Of course, I warn them I am going to be picky.

PARTNER AND GROUP WORK

1) With a partner, one be the horse and one hold the "reins."

2) With a partner, using no hands, make a triangle out of your rope and go somewhere. Take the rope away and see if you can get your bodies in the same positions. Go somewhere again.

3) With a partner get your rope as round as possible. Spin. Do the same without the rope.

4) In groups of 3 (each group gets one rope) make a star shape out of your rope. Rise and fall.

5) In groups of 4, 3 people get ropes. These ropes are stretched across and through one another until a maze is created. The 4th person jumps in and out of the maze without touching a rope. If he touches, it is someone else's turn to jump and the first child takes a turn holding a rope. The maze can be slightly stretched and contracted at the same time the child is jumping.

STRAIGHT ROPES
  Good for: 1) Large muscle coordination.
                2) Partner work.

The 3 things I like to do most with straight ropes are "Tangle," "Twirl," and "Moveable Maze jump." (I prefer nylon ropes, about 6 feet long, without handles. However, almost any kind of ropes will do.)

  TANGLE

    The main rule in Tangle is that the rope cannot immediately double back on itself; the rope can only double back if it has gone around a different part of the body. With that as a given, the children are asked to tangle themselves up in their ropes. The rope must be taut at all times. It is great to see a class completely tied up. (You will be tempted to leave them this way.) The children stay tangled and go somewhere, change levels and go somewhere, roll, wiggle. They tangle themselves up with a partner or a group of 3 and move somewhere.

  TWIRL

    This is simply winding in and out of the rope. The children are in partners. One child holds one end of the rope; the other child holds the other end and turns into the rope, wrapping it around his waist. (Not neck!) The child that has been wrapping the rope around ends up like a coiled top next to the child holding the other end. The child holding the end then pulls hard, uncoiling the "top" very quickly. Two children can coil together; with one at each end, they meet in the middle and spin out.

  MOVEABLE MAZE JUMP

    The hardest part of this is getting it set up. Children are in partners; each child holds one end of a rope, keeping it taut at all times. The 2 children move the rope up and down like a teeter-totter, one lifts his end up while the other lowers his end. Once this is clear, cross several ropes in a maze-like pattern. Each rope is its own teeter-totter.

    This maze will take about half a class, approximately 8 ropes, 2 children working with each rope. The other half of the class jumps in and out of the rope maze without touching the ropes. The hard part is keeping the ropes evenly teeter-tottering while children are jumping. The key to keeping them even is keeping them taut. I do not use any penalties for touching a rope, but it could be made into a competitive game. The sides, of course, switch.

HULA HOOPS

HOOPS AS AN INDIVIDUAL PROP
   Good for: 1) Coordination.
                  2) Sequencing and memory skills.

Even if I have enough hula hoops for one per child, I usually have half the class work while half watch, because hoops are noisy and potentially dangerous.

The children stand in Perfect Spots. I give each child his preferred color hoop. The children have 5 to 10 minutes of free time. Most often they just spin the hoop in the traditional around-the-waist way.

I then ask for different ways of moving the hoop:

1) Around the neck.

2) Around a arm.

3) Around a leg, other leg hops over the twirling hoop. (See illustration at right.)

4) Over the body, like a stiff jump rope.

5) Upright like a wheel. There is a way to do this spin so that the hoop rolls away and then comes back. I cannot do it, but most of the children can.

6) Upright like a wheel. The child goes through it while it is moving.

7) Flat on the floor. The child jumps, hops, skips in and out of the hoop.

8) Any of the above using different levels.

The children then pick 5 different ways of moving the hoop and put them in a specific order. This is a good study in itself. In addition, I ask the children to do their pattern again without the hoop. What I look for is muscular memory of exactly what the body did, but without the prop.

HOOPS AS A PATTERNING PROP
   Good for: 1) Coordination.
                  2) Patterning skills.
                  3) Sequencing and memory skills.

Hoops usually come in 3 colors, yellow, blue, and red. Place them in a color sequence on the floor with each color representing a movement. The children work out the resulting movement pattern. (One possibility is diagramed at right.)

RED · RED ·YELLOW·YELLOW·BLUE · BLUE · RED ·YELLOW· BLUE · RED ·YELLOW·BLUE

STEP · STEP · HOP · HOP · JUMP · JUMP · STEP · HOP · JUMP ·STEP · HOP · JUMP

Two tips: 1) This is harder than it seems, so make the color pattern simple and obvious. Try it yourself first. 2) Put the hoops very close together and tape them down. This initial effort will pay off in not having the hoops scattered by a faulty hop.

Usually I use hoop patterning within an obstacle course. It is fine to use these patterns by themselves, especially across the diagonal. Once the children know the pattern, ask them to do it without the hoops.

BALLOONS

UNBLOWN BALLOONS
Good for: 1) Coordination.
2) Sequencing and memory skills.
3) Abstracting movements.

For unblown balloon activities, the least expensive balloons work just fine. Each child picks his preferred color. "How many ways, without tying them, can you make the balloon move?" The children will stretch them in various ways, blow them up and let the air out, make them "squeek," and, best of all, will blow them up and let them "fly." I let the class have 5 to 10 minutes free time with the balloons, depending on how long I can stand the "flying."

GUIDED MOVEMENTS

I then ask the children to imitate the balloon movements with their bodies. This will not work if they are still playing with their balloons, so I ask them to put their balloons in their pockets or somewhere where they can find their own. I use one balloon as a demonstrator.*

1) Stretch the balloon long and let it snap. What I am looking for in the children's movements is a long, narrow stretch and a quick snap contract. This is done with isolated body parts, arms, legs, torso, neck, and then with the whole body. The whole body stretch and snap is done on different levels.

2) Blow the balloon up and slowly let the air out. Since it takes several breaths to fill the balloon with air, I expect a jerky, wide stretch and then a slow, even release. This is done with various wide shapes, on all levels.

3) Blow the balloon up and let it "fly." At first most children just shake wildly. I ask them to stop and actually look at the path of the flying balloon. The balloon usually spins several times, leaps up, and dives down. We talk about how we could approximate these movements in our bodies. Then I set the flight pattern. For example: "Three spins, leap up, land"; or, "Spin twice, bounce off the floor and slide land"; or, "Loop around, hit a wall, bounce off the floor, leap up, and land." In other words, we watch the balloon a few times, talk about its typical flight pattern, and then follow the verbal pattern that I call out. These flight patterns are done in as much space as possible, as little space as possible, as fast and slow as possible, and with and without vocal sounds.

------

* "Since they are used for such a short time, why bother giving each child his own balloon?" It works better. That period of free time before imitating the balloon makes the movements come alive.

STUDIES

- A) 1) Stretch long and snap contract, lowest level. 2) Blow the balloon wide and slowly let the air out, standing level. 3) Blow the balloon up again and let it fly: spin, spin, leap up, and land.

- B) 1) Stretch and snap contract 5 different parts of your body. Each stretch is 8 beats long and each snap is one beat long, hold one beat. 2) Stretch wide and then slowly release. Do it twice, each on a different level. Each stretch and release is 13 beats long. 3) Stretch again, in 8 beats, and let the balloon fly. Make up your own set, flight pattern, 16 beats long.

- C) "Divide into groups of 4. Pick 5 movements your balloons did and put them in a pattern. Use your voices sometimes if you want." All group members do not have to do the same movement at the same time; it is interesting to juxtapose 2 different movements, for example, 2 people "fly" while 2 people stretch and snap arms and legs. However, I do require that the group as a whole has a remembered pattern.

BLOWN UP BALLOONS
  Good for: 1) Large muscle coordination.
            2) Eye/hand and eye/foot coordination.
            3) Sequencing and memory skills.
            4) Class tone.

Blown up balloons are even more exciting than flat ones. It is worth using more expensive balloons in order to reduce the number popped in class. Any size or shape will do, although round balloons are a little easier to work with than long balloons.

A few miscellaneous balloon tips: 1) Blow the balloons up yourself or use some *reliable* help. Even older children who say they can blow up balloons often cannot, and you are stuck with flat, wet balloons. 2) Devise in advance a place where you can keep 35 blown up balloons enclosed. The best place is a stiff mat stood up like a "house." A table laid on its side and a piano placed diagonally across a corner also works. 3) Do *not* put the balloons near a heating vent. (I smile as I write these tips, thinking of the situations that brought them to mind.)

FREE TIME
   I usually have the children pick their own balloons: "When I tap you on the head go carefully into the balloon house and pick one." The children then have 5 to 10 minutes free time.

   About popping balloons: I tell the children that if their balloons should accidentally pop, they are to pick up the pieces, throw them away, and take another balloon (I have about 5 extra). "If, however, I even suspect that you made it pop, you will not get another."

GUIDED MOVEMENTS
   The children will come up with marvelous ideas during free time. Here are a few more:

1) Jump as you hit the balloon in the air and see if it can touch the ceiling.

2) Drop your balloon on the ground. Move it *without touching* it. (It is delightful to see kindergarten children puzzling over this problem.)

3) Kick the balloon like a football. Keep it in the air with only your feet.

4) Put your balloon between your feet and spin on your seat.

5) Keep your balloon up with just your head. (This is an especially good coordination problem.)

6) Keep your balloon up using all different parts of your body.

7) Rub your balloon on your head and see if it will stay up on the wall.

8) Carry your balloon without using hands. (When I was pregnant, guess where most children decided to carry theirs?)

9) See if your balloon bounces.

10) Place the tied end of the balloon in your lips, not teeth, put your hands behind your back, and see if you can shake someone else's balloon out of their mouth with your balloon. (Of course, you cannot do this if you are planning to use the balloon again with another class.)

STUDIES

A) 1) jump, hitting the balloon as high in the air as possible. 2) Move the balloon on the ground without touching it. 3) Keep the balloon in the air by kicking it. 4) Keep the balloon in the air with just your head. 5) Put the tied end of the balloon in your mouth and shake other balloons.

B) "Pick 3 to 7 things to do with your balloon and put them in a remembered pattern."

C) An especially effective balloon study is the Balloon Round. The children learn 3 phrases, each 8 beats long: 1) Keep the balloon in the air using different parts of the body. 2) Move the balloon on the ground by blowing it. 3) Sit and spin with the balloon held between the feet.

So far, it is very simple. Now put the pattern in a round. (The children must know the phrases perfectly, with just counts, and they must change phrases immediately on count number one.) Divide the room in half, marked with a line of tape, place half the class on one side and half on the other. I ask the children to stay on their own side as much as possible. The children start very still, holding their balloons either in their hands or with the tied end in their mouths. One side begins the pattern and the other side begins one phrase later. The pattern is repeated 2 times. (For older classes, divide the room into 3rds and make it a 3 part round.) The clarity of the round structure amid the festivity of the balloons makes this study very effective.

SCOOTERS

WHAT ARE THEY?
    Good for: 1) Coordination.
                  2) Perceptual skills.
                  3) Partner work.

Scooters are square skate boards. They range from one to 2 feet square and are made of wood or plastic. Scooters are available from most sporting outlets. Although they are expensive, you do not need many. For a class of 30 children, 6 scooters are workable and 10 ideal. Any size and type of scooter will work fine.

Traditionally scooters have been used in sensory motor classes for children with severe problems but lately they are coming into general use. This is great because they are an excellent perceptual-motor coordination tool and the children love them. Scooters rival the parachute as the children's most favorite prop.

FREE TIME AND GUIDED MOVEMENTS
    Yes, even with scooters, I allow free time. The trick is to have enough space for them. If the room is small I will use perhaps 8 scooters at a time, even if I have more, to insure enough space. The children are given 2 inviolable rules: no standing, and no rough play. After that they are on their own. (Because scooters are so popular I keep close watch that everyone has exactly the same number of minutes, usually 3. A timer is handy for this.)

While the children play with their scooters, I casually mention some ideas:

1) Move your scooter while laying on your tummy, while sitting, while kneeling, while laying on your back.

2) Spin as fast as you can.

3) Push off a wall and see if you can balance on just your tummy, seat, or knees, no hands or feet touching.

SCOOTER LINE
    Tape a large design on the floor with masking tape.* Use both loops (ℓ) and uncrossed circles (Ω) in the design. (See sample design at the top of page 137.)

The children follow the line while on their scooters. The idea is simple; the organization takes a little planning. In the example at the top of the next page I have the class sit on one side of the room. The first children with scooters line up before the start of the line. Each child goes when the one in front of him has passed the table "tunnel." (This long spacing avoids most traffic jams.) As the children finish the design they *hand* their scooter to the next waiting child.

Some young children have a lot of trouble with the scooter line. These children need a great deal of work with perceptual-motor coordination. Have the children do many

---
* After a couple of days, or even a couple of hours on some floors, the masking tape will be almost immoveable. This is not to scare you, but to warn you. Putty knives and elbow grease work well.

different locomotor movements (without scooters) on the line and then try it with the scooters. Even if they are not having difficulty, most children like to move on the tape line doing different locomotor movements. A good class progression, therefore, is to do locomotor movements on the line as a warm-up activity; do something different like a pattern in Perfect Spots; then do the line with scooters.

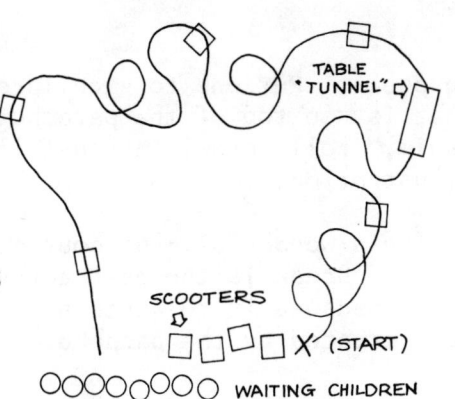

SCOOTERS WITH PARTNERS

This is another activity that will raise your blood pressure. The children get partners and each pair gets one scooter. They are told to push or pull their partners on the scooters. I point out that the person guiding the scooter is completely responsible for his partner's safety.* Any rough play is penalized by the guiding partner sitting down, but this rarely happens. Mostly the children are careful while having a very exciting time.

PARACHUTE

INTRODUCING THE PARACHUTE
   Good for: 1) Class tone.
                   2) Coordination.
                   3) Perceptual skills.
                   4) Partner work.
                   5) Concept review.

When you introduce the parachute you need to be ready for 2 repercussions: 1) for the rest of the school year you will get daily requests for it, and 2) while using the parachute your class will be in controlled chaos; the parachute is so exciting the children's excitement verges on the volcanic.

Almost any kind of parachute will do, except for the cargo kind, since it is not a continuous piece of material. For younger grades, thin, light parachutes are better, but not mandatory. I prefer a small (12 feet in diameter) parachute for Ms. Monster and Rocks and Waves and a large one (24 feet in diameter) for all the other activities. However a large parachute will work for all the activities.

Following are some activities I have found to do with a parachute. Without doubt your children will come up with more ideas.

OCEAN
Spread the parachute out and have the children spaced around it, holding the edge. The children shake the parachute vigorously. It will billow and shake like waves in

---

* Scooters in partners works best if the class has done some partner activity earlier in the lesson. They seem to be more careful of each other.

an ocean. Put one to 4 children "in the ocean," that is, on top of the parachute. They can walk, "swim," roll, crawl, or just lie there. (See illustration.)

It feels wonderful! Of course, the children take turns. Ocean is the best activity with which to start because it releases a lot of the tension-excitement created by the parachute.

WHOOSHING

"Whooshing" is not so much an idea by itself but rather a basis for several other ideas. The parachute is spread out; children stand around it, holding the edge. The parachute needs to be loose rather than stretched taut, or it will not go up as high. With the count, "1, 2, 3, Whoosh!" everyone lifts the parachute so that it mushroom-clouds up.

At this point the children will want to: 1) Let go---this will cause the parachute to flutter away to one side. 2) Move back as they hold on---this will cause the parachute to lose its billowy fullness and just stretch taut. Therefore *before* trying the whoosh, impress on your class: *"Hold on and stay put."* The children will need some practice in whooshing and in letting the parachute gently float down at its own speed.

Kindergarten children will have quite a bit of trouble with whooshing. Why not invite some 5th or 6th graders to help? Older children usually love to help and the kindergarteners can "ooh" and "ahh" at some magnificent whooshes. Also they will learn how to do it. For beautiful whooshes you will need 4 to 6 older children.*

HAMBURGERS AND FRENCH FRIES

The parachute is spread out; children stand around it, holding the edge. I divide the class into alternating groups by calling half "Hamburgers" and half "French Fries." The children whoosh the parachute up. When it is up, the Hamburgers let go of the edge and go under the parachute. They do whatever they want, staying under as long as they can, but have to get out to their *original places before* the parachute lands on them. It is important that they go back to their original places so that children are always spaced evenly around the parachute and therefore can give it a good whoosh. It is then the French Fries turn.

Variation #1 on Hamburgers and French Fries. Hamburgers go under the parachute when it is whooshed up, and stay there letting the parachute land on them. *After* the parachute has covered them up (not before, so we can be surprised) they take a strange shape. The French Fries and I then whoosh the parachute up and see what they look like.

---

* I might mention that recently I have asked for more help from older children. They are wonderful aids when working with the parachute, gymnastics, and some small group work. Generally, it works out fine if the older children are the "trouble makers" in their own classroom. This is an extraordinary situation. When they come into a movement class of kindergarten children they are not only older and wiser but they are successes. They can do things that the little ones cannot do yet. For many of these older children the admiration they get is unfortunately rare, and fortunately very effective. They come through. Most of the time they turn out to be not only good helpers but good teachers and example-setters as well. I had one child, the biggest and toughest of the rough crowd, help with head-stands and parachute activities. Stone (his real name) taught with such firm gentleness and such care that I was truly inspired.

The children stay in their weird shapes as long as they can and then scramble out before the parachute lands on them again.

Variation #2 on Hamburgers and French Fries. After the parachute is whooshed up, Hamburgers go under and see if they can run around the parachute (while underneath it) 3 times before it lands on them. I indicate the direction of the run before the whoosh.

What about children that stay under the parachute? If the children are accidentally caught and the pace of the activity is going well, I ignore them. If the children deliberately stay under the parachute, slowing down the fun for the rest of the class, I establish the rule that if they are caught they will lose their next turn.

MERRY-GO-ROUND
This idea came from a first grade class. The parachute is spread out; children stand around it, holding the edge. Two to 4 children get in the middle, on top of the parachute. The rest of the class pulls the parachute taut and runs as fast as possible in one direction. This turns the parachute around like a merry-go-round. The children in the middle can try to walk against the turn, or crawl, or just sit there. Merry-Go-Round is best alternated with Ocean so that neither activity gets too tiring.

BAG THEM UP
This idea came from a teen dance class. The parachute is spread out with children around it. One or 2 children get in the middle, on top of the parachute. The rest of the children "bag them up," that is, put all the rest of the parachute material on top of them so they are in a "bag." Then one person makes up a commercial, something like, "Ladies and gentlemen, this is the biggest, squishiest roll of toilet paper in the world." The people that are bagged have to become the product. When they are unbagged they move in the way indicated by the commercial.

MS. MONSTER
This idea is as much fun for the people watching as those doing it and therefore is a good one for school demonstrations. I divide the class in half; one half is an audience and the other becomes Ms. Monster.

Ms. Monster results when 5 to 15 children go completely under the parachute and, as a unit, begin to move about the room. It works best if the children move on lower levels, knee, sitting, lowest. Ms. Monster comes out from behind pianos, from in back of the stage, or from a closet. She moves to the center of the room (or stage). This procedure of moving together under the parachute is an excellent social problem for the children; they must cooperate or the maneuvers simply will not work.

In school demonstrations I often combine Ms. Monster with a concept review. I say: "Thank you Ms. Monster for showing us the concept 'locomotor,' moving from there to here. Could you show us the concept 'level'?" The children stay in place and slowly move from standing to lowest level, then back to standing. They move at their own speeds rather than as one unit, but they are still all under the parachute. The effect is like a billowy cloud or a family of ghosts. Sometimes I ask for appropriate noises.

"Thank you, Ms. Monster. Can you show us the concept 'nonlocomotor'?" For nonlocomotor the children, still under the parachute, sit or lie down and stick one leg out from the edge of the parachute. They hold their legs high and do a nonlocomotor movement, shake, twist, contract and stretch, whatever. It is extremely funny looking.

Sometimes I will ask them to keep doing their nonlocomotor movement and try to move somewhere too. This usually just breaks down in giggles.

"Thank you. How about the concept 'direction'?" This one needs a little more organization. One child at a designated front of the parachute sticks out his head; one child at the back of the parachute sticks out his seat; one child at each side sticks out his side or arm. Then, as a unit, the parachute moves forward (head leading), backward (seat leading), and sideways (sides take turns leading). I have never attempted turning direction, but am warming up to the notion.

"Well thank you so much, Ms. Monster. For one final concept could you show us 'focus'?" All the children under the parachute stick their heads out the edge. They focus on something or someone in the room and slowly start to move in any locomotor movement they want toward their focus point. This, I must admit, is just a sneaky way to get them out from under the parachute. Right about this point I will stop them and have the other half of the class do Ms. Monster.

FLYING
If 2 or 3 children take one side of the parachute, lift their arms high, and run very fast, the whole parachute will lift and billow and look very beautiful. If you have a clean, dry, outside area, it is fine to fly the parachute there. If not, a multipurpose room is just as good. If you only have a small room available, it will not work.

ROCKS AND WAVES
The children are frozen in bizarre shapes all around the room; they are the rocks. Two children fly the parachute (the wave) over the rocks. As they do, the rocks quickly change their shapes while the parachute is fleetingly over them so, from one shape, they miraculously become another. It is exciting to watch and a lot of fun to do. However, it takes work to get there.

I begin without the parachute. I ask the children to get in Perfect Spots, on lowest level, in rock-like shapes. This might take some time, talking about what makes a rock shape, how a body could look gnarled or craigy.

"I will say '1, 2, 3, Change!' On the word 'change' you change your shape *and* change your level." The level change is important, otherwise the shape change will not appear very distinct. We practice level and shape changes for a while, moving quickly and freezing immediately. This might be a lesson by itself. It certainly is a great review of levels.

"Now that you can change levels and shapes so well, I will not tell you when to change, the parachute will tell you. When the parachute goes over you, change levels and shape. So, we will see you one way, the parachute will hide you for a second, then we will see you a different way." I walk around and glide the parachute over the children, reminding them to change. After they get the idea I ask 2 children to fly the parachute over the rocks. If the parachute goes over only a part of the rock, only that part changes shape.

Later I ask the children to get a partner and make one rock shape out of the 2 of them. When the parachute goes over them they have to change level and shape simultaneously, but each may wind up on a different level. It is at this point that I have gotten some of my greatest rewards as a teacher. Not only have the shapes been marvelously creative, but the partner work, the freedom of touching, the closeness, the cooperation, and the joy on the childrens' faces assure me it has all been worthwhile. Often I will ask these partner-rocks to join and make rocks out of 4 people; then 8, and so on, until everybody is one big rock, with the wave continously making changes.

At the end I sometimes add a variation. The rocks become individual rocks again. I become the wave, that is, I hold one end of the parachute high, ready to fly. As I go over a rock the child gets up and comes *with* me under the parachute.

He cannot use hands to slow the parachute down. I start very slowly, "picking up" one child at a time and then speed up until the whole class is running, trying to stay under the parachute as I fly it around the room. Exhausting and exciting. I like Rocks and Waves a lot, I suppose because when we are doing it I feel like one of the children. (See illustration above.)

LIFTING
This idea is not for the faint-hearted. It is scary. Not for the children, for the teacher. It can only be done with a large, heavy parachute and works best with 2nd to 6th graders (or a young class with 5 or 6 helpers). The parachute is spread out; children hold the edge and gather the material in, so that they are holding a clump of parachute at the edge. One child gets on top of the parachute in the exact middle. The rest of the class whooshes the parachute and child *off the ground*. (See illustration at right.)

I have seen children get thrown as high as 3 or 4 feet! Of course, I use mats, double thickness, on the floor under the entire middle area. A few older classes even got me into the air. It is great fun.

One side benefit of Lifting is that the little children in the class are in great demand because they go the highest. In a society where biggest is considered best, this is great. On the other hand, it might be embarrassing to any fat children in the class. I certainly respect their choice not to do it, or I remark that it feels nice to have the parachute whoosh all around you even if you do not go into the air---like me, since the children usually cannot lift me.

In any case, Lifting is one of those activities where the children look at me as if to say, "Are you really letting us do this?"

MUSHROOM
This is a favorite of mine. The children whoosh the parachute up. At its peak they quickly pull it down *behind* them and sit on the edge. With the whole class under the parachute, sitting on the edge, the air is captured. The children immediately scoot toward the middle. This pushes the parachute up into a tent-like house or mushroom. The feeling inside the Mushroom is marvelous: it is safe, warm, united, and beautiful. As one child said, "It feels like church."

PUTTING THE PARACHUTE AWAY
   With the parachute, it is essential to plan how to put it away. The children will not
want to give it up. Their reactions will range from moans, to diving under it, to just
holding on. Plan ahead. Here are some ideas, from the mundane to the sneaky.

1) The children roll the parachute from the edge into the middle.

2) "Drop the parachute, take one step away, and sit down." The children sing and sway
   to the Rocking Song on the sitting level. I ask them to do it again on a different
   level *while I pick up the parachute*. The children calm down with the song and I
   have a moment to get the parachute in its box.

3) "Sit down around the parachute...Now boys and girls, it is time for your nap. Pull
   your blankie up and go to sleep." Children pull the edge of the parachute up, like
   a blanket. After a moment, "Now I am going to pull the blanket off and you show me
   how you were sleeping." I pull the parachute away (quickly stuffing it in its box)
   and the children remain lying on the floor.

   Children love the opportunity to act younger. Third to 6th grades especially, when
   they feel safe, adore acting like babies. They pout and cry about their blankies
   being taken away, suck their thumbs and wave their arms and legs. I think it is
   good for them to act baby-like. So much of the intermediate grade years are spent
   "being cool" and acting older, that it is nice for them to have time to act younger.
   I am tolerant of much of the commotion but still insist on putting the parachute away.

4) Play Rock and Wave. Fly the wave right into its box.

5) Play Variation #1 of Hamburgers and French Fries. One half of the class lifts the
   parachute up and the other half goes under, stays there, and takes a shape after
   the parachute lands on them. When the 2nd half of the class is under, I say: "*Instead* of whooshing the parachute up, we are going to *pull* the parachute off to see
   what you look like. You stay frozen and the French Fries and I will 'unveil' you."
   (Quite a hodge-podge of metaphors!) This gives us a purpose for pulling the parachute
   off and into its box.

   If you have a rather gentle class you can ask all the children to step under the
   parachute and take a statue shape. Then unveil them all. This unveiling technique
   is the most consistently easy method for putting the parachute away.

OTHER PROPS

WHAT CAN BE USED AS A PROP?
   Almost anything can be used as a prop, whatever strikes your fancy, whatever you have
available. If you are not sure what to do with a prop, follow the basic formula: 1)
Free time. 2) Guided movements. (If you have no specific movements in mind, guide in
general ways: different levels, directions, locomotor or nonlocomotor movements, size
of movements, tempos, use of different parts of the body.) 3) Study. With this formula,
your only limitation in props is storage space and money. Here are a few miscellaneous
props I have used.

MARBLES
   Good for: 1) Coordination.
              2) Sequencing and memory skills.

It all started with an enormous marble craze at school. I had encountered a pocket full of marbles spilling on the floor, some shattering, and a child getting glass in his foot. So, in self protection, I ruled that the children were to leave their marbles in their shoes and that any marbles I saw or heard in class were mine. In a few months I had collected hundreds of marbles. It was time to do something with them.

I handed each child a marble. Free time carried the restriction that the marbles had to stay on the floor to prevent dropping. For guided movements, the children moved the marbles on the floor in various ways: they used different levels, different parts of the body (an excellent foot exercise is to grab a marble with just the toes), different locomotor movements in different directions, and different tempos. Studies were done in groups of 4: "Pick 6 different ways to move your marbles and put them in a pattern."

At the end of class each child took the marble he had worked with. I felt a little like Robin Hood equalizing the marble wealth.

FEATHERS
   Good for: 1) Coordination.
              2) Abstracting movements.

When you can find them, feathers are great. They are available at some natural craft and bead stores (and from shedding birds). It is nice if you have enough for one per child.

Again I use the basic formula. Feathers are the type of prop where children find both different ways of moving the feather and different ways of imitating the feather's movement. When imitating the feather, have the children use isolated parts of their bodies: "Make just one leg fall like the feather fell. Make one arm stay in the air, the way the feather did when you blew it up. Make your torso spiral down like the feather." Then have the children extend these movements to different speeds, sizes, locomotor and nonlocomotor movements. This is a pretty, quiet, prop.

NEWSPAPERS
   Good for: Class tone.

When I was in my experimental dance phase, I brought in stacks of newspapers and asked the children to rip them, wad them up, throw them, and so on. It was not an especially successful prop in that the children's movement imagination did not seem to grow, but it was fun for one time. News print, however, is very hard to wash off.

PLASTIC GARBAGE BAGS
   Good for: Coordination.

If they were not so expensive, large plastic garbage bags would be great. Children run, filling the bags with air. The bags make strange, indescribable noises, depending on how they fill with air. They also can be punched, jumped in, and so on. The obvious restriction is that the bags do not go near the children's heads. My objection to the bags is the expense. No matter how well they hold up to garbage, they do not last long with children.

CHAIRS
  Good for: 1) Coordination.
            2) Review of relationship words.
            3) Sequencing and memory skills.

Ordinary chairs are the base for marvelous studies. Any kind of chair will do. (If the chairs fold, spend a few minutes talking about safety.) The basic things to do with a chair are 1) move it, and 2) let it be stationary and move on, around, under, and through it.

Chairs are so taken for granted that children are at a loss thinking of what to do with them. I therefore skip free time and go right into guided movements: "Move your chair from one place to another...Move it with no hands...Use a different locomotor movement and move it...Use a different level...Fold your chair...Now find a different way to fold it...Shake your chair...Find a different way to position your chair (lay it down or turn it over)...How many different ways can you move under, around, over, and through the chair?...Use the chair to find a strange way to contract...Use the chair to stretch...Now contract and stretch on every level using the chair." (I do not allow air level on top of the chair; if I use air level at all, the children hold on to the chair and jump.) After working with guided movements, a few minutes of free time is appreciated.

One beautiful chair study came from a simple structure. Each child sequenced a contract and stretch on each level, except air level. For example, a child could have 1) sitting level contract and stretch, 2) knee level contract and stretch (see illustration #1), 3) lowest level contract and stretch (see illustration #2), and 4) standing level contract and stretch. Each movement used the chair in some manner.

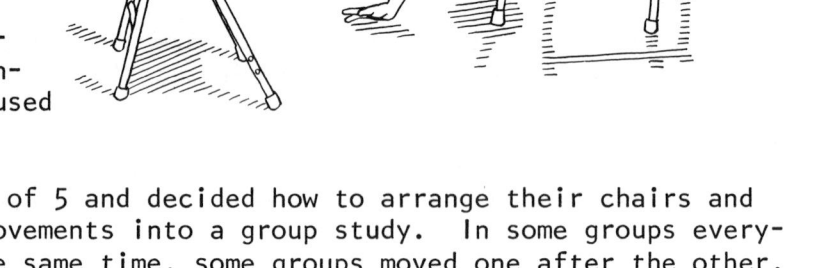

The class then divided into groups of 5 and decided how to arrange their chairs and how to organize their individual movements into a group study. In some groups everyone contracted and stretched at the same time, some groups moved one after the other, and other groups contrasted the movements so that some children were contracting while others stretched.

I have used chair studies several times for demonstrations because they are impressive even on a small stage. Here are some other chair studies:

1) In groups, pick 7 things to do with your chair and put them together in a study.

2) Each child finds a way to move the chair from the side to the center of the room; he does 5 different movements using his chair, and then moves the chair back to the side of the room. The class does the pattern all together, once using the chair and once attempting the movements without the chair.

3) The class divides into groups and puts their chairs in any arrangement they want. They do different locomotor movements around the chairs without touching them; they move through the chairs in different ways; they move over the chairs in different ways; finally they hide under their chairs. "Now put one 'around,' one 'through,' one 'over,' and one 'hide' into a group study."

COSTUMES
  Good for: 1) Class tone.
             2) Fantasy play.

There is not much to say about costumes except trust your class or do not use them. I have used costumes in only a few of my school classes but most of my dance classes. I have to know that they will be handled carefully without my constant scrutiny and that the children are sophisticated enough to do something with the costumes other than giggle.

What to use for costumes is completely open. Most teachers are collectors at heart; this is just another area to think about. In my costumes suitcase: old party dresses, the leopard-skin one-piece pajama my mother sent, army boots, ballet shoes, the grass skirt my sister sent from Hawaii, liederhosen, a fringed bikini, football shirts, a merry widow, some harem pants, red statin boxing shorts, various masks, costume jewelery, a dull machete, and all sorts of hats.

In addition, I bring my scarf box, a box of safety pins, and an inexpensive full length mirror, if there is not one available at school. It is important that there are enough costumes for everyone. Ideally I try to have half the class at a time that day.

On costume day I say, "Try on as many different combinations as you want. How does each costume make you feel like moving? Let me see even a short movement pattern before you exchange your costume." *Then* I open the suitcase. Do not expect to be able to give any instructions for at least 15 minutes after you open the suitcase.

It is possible to set some of these movement patterns into studies. (Once, a delightful play spontaneously grew out of the costumes.) Usually however, I see costumes as a one time improvisation.

With costumes, I have 3 recommendations: sit down, ignore how fast your grass skirt is shedding, and enjoy watching your children.

PROPS THAT MOVE--BEGINNING ABSTRACTIONS
  Good for: 1) Focus of attention.
             2) Abstracting movements.
             3) Sequencing and memory skills.

Most props are "passive," that is, the children's movement consists of making the prop move, for example, "Keep the balloon in the air." Some props are "active" and inspire imitation, for example, "Stretch like the balloon being blown up and fly like the balloon being let go." Imitating movement and then abstracting it to create new movements is the essence of choreography.

We touched on imitative movements when using unblown balloons, feathers, and balls. These were casual foreshadowings. Some time you might want a more direct approach to imitative movement and subsequent abstractions. Props can be found specifically to excite imitative movements. Anything can be used as long as it moves and it captivates attention. In my bag of moveable props: a book, a wind up car, several moving bath toys, a plastic squeeze toy that, when poked, "contracts," the gears of a clock, a bottle of spray cologne, a push button bottle of hand cream, a bottle of soap bubble maker, a spoon that fits a particular bowl in such a way that the spoon balances and twirls, and (my favorite) a pronged olive picker--when the handle is pressed, 3 wire fingers come out and grab an imaginary olive.

The children gather near me on the floor. We begin with a demonstration; most often I use a book. Opening and closing it, I ask, "Can you move like this?" The children come up with numerous examples. We explore the hinge-like movement with isolated body parts, with the whole body, with a partner. I make sure the children note that they are using different levels, locomotor and nonlocomotor movements, different sizes, and tempos.

The next step is to demonstrate how to combine a number of these movement ideas into a pattern, choreography if you will. Using as many variations on hinge movements as possible, I direct a short study. Here is an example:

1) The children move toward the center of the room, each doing a different hinge movement, for example, both arms opening and closing, hinging at the elbow, hinging at the knee, hinging at the hip joint.

2) When they reach the middle of the room, the children assume positions using different levels and hinge robot-like from the hip joint. They move at their own speed.

3) One by one, the children "break loose" from the robot-like hinge movements and do large locomotor movements plus hinge movements with their arms.

4) They regroup in partners and do a paired hinge movement that takes them off to the side of the room.

In this example, I direct the class by calling out the changes. My purpose is to give the children the idea of how to use many different hinge movements and how to organize them into a group study.

The children then divide into groups and pick their own moveable prop. They experiment with imitative movements and create a study based on that movement. This is only for older classes, probably 4th grade and up, although mature, experienced, younger classes will be able to handle it.

The beauty of using moveable props for group choreography is that it stimulates problem solving and imaginative thinking. How does one burst like a soap bubble or advance like a 3-pronged olive picker? Such questions are stimulating challenges and, occasionally, result in beautiful dances.

CONCLUDING

ABOUT CRITICIZING CREATIVE WORKS
A great deal of the work with props concludes with the children creating a pattern. When the children show me their creative efforts I am free in giving my choreographic criticisms. I do not think it "stifles creativity" in the least. All of us need to have our creative energies pushed now and then; if movements are dull it does not help to say "How wonderful!" Plus that, one new idea often inspires another.

However, I do 2 things to lighten my authoritative hand: 1) 99% of the time I recommend with the understanding that the children do *not* have to follow my recommendations, and 2) the tone of my class is such that I welcome a group saying "Don't watch us now," or "We don't want any ideas now." As long as they are working hard, I hold my tongue.

When they are ready for ideas, I give them. Generally what childrens' choreography will need is diversity: a group will get stuck with all locomotor or all nonlocomotor movements or with the movements all on one level, or with one configuration. Most children need to be told to use more space, and almost all will need to be told to use different parts of their bodies. Occasionally a group will need to repeat some movements so that the pattern is a tighter unit, but usually the patterns will need greater variety.

ABOUT FUN

You can have a sound movement program without props but it will not be great. Props are wonderful tools for working on basic skills: memory, sequencing, large muscle coordination, eye-hand coordination, eye-foot coordination, and abstraction. Equally important, props are just fun.

"Try on a costume and see what you look like." "I'll lay the parachute out and group one get as tangled as you want in it." "Let's play with the balls for the last 10 minutes of class." This kind of "unpurposeful" fun is important to children. It makes them feel good. It brings them closer to you. It says to them, "I like you and I like seeing you have a good time."

PART 9
MOVEMENT AS AN ACADEMIC TOOL

USING MOVEMENT TO TEACH SKILLS

TECHNIQUES PRESENTED
Movement is an excellent tool for teaching academic skills. Throughout this book we have touched on general skills such as sequencing, memory, concentration, and visual awareness. In Part 9 we shall focus on specific language and math skills. My hope is not so much to cover all possible needs of a class, but to present the techniques with which to apply movement to whatever needs arise.

WAYS THAT MOVEMENT CAN BE USED
There are 2 ways that movement can teach academic skills. First, movement can provide concrete experiences involving the skill, for example, getting into groups of 3's and seeing a remainder of one. Second, movement can link a desired skill into a rhythmic framework that facilitates memorization, for example, spelling "necessary" outloud while skipping across the room. Because these methods are concrete and experiential, the lessons taught through movement are usually remembered and internalized. In any case they are fun.

LANGUAGE DEVELOPMENT

LETTERS

BODY SHAPE LETTERS
   Good for: 1) Recognizing letters.
                2) Distinguishing letters.
                3) Sequencing and memory skills.

Almost everyone involved with children has, at one time or another, made letters out of body shapes. "Make your body into an 'A' (usually make by one arm crossing at the knees)...Make your body into a 'B' (rounded arm and rounded leg)." It is not a bad idea and certainly worth doing. (But not over-doing.) I have a few recommendations for using body letters:

1) Make sure the letters are right. The only value in making letters is to teach them to children. If the children form a letter incorrectly there is no value in doing it. There may be several correct ways of making an individual letter but check to see that the rationale behind each variation is appropriate.

2) Do only a few at a time and do them fully. Maybe just do "A, B, and C," or "X, Y, and Z," or "p, d, and q."* Try them on different levels: "Make an 'X' on standing level...On lowest level...On knee level...Can you make an air level 'X'?" Ask the letters to move somewhere: "Make a 'Y' on standing level and go somewhere... Don't let the stem come apart...Make a 'Z' on knee level and crawl...Make a 'P' air level and go somewhere." Make letters with a partner: "Get a partner and the 2 of you make one 'E'...Stay like that and go somewhere."

3) Start combining letter shapes into a study. Here are 3 examples of studies: a) In groups of 4, pick 4 letters and make each one on a different level. Be able to move smoothly from one to the other with no stops or hesitations. Remember your sequence. b) With a partner, pick 3 letters and make them together, that is, one letter out of 2 people. In between each letter you will have 8 beats of free locomotor movements. On count 8 be back together because you will only have 2 beats to get into your letter shape. After you get your shape, freeze. Remember your pattern. c) Make 3 letter shapes out of your body. Stay in each shape and do a locomotor movement. Remember your pattern.

OUTLINING LETTERS
Good for: 1) Recognizing letters.
           2) Distinguishing letters.

Making letters by outlining them in the air is coming back into style. Children draw the shape on an imaginary chalk board. When I introduce this technique I have the children hold their hands together so that I can clearly see the shape they are attempting. I ask for very large shapes stretching as high, as wide, and as low as possible. Also, I insist that they be done the same way as they would be literally printed, for example, an "A" starts at the top and goes diagonally down to the left, backs up to the top and down to the right, then crosses from left to right.

Once the children are at ease outlining letters with their hands in front of them, I ask for 2 types of variations: 1) a different part of the body, and 2) a different plane in the air. For example: "Outline a 'B' with your hands clasped in front of you...Again with your hands, outline a 'B' on the floor...With your hands outline a 'B' on the ceiling...Show me a 'D' with your toes as the pencil...Make the 'D' in front of you, on the floor, on the ceiling...Can you outline a 'D' with your toes in back of you?...Outline an 'S' with your elbow, your head, your seat, your little finger."

Gradations in size are also possible: "Use your nose to make the biggest 'S' in the world...Use your right knee to make the smallest 'S' in the world...How about a medium sized 'S' with your tummy?"

When using body parts like the seat, tummy, torso, eyes, and shoulder, the letters are difficult to distinguish and I am not fussy about the resulting letter outline. These are mainly for fun. When using hands, arms, elbows, toes, and heads, I am medium-fussy; at least I am on the look out for scribbling.

FLOOR PATTERN LETTERS
Good for: 1) Recognizing letters.

---
* For "p, d, and q," make sure the children see the room as if it were a piece of paper, with a clear top and bottom, so that the relation of circle to stem in the letters is correct.

2) Distinguishing letters.
3) Sequencing and memory skills.

My favorite way to reinforce letters is through floor patterns. It is best to introduce letter floor patterns after the children have had some experience with straight and curved lines. Like other floor patterns, we begin with a room representation. The pattern then moves the same way as the letter is formed on paper. For example, a "B" starts down with the straight line, backtracks up, and then curves twice. (See diagram #1.)

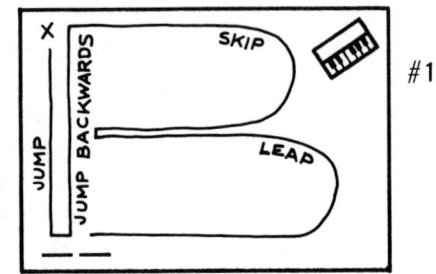

Most of the time I make the letters room size. Sometimes we play with size gradations: "Make a 'B' as big as the entire room...Make a medium-sized 'B'...Keep the 3 locomotor movements you used and make a tiny 'B'."

These floor pattern letters are an unlimited source of studies. 1) Put letters together to make a word or name (see Part 6). 2) Pick 4 letters and make each a different floor pattern, using different locomotor movements on different levels in different directions. 3) For older classes, pick a word and do one cursive floor pattern. (See diagram #2.)

COMBINING TECHNIQUES
   Best of all is combining these 3 letter forming techniques (body shapes, outlining, and floor patterns) into one study. Here are a few examples:

1) Beautiful studies came from this simple structure: "Pick a word; make each letter in a different way." (Although there are only 3 basic letter forming techniques, each can be done in various ways. For example, body shapes can be done on different levels, outlining can be done with different parts of the body, and floor patterns can be different sizes.) "Move smoothly from one letter to the next so that the pattern becomes one fluid dance." These can be truly lovely, especially if the children include different tempos and dynamic qualities. One would never guess the academic origins of the outcomes.

2) In groups, find a word that has the same number of letters as the group size, for example, a group of 5 has to find a 5 letter word. Each group member makes one letter in his own, unique way. Make the letters one after the other, then make them all at the same time.

3) Pick 3 letters, make each letter 3 different ways. Do the whole thing without stopping or hesitating.

4) "Move your name."

5) "Using voice and movement, tell the class a message."

WORD COMPREHENSION

USING MOVEMENT TO TEACH WORDS
   With letter patterns we begin to overlap into the area of words. Movement is a master at teaching words. A movement lesson can teach almost *any* word, even if it does not move. I made this claim once at a teacher workshop and one of the participants called me on it. "Alright," she said, "if movement can teach almost any word, I'll

pick a word and you create a lesson." I accepted the challenge with trepidation. She picked the word "and" and I sighed with relief. I shook one arm, "I am shaking my arm *and* (lifting a shaking leg) shaking my leg." "I am twisting my head *and* bending my knees." "I am swinging my torso *and* wiggling my fingers."

I was lucky; I had put myself on the spot. I do not believe movement can teach any word, but it can teach and develop a surprising number of words. Following are movement ideas for 1) relationship words, 2) problem words, 3) inclusive/exclusive words, 4) emotion words, and 5) homonyms and antonyms. These examples may be useful in themselves, but more importantly, they will help develop your own ideas about using movement as a language tool.

I believe education is at least 50% teaching words, their meaning and use. When a child knows a word in his body, that word becomes a reality; it becomes a usable, internalized part of his world.

RELATIONSHIP WORDS
Relationship words describe the juxtaposition of one object to another: "over," "under," "around," "between," "off," "on," "in front of," "behind," "beside," and so forth. These words become the glue that ties ideas together. They are crucial for text comprehension, for following instructions, and for testing skills.

The best way to teach these words is by asking children to demonstrate them in the relationship of their bodies to physical objects. For example, crawling under a table to demonstrate "under." An efficient teaching device for this type of demonstration is an obstacle course. An obstacle course can reinforce almost any relationship word: "over" the table, "under" the chair, "around" the piano, "on and off" the foam, "in and out" of the box, "between" the bookcases. The children enjoy themselves tremendously while mastering these words.

I usually plan an obstacle course as the first activity of a lesson so that I can have it ready when the children enter the room. It is important to vary the courses so that the relationship words are not always associated with a particular object; the words should have a wide range of applications.

In addition to obstacle courses, specific lessons can be planned for work on specific relationship words. As with obstacle courses, I set up any equipment before the children enter and use these activities as lesson warm-ups.

"On and "Off"
   Good for: 1) Teaching words.
              2) Control of movement.

   Place mats around the room, close enough so that a child can jump from one to another but far enough apart so that it is a long jump: "Jump only 'on' the mats, don't touch the floor...Jog 'off' the mats...Hop 'on' the mats...Sit 'off' the mats and swing...Roll 'on' the mats...Skip 'off' the mats."

   The mats are fun because while on them the children are very close together holding on to each other "so they won't fall off," giggling, and carrying on. Off them they have room to move freely with a lot of energy. For safety, pick movements that are rather small for "on." For energy release, pick large movements for "off."

What happens to the child who is "off" (when he is supposed to be "on")? It depends on why. Once in a great while a child will truly not understand. He needs individual help with a myriad of "off" and "on's": "Put your hand on the piano...Take it off...Put your foot on the chair...Take it off...Put your head on the desk...Take it off." I do this one-to-one work outside of class.

Most often mistakes with "off" and "on" are caused by carelessness. This is when I revert to a competitive game: "Anybody 'off' when they are supposed to be 'on,' or 'on' when they are supposed to be 'off,' will sit down this round. You'll be able to play the next round." I start a new round when about half the class is "out." We usually play 3 or 4 rounds during a 10 or 15 minute warm-up.

"In" and "Out"
Good for: 1) Teaching words.
           2) Group work.

Large boxes (from furniture or appliance stores) are wonderful for work with "in" and "out." Have the children divide into groups of 3 to 5 and have one box for each group. "One child 'in'...Come 'out'...Three children 'in'...Two come 'out'...Three more go 'in.' How many children are 'in' the box now? (Oops, off on an arithmetic lesson.) One child go 'in' and the rest of the group give him a ride. (Take turns so that everyone has a ride.)....Everybody get 'in' your box...Can you stay 'in' and go somewhere?"

Going in and out of boxes has produced some spectacular studies. These studies resulted from this simple structure: "Your box has to go from one side of the room to the middle, do something, and go to the other side of the room. Use some parts of your bodies 'in' and some 'out' of the box."

I gave this study to grades 3 to 6. The results were incredibly funny. One box started from the side of the room with just feet, pointed every which way, showing from the bottom. In the middle of the room the box, with children in it, turned itself over so that the open side was on top. Disjointed arms, legs, and elbows emerged, preceeding to put on a show full of remarkably identifiable personalities. The box turned back over and walked off as it had come in.

In other studies, children cut holes in their boxes so that they could stick parts of their bodies out; the boxes looked grotesquely human. These studies certainly grew much larger than the original intention of working with "in" and "out."

For younger children, mats can be used to differentiate between "on and off" and "in and out." Stiff mats can be made to stand up and form little "houses." (See illustration at right.)

Ask the children to stand the mats up and go "in" the house; come "out" of the house. Have the children knock the houses down and stand "on" them, then "off" them. This game can be repeated innumerable times; young children do not seem to tire of it. Their favorite part, of course, is knocking the houses down.

"In Front Of," "Behind," and "Beside"
Good for: 1) Teaching words.
           2) Problem solving.

For young children I only introduce "in front of" and "behind"; later I include "beside." For older classes I work with all 3 at once. Generally children who understand front, back, and side on their own bodies (see Part 6) easily transfer these directional planes to objects. I explain that just as our bodies have front, back, and sides so do many objects. "If you stand by the front of something, it's called 'in front of'; if you stand by its back, it's called 'behind'; if you stand by its side, it's called 'beside.'"

We work with "in front of," "behind," and "beside" somewhat in the same way we worked with "near" and "far" to get Perfect Spots. "Go 'in front of' the piano... Go 'behind' a chair...Go 'beside' my desk...Go 'in front of' the chalk board... Go 'behind' me...Go 'beside' Andrew." The only trick is to pick objects that have a clear front and back, and to make sure they are possible and desireable.*

Once the children get these one-part instructions try 2 parts. The 2-part instructions can either combine 2 objects or an object with the child's body. Here is an example of 2 objects: "Go 'behind' the piano *and* 'in front of' a chair... Go 'in front of' me *and* 'beside' my desk...Go 'behind' Joe *and* 'behind' the green box." Here are examples of an object combined with the child's body: "Put your *back* 'beside' my desk...Stand with your *front* 'behind' the piano...Stand with your *side* 'in front of' the stage."

"Between"
Good for: 1) Teaching word.
           2) Coordination.
           3) Group work.

To introduce "between" I scatter objects throughout the room (tables, chairs, mats, my desk, the piano, traffic cones) and ask the children to stand between 2 objects: "Stand 'between' a table and a chair...Stand 'between' my desk and a mat...Stand 'between' a traffic cone and the piano."

To make it more of a game, the children have only a certain number of seconds (usually 10) to get to their designated spot. Those that do not make it are out for the round. (This game is very similar to the In and Out Game which follows.)

Another way to reinforce "between" is with locomotor movements. I ask the children to get into groups of 3's, ready to move on the diagonal. "If you line up side by side in your groups, there are 2 people on either side and one person 'between' them. First group, the person that is 'between' 2 people raise your hand...That's right, Greg, you are 'between' Antoine and Mark. Now rearrange yourselves so that Antoine is the 'between' person...How would you be arranged for Mark to be the 'between' person? Good."

When the children are clear as to who is "between," we do a series of movements where the "between" child does something special or different. The children take turns being the "between person." If the movement is especially fun we do it 3 times so that everyone has a turn.

---
* Here are some instructions I wish I had never said: "Go behind the front door." (They all left.) "Go behind the chalk board." (It is nailed to the wall.) "Go behind the stage." (Clutered with lighting equipment.)

1) Carry. (This is the all time "between" favorite.) The 2 side people make a hand square. This is done by each child holding his own left wrist with his right hand, and then holding his partner's wrist with the left hand. (See page 51.) The "between" person sits on the hand square and gets carried across the diagonal. Obviously, this locomotor movement has to be done 3 times.

2) Directional Can-Can. Children hold on to each other's shoulders. The 2 side people kick forward and the "between" person kicks backwards.

3) Galloping in a Basket. The 2 side people hold hands and side-slide. The "between" person gallops within the arms of the side people.

4) Directional running. The 2 side people run forward and the "between" person runs backwards, while all hold hands.

5) Directional skipping. The side people skip forward, the "between" person skips turning around, and they all stay together.

6) Hop-jump. The side people hop and the "between" person jumps while all hold hands.

7) The Stretcher. The side people walk sideways, each holding one arm and one leg of the "between" person. The "between" person relaxes and enjoys the ride.

8) Counterpoint. All the children learn a simple, even-beat pattern, for example, walk 4 beats, jump 4 beats, skip 4 beats. The side people do the pattern in the original order while the "between" person does it in reverse order, for example, skip 4 beats, jump 4 beats, walk 4 beats. (In this example the jumps of all 3 coincide; this helps keep the pattern together.) The children have to stay together. This is a good exercise in thinking for oneself.

9) Opposites. Each group picks one opposite relationship, short-tall, fast-slow, big-little. The "between" person does one word and the 2 side people do the opposite, while they all stay together.

The Unbeatable In And Out Game
Good for: 1) Teaching words.
            2) Coordination.
            3) Class tone.

This game is one of the best ideas in this book. The game reinforces all the previous relationship words plus some, and the children love it so much they request it more than the parachute. Amazing.

Here is the set up: I place 3 stiff mats standing up (like houses) in different parts of the room. I place 3 soft mats randomly on the floor. Then I scatter pieces of foam, tables, sturdy (not collapsable) chairs, my desk, a box with a clear front, hula hoops, and traffic cones. Finally I pull the piano out from its corner so that children can easily move around it. The room looks like a complete disaster. (See diagram at right.)

The game is simple: I call a relationship word and the children demonstrate it within a prescribed time. The words I use are "in," "over," "around," "between," "on top," "under," "in front of," "behind," and "beside." For the word "in" the children go in the stand up mats or stand within a hula hoop. "Under" may be under anything in the room, under soft mats, pieces of foam, tables, chairs, traffic cones. "Around" is shown by running circles around any one object. For "between" I specify what the children should stand between, for example, "stand 'between' 2 hula hoops," or "stand 'between' a table and a chair." "In front of," "behind," and "beside" are done to specified objects, for example, "stand 'in front of' the green box," or "stand 'beside' a chair." For "on top" the children stand or sit on any object. "Over" is a little different; the children jump or leap over objects without touching them. For "over" the children do not have a set number of seconds; rather, I play the piano and they continuously move over different objects while the piano sounds. All the other words are done within a prescribed time limit.

It is this time limit that makes the game exciting. When the game first starts I use a 10 second limit but as the game proceeds I cut it to 5 seconds. Anyone not doing the word at the end of the time is out for that round. A round ends when there are only a few children left and I declare them the winners. I keep the game moving very fast and we might play 5 rounds in 20 minutes. The children would like to play 50 rounds. I have played the In and Out Game with kindergarten through 6th grade and the response is unanimous: they love it.

A few additional points: When the children go "in" the stand up mats, I include the rule that if they knock the mat down, they are *all* out. Instant cooperation. As in most referee games, I announce that the umpire's word (mine) is final. If a child argues too much he is out for another round. In older classes, when there are just a few children left and they are not getting out, I sometimes give 2 instructions to do within the 5 second limit. For example, "Go 'on top' of the stage and then 'under' something," or "*At the same time*, show 'on top' and 'under.'" (The latter could be done with one part of the body, a leg, under an object while another part, an arm, is on top.)

Here are a few typical calls: "In, 1-2-3-4-5-6-7-8-9-10...On top, 1--10...Under, 1--10...Over (I play the piano and the children move until the sound stops.)... Beside my desk, 1--10...Around, 1--10..." When about half the class is out, I cut the time limit in half: "OK, you are too good at this, now you'll only have 5 seconds. In front of a chair, 1--5...Under, 1--5...Around, 1--5..."

How does the room get back in order? The most efficient method I have found is this: I sit the children in the middle of the room. One or 2 children at a time are given a clearly defined task. When they finish they *sit back down with the rest of the class*. This avoids the chaos of too many children trying to do too many things at one time. Also, it is often a good lesson in following verbal instructions. For example, "Albert, fold this blue mat and put it on the floor in front of the stage. Mary and Jane push the piano back against the wall. Henry pick up all the foam pieces and stack them on the table next to my desk." In this way the room can be picked up within 3 to 5 minutes.

There is no way I can describe how exciting the In and Out Game is. I hope you will take a leap of faith and try it. The children adore it. Considering its academic importance, it is something like children choosing to spend their allowances on broccoli.

PROBLEM WORDS

Problem words are those particular words with which a class has difficulty. Each class has its own unique problem words. Here are a few examples of movement lessons used to teach word comprehension. These examples demonstrate 4 techniques of working with problem words: progression, opposites, vignettes, and physical objects.

Progression--"Horizontal" And "Vertical"
Good for: 1) Teaching words.
2) Coordination.
3) Group work.
4) Sequencing and memory skills.

We begin with a short verbal definition, and then explore these 2 words with isolated body parts: "Make your hand 'horizontal' to the floor...Make your hand 'vertical' to the floor...Make your arm 'horizontal' to the floor...Make your arm 'vertical'..." So on with legs, torso, feet, back, and head. "Can you make your seat 'horizontal'? 'Vertical'?"

After working with isolated body parts we move to whole body positions on different levels: "Make your body 'horizontal' on the lowest level...Sitting level... Knee level...Standing level." For sitting, knee, and standing levels I accept any part of the body horizontal, for example, on standing level a child might bend his torso straight forward, or even better lift a leg back as he bends his torso forward. (See illustration at right.)

"Can you make your body, or part of it, 'horizontal' in the air level?" "Vertical" is easier, and we do it on all levels. For lowest level vertical position I accept shoulder stands or prone torsos with raised legs and arms.

Now we are ready to play with the words: "Make your body 'horizontal' on any level you want...Keep the shape and move locomotor, backward direction...Make your body vertical and change levels...Keep changing levels and go somewhere." Best of all: "Get into groups of 3. Lift one person so he is completely 'horizontal' off the ground. (The children take turns.) Lift one person so he is 'vertical' off the ground."

Finally a short study: "In groups of 3, make up 4 different ways to show 'horizontal' and 4 different ways to show 'vertical.' Alternate them. Move smoothly from one to the other so it is a continuous pattern, and remember your pattern."

The progression used to teach these words is one I use often: 1) initial definition, 2) explore the idea with isolated body parts, 3) explore the idea with the whole body, 4) play with the idea, adding other known concepts, and 5) create a remembered study. The sequence moves from little to big, from less to more freedom, from a literal to a more expanded view of the idea. This progression is very adaptable and can be used to teach just about any word.

Opposites And Vignettes--"Comfortable"
Good for: 1) Teaching words.
2) Group work.
3) Sequencing and memory skills.

One teacher mentioned that her class had trouble with the definition of the word "comfortable" and asked me to work on it. I tackled the problem by starting with "uncomfortable": "Twist so hard that you are 'uncomfortable' or strained or hurt a little...Relax the twist so that you are 'comfortable' or at ease... Contract so hard that you are 'uncomfortable' or tense or hurt a little...Relax the contraction so that you are 'comfortable' or at ease...Stretch so hard that you are 'uncomfortable'...Relax so that you are 'comfortable.'"

Later in this 5th/6th grade class we talked about "comfortable" and "uncomfortable" as they related to social situations. The children identified with these problems easily. "Walk as though you were 'uncomfortable' or ill at ease, in a brand new school, a scary place, among a group of kids that don't like you... Walk as though you were 'comfortable'...Sit 'uncomfortably'...Sit 'comfortably.'"

Have you ever done move-freeze vignettes? The children place themselves in a "frozen picture" depicting some idea. (In the case of "uncomfortable" 4 children might sit pointing accusingly at one startled child, or they might stand very crowded together as if in a crowded elevator.) The pictures are set so that each child knows exactly where he stands and exactly what position he is in. The children move instantly into these "pictures" and freeze until I ask them to go on to the next.

Vignettes are a great structure for words that can be visualized. In this example, I asked groups of 5 children to set up 2 vignettes showing something "comfortable" and 2 showing "uncomfortable." We put them in a sequence and performed them on stage. They were terrific!

Physical Objects--"Reverse"
Good for: 1) Teaching words.
           2) Sequencing and memory skills.

We used physical objects when working with relationship words; objects can also be used to teach other words. Here is an example of using objects to teach the word "reverse."

I work with the word "reverse" in a specialized sense, that is, in a sequence, going from the end to the beginning. In this way "reverse" and "backward" are differentiated. "Backward" is used to mean a direction of the body, the back leading; "reverse" is reserved for opposite ordering. The best clarification of this differentiation comes from working with an obstacle course. I set up a standard course such as the one diagramed at right.

The children learn the course quickly. I then add backward direction. When I stop the piano the children stop and I call either "forward" or "backward." The children continue the course in that direction. They are, however, still taking the obstacles in the same sequence.

I then introduce the idea of "original order" and "reverse order." For "original order" the children do the course in the order first taught, first the somersaults, then the foam jump, etc. For "reverse order" the children turn, wherever they are in the course, and go the other way in the sequence.

When I first introduce "original order" and "reverse order" the children do them only in the forward direction. Later I combine "original and reverse order" and "forward and backward direction." When I stop the piano, the children "freeze" and I give dual instructions: "Go the original order, backward direction." "Go the original order, forward direction." "Go the reverse order, forward direction." "Go the reverse order, backward direction." This is pretty much self corrective because someone going the wrong way is met by a rush of children going the other way. I speed up the change of instructions, going faster and faster, until the whole thing falls apart in laughter.

For young children the distinction between "backward and reverse order" can be made by using a simplified obstacle course or by using a simple locomotor study. A locomotor study might be: "Skip one side of the room, jump one side, run one side, and crawl one side. Do the pattern...Do the pattern, backward direction... Do the pattern reverse order, that is, the crawl side first...Do the pattern reverse order, backward direction."

INCLUSIVE AND EXCLUSIVE WORDS

Inclusive and exclusive words, "only," "both," "everybody," and "nobody," demand physical attention because they are so abstract they are sometimes nonfunctional. I am sure we have all experienced the hair pulling frustration of saying "Everybody get a ball," with one child asking, "Do I get a ball?"

"Only"
Good for: 1) Teaching words.
           2) Control.

"Move only your fingers." (I am strict that nothing else moves. This is good muscular coordination as well as mental concentration.) "Move only one shoulder...Move only your toes...Only your head...Only your eyes...Only your hips... Only your leg."

"Take only one jump...Only 3 skips...Only 2 hops...Only one leap."

"Only the boys move...Only the girls...Only the children with black hair...Only the children wearing red..." Simple, but workable.

"Both"
Good for: 1) Teaching words.
           2) Coordination and control.

After "only" is established I use it as a contrast to "both." "Move only one arm...Now move both arms...Move only one leg...Now move both legs...Move only your head...Move only your hips...Now move both your head and hips...Move only your fingers...Move only your toes...Now move both your fingers and toes."

I find that it works best to use 2 "only's" before a "both" so that the "both" results in precisely 2 movements rather than a jumble of activity.

With a partner: "Only one of you skip...The other person gallops...Now keep your own movements, hold on to one another, and 'both' of you move. Only one of you jump...Only one of you roll...Now stay together and 'both' of you move."

"Everybody" And "Nobody"
Good for: Teaching words.

"Everybody" and "nobody" are best done together, like a game. "'Everybody' stand in Perfect Spots and swing...'Nobody' swing." For the "nobody" instruction the children stand still. This has to be initially pointed out: "If *no* body is swinging then you don't swing." (If the children do something else instead, like shake or spin, I accept that since no one is swinging. But that is quite sophisticated and rarely happens.)

"OK 'nobody' jump, come on 'nobody' jump." (I ham it up as if I expected them to jump and am surprised they are not.) "'Everybody' jump...'Everybody' skip... 'Nobody' skip...Now 'nobody' run. Oh oh I fooled you. Now 'everybody' run."

EMOTION WORDS
Good for: 1) Teaching words.
2) Expanding movement vocabulary.
3) Group work.

Emotion words would seem to be a natural part of movement class. The basis of a great deal of dance is emotional expression in physical form. The trouble with using emotion in the classroom is that it often ends up so trite. "Sad" is a limp head with a frown, "happy" is a wide palm skip. I must admit that I have sometimes neglected emotion words just because I could not bear the results.

I do not have a solution for this stereotyping. However, I do have 2 conclusions: 1) Emotional expressions turn out trite because they are untrue, not from the gut level. Either the children are not in touch with their feelings or they are afraid to let them out. Dealing with the children's inhibitions creates a teaching dilemma: I do not want to criticize but I do not want to accept their superficiality. Generally, I attempt to be moderate and to use a little of both. 2) The children need hundreds of good examples: pictures, movies, performances, and, if possible, their teacher's gut level demonstrations.

However, the problems of doing emotion words should not preclude using them. The meaning and spelling of emotion words will be learned through movement activities, even if the feelings are not real.

It is best to begin emotion words in the Free Traveling Structure so that all the children are moving at once and none feel too exposed. The children move as though angry, happy, scared, lonely, tired, excited, and so on. (For older classes use more sophisticated feelings: melancholy, exuberant, astonished, guilty, exasperated, sullen, proud.) As much as possible I introduce the word within a complete emotional scene. The children sit or lie down with their eyes closed: "You are walking to school by yourself. Another kid comes and purposely pushes you down. On top of that he takes your homework paper and won't give it back. He runs off laughing and you can't catch him." (When setting an "angry" scene it is important that the other child runs off and is *not* caught, otherwise all the resulting movement will simply be a fight.) "You are mad, furious, angry. With your eyes still closed, show how you would look. Open your eyes, how would you walk?...Run angry...Sit angry...Contract angry...Stretch angry...Skip angry...Twist angry...Turn angry...Move any way you want angry...Do as many different angry movements as you can."

Do give the children specific movements to do before they move any way they want. This broadens their perspective from a stereotyped anger (usually a chest out bully stand). Furthermore, ask for movements that are not usually associated with the particular emotion, for example, skip is not a typically angry movement. This again provides a broader scope.

Working with emotion words will be better the 2nd or 3rd (or 5th or 6th) time you do it. Children need the time to build up confidence in themselves and trust in the class. As I mentioned, I do few corrections. When I do, I use a light hand: "How could somebody who is angry giggle so much? Your 'happy' and your 'sad' look an awful lot alike. Do that 'joyous' on different levels. Use some locomotor and some nonlocomotor movements. Can you show me a backward 'excited'?"

After exploring emotion words in the Free Traveling Structure, we do them on the diagonal. When working on the diagonal, I will often ask for the same locomotor movement or pattern done in different ways: "Skip as if you're happy, skip sad, skip proudly, skip determined." We are then ready for studies using emotion words.

1) Teach a simple pattern, for example, walk 4 beats, contract 4 beats, stretch 4 beats, gallop 4 beats. The children divide into groups. Each group picks an emotion and does the pattern appropriately.

2) Teach a simple pattern, for example, run to the middle of the room, turn, fall, and roll. The children form groups. Each group picks 3 emotions and does the pattern 3 times each a different way.

3) Each group is given an emotion word on a card. They show that emotion in 5 to 10 different movements and put the movements together to form a continuous pattern. The children are instructed to use all known movement concepts: different levels, locomotor and nonlocomotor movements, directions, and floor patterns.

HOMONYMS AND ANTONYMS

Homonyms and antonyms can be an academic bore. In movement class these word skills become the basis for several games and are easily understood and remembered.

Homonyms
Good for: 1) Teaching words.
            2) Class tone.
            3) Sequencing and memory skills.

Let us take a frequently tested homonym: "skip." We begin with a verbal introduction:

"What does 'skip' mean?"

"To skip around."

"Yes, that is locomotor movement skip. Good. What other kinds of 'skips' are there?"

"The guy that runs a boat." (A skipper.)

"Someone's name."

"Skip it."

"Great. The word 'skip' has a number of meanings. You already know the locomotor movement skip. We are going to work with the kind of 'skip' that means to pass over, like 'skip it.'"

I ask the children to line up on one side of the room and then pick a volunteer. "Tina, shake hands with the first person in line...Now 'skip' 9 people and shake hands with the next...'Skip' 15 people and shake hands with the next...'Skip' one more person and shake hands with the next...Good. Can I have a new volunteer? Rich, 'skip' the first 7 people and twirl the next person...'Skip' the next 20 people and twirl the next..." And so on. The children "skip" certain numbers of people, shaking hands, shaking feet, twirling people, patting backs, and once in a while even hugging.

We then go on to a more abstract by-pass "skip." In the above example it was visually clear what was "skipped." Now the children will "skip" sections that they can not see. The children learn a simple, medium long pattern, for example, jump 4 times, walk 4 times, skip 4 times. They form groups and practice the pattern on the diagonal until it is clear.

"Group one, do the pattern but 'skip' the jump part." To do this I ask group one to stand still for the first 4 beats, then resume the pattern with the walk and the skip sections. "Group 2, you 'skip' the walk part." (Group 2 jumps 4 beats, stands still 4 beats, and skips 4 beats.) "Group 3, you 'skip' the skip part."

Another technique useful for most homonyms is pantomine. Generally I do not like pantomine in movement class.* However, it is a fast and efficient way to see if a class understands the difference between 2 similar sounding words. Here are a few examples. In all cases I show the words on a card.

"Aisle" and "isle" present a good spelling problem. For "isle" the children essentially find Perfect Spots and pretend to be islands. For "aisle" the children line up in 2 rows leaving an aisle between them. (Sometimes I ask 2 children to "walk down the aisle.")

Another spelling differentiation is "fowl" and "foul." When the card "fowl" is held up, the children act like chickens. For "foul" they enact a ball going out of fair play.

In the case of "row, row, and row" I show the words on cards and verbally distinguish them. "Row, the boat kind." The children pretend to be using oars.

---

* Too often children spend a lot of time jumping like frogs, growing like flowers, and swinging like elephant trunks, but they do not go anywhere from there. I suspect I have overreacted. My fear is that too much energy devoted to superficial immitation will sacrifice the energy needed to experiment with the children's own movement. True pantomine begins only after extensive training and requires an enormous movement vocabulary and fluency. It is an art form I greatly admire. But elephants that look like dogs that look like mice are not close to true pantomine.

"Row the line kind." The children quickly line up. "Row." (The fight kind of "row" has a different pronunciation, therefore, I do not verbally distinguish it.) For this one the children gleefully *pretend* to have an enormous brawl.

Antonyms
Good for: 1) Teaching words.
2) Partner work.
3) Problem solving.
4) Class tone.

We begin with a verbal introduction of the word "opposite": "Opposite means very different. What is the most different, or opposite, of 'yes'? day? left? wrong? high? big? happy? rich? ugly? messy? wonderful?"

At this point, in young classes, I bring out Ms. Opposite. Ms. Opposite is a large cardboard puppet with one eye open and one shut, half of her mouth happy and half sad, short light hair on one side and long dark hair on the other, half her torso covered with bumpy corderoy and half smooth silk, half her skirt is red and half green, one foot has a shoe on and one off. (Young children love her.) The joints are made moveable by using butterfly tacks. We therefore can use Ms Opposite to show opposite positions: bent arm and straight arm, contracted leg and stretched leg, high and low, and so on. All these positions are, of course, transferred to the children's bodies.

There are numerous movement activities possible with opposites. The 2 best activities are Partner Opposites and The Opposite Game.

Partner Opposites. The goal of Partner Opposites is for the children to stay with their partners while demonstrating an opposite relationship. The children hold hands and show high and low, forward and backward, pretty and ugly, crooked and straight, heavy and light, and for older classes, stereotyped boy and girl. A good logic problem is to ask the children to stay together (not necessarily hold hands) while demonstrating fast and slow. (One child can run circles around a slow moving child, or one child can run fast but almost in place while the other child moves slowly.)

The Opposite Game. The children divide into groups and line up ready to move on the diagonal. "This is your chance in a lifetime! Have you ever wanted to do the opposite of what a teacher told you to do?" (Resounding "Yes!") "Well, this is the time. Whatever I tell you to do, *you do the exact opposite*. However, there are 2 rules: 1) When I say 'game's over' *the game is over*. 2) When I tell you to move on the diagonal in a certain way, *do* move on the diagonal and *do* stay in your groups, but make the 'certain way' opposite."

The joy of this game depends entirely on teacher "haminess." "OK boys and girls, everybody stand up." (They all sit down.) Smiling with nervous embarrassment, "OK all of you up, come on, with energy and spirit." (They lay back languidly.) "What's the matter with all of you?" I feign anger, "Why are you just sitting there like lumps? Get up! I say up!" (Gleefull giggles.) "OK stay seated then." (They get up.) "My goodness what a strange class. Never mind. Let's start on this side of the room." (They all run to the other side.) Acting more and more angered, "Alright, let's start on this side." (They run to the other side.) "This is the last time! Let's start on this side!" (They run to the other side.) Alright! Group one, move across the diagonal as slowly as possible." (You will probably have to remind the children that they are to stay in their groups and move on the diagonal.) "No, no, *slowly*. That's not slow! (All the groups try it.) OK, this time I want you to move across the diagonal as straight as possible, no bends or twists in your bodies...No, no, you're all crooked. What a terrible class!"

We go on like this for whatever time is available. I ask them to move a certain way, the children move the opposite way, and I complain, rant, and rave about it. I ask the children to move across the diagonal low, fast, light, happy, forward, crooked, little, smooth. I like to conclude with the opposite of silent. If your neighbors can stand it, the children love it.

The children request The Opposite Game often. In one dance class, at the children's pleading, we did it for visitors day. On this day, parents, friends, and relatives come to watch the class. After a normal introduction, the class and I played The Opposite Game without telling the visitors what we were doing. I could see some parents getting upset at their "unruly" children. I had to pretend to cough many times to keep from laughing and giving the game away. After a short while everyone caught on; it was great fun.

SPELLING

RHYTHMIC SPELLING
The spelling problems that movement solves best are those pure memory words that do not fit the rules. Do you remember how most of us learned to spell "Mississippi"? We put it into a sing-song pattern and learned it by rote. By using movement, the spelling of a word becomes rhythmic and therefore more easily remembered.

EXAMPLES OF SPELLING
Good for: 1) Teaching words.
           2) Partner and group work.
           3) Memory skills.

Following are examples of using movement to teach the spelling of "said," "turn," "friend," and (believe it or not) the thirteen original colonies. These words will exemplify the techniques of strict memory spelling, spelling connected to word comprehension, and spelling through puns.

Since there is no spelling rule involved I treated the word "said" strictly as a memory exercise. "One by one, run across the diagonal, shouting 's-a-i-d'; next person start as soon as the person ahead has said the 'd.'" "S-a-i-d" shouted 36 times can make a pretty indelible impression. Further, each child had to spell "said" quickly *while* he was in the air, jumping over the foam.

The words "turn" and "friend" can connect spelling and meaning. For "turn" the children picked 5 different ways to turn; each turn was accompanied by a vocal "t-u-r-n." "Friend" was approached through partners. Each pair moved on the diagonal in a "friendly way" shouting the spelling together. Some results: One child gave another a piggy back ride and they both shouted the spelling simultaneously. Two children held hands and took turns jumping; with each jump, the children shouted the next letter of the word so that the spelling of "friend" was done by alternating letters. One pair did leap frog and the person jumping over spelled "friend" quickly while he was in the air.

The spelling of the 13 colonies was tackled through pantomine and puns. I divided this 6th grade class into 13 groups. Each group got a card with the name of a colony. Their instructions were simple: "Do the spelling of your colony so that it will be remembered." The only other suggestion I made was to divide large words into smaller pieces. One of the most ingenious results came from the word "Connecticut": Two girls put their arms over each other's shoulder and shouted "connect -- c-o-n-n-e-c-t"; they then pointed to their eyes and shouted "i"; pretending to cut, "cut -- c-u-t." (Even I remember how to spell it, which is saying a lot.) Another good example was for the word "New Hampshire": 3 boys strolled out pretending to display new clothes, "new -- n-e-w"; acting and sounding like pigs, "ham -- h-a-m"; pretending to spray their underarms (as in a TV commercial for a deodorant called "Sure") "sure -- p-s-h-i-r-e." Yes, the pronunciations were a little strange and the syllabification was way off, but the results were memorable.

MATH

NUMBERS

BODY SHAPE NUMBERS
  Good for: 1) Recognizing numbers.
  2) Understanding quantities.
  3) Sequencing and memory skills.
  4) Group work.

I ask the children to make their bodies into a "1," "2," and so on. With numbers, I like to use the quantity as well as the shape: "With 2 people make a '2'; with 3 people make a '3'; with 5 people make a '5'; with 10 people make a '10.'" As with letter shapes, check to see that the numbers are formed correctly.

The larger numbers are formed by lining children up and seeing the number as if from above. With young children these large numbers need teacher assistance. (See illustration at right.)

Interesting patterns come out of number shapes plus quantity. For example, "In groups of 6, make one '6' out of all 6 of you. Now divide up the 6 any way you want. You can have 6 separate '1's,' three '2's,' each made by 2 of you, two '3's' each made by 3 of you, a '4' and a '2,' and so on. You have to make the numbers equal 6 and you have to use the same number of people as the number you are making."

We put the pattern into an ABA form. The 6 children began with their "6"; they divided up and showed one or 2 divisions, for example, "3" and "3," and "5" and "1"; then they formed the composite "6" again. This can be done with any number group, and can be done before the children know division.

OUTLINING NUMBERS
   Good for: 1) Recognizing numbers.
              2) Understanding quantities.

Like the letter shapes, the children begin outlining in front of them with both hands clasped together. They then move on to different parts of the body outlining numbers on different planes.

With number outlines I ask the children to make the outline the same number of times as the number, therefore we outline a "3" three times, a "5" five times.

FLOOR PATTERN NUMBERS
   Good for: 1) Recognizing numbers.
              2) Understanding quantities.
              3) Sequencing and memory skills.

Floor patterns are as useful for number shapes as they were for letter shapes. (See diagram at right.)

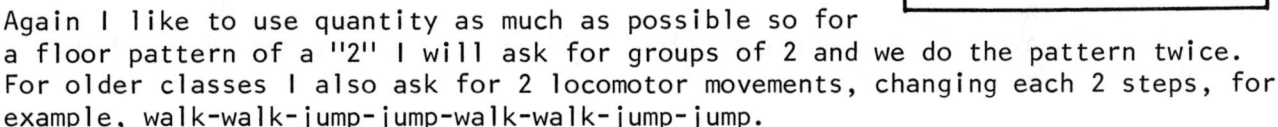

Again I like to use quantity as much as possible so for a floor pattern of a "2" I will ask for groups of 2 and we do the pattern twice. For older classes I also ask for 2 locomotor movements, changing each 2 steps, for example, walk-walk-jump-jump-walk-walk-jump-jump.

COMBINING TECHNIQUES
   Like the letter patterns, great studies result from combining these 3 number shape methods.

1) "Do your telephone number, each number done a different way."

2) "Do your address."

3) "In groups of 5, form a '5' out of all 5 of you, break up and each of you do a different number, then rejoin and make the '5' again."

4) "In groups of 3, figure out a way to make a '1' in one beat; a '3' in 3 beats, a '7' in 7 beats, a '13' in 13 beats."

5) "In groups of 4, pick a number and do it in as many ways as possible."

GEOMETRY

GEOMETRIC SHAPES
   Good for: 1) Teaching words.
              2) Understanding shapes.
              3) Memory skills.

Again we find the ubiquitous floor pattern. Floor patterns are great for teaching simple shapes such as squares, rectangles, triangles, and circles and for teaching more complicated shapes such as trapazoids and hexagons. (See sample floor patterns at the top of page 166.)

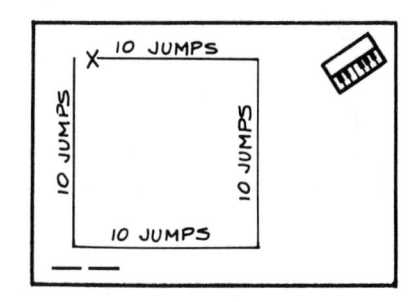

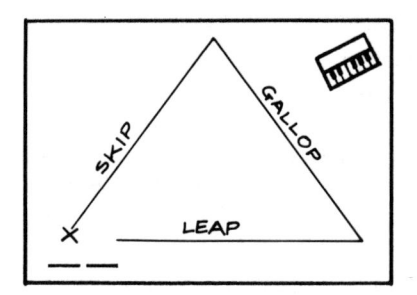

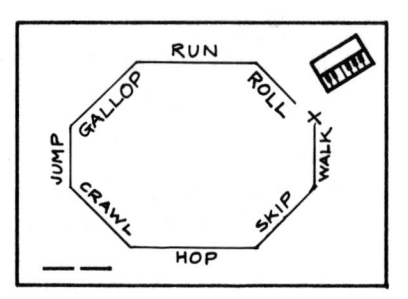

The shapes must be correct and exact or they will all blur together. I am fussy that the corners are sharp and ask for "military corners."

Floor patterns are especially good at teaching the idea that a square has to have exactly the same length sides. When children have to count the same number of steps for each of the sides, the idea becomes very concrete.

"CIRCUMFERENCE" - "DIAMETER" - "RADIUS"
Good for: Teaching words.

These 3 words are long and uninteresting until related to one activity children love: the parachute.

We lay the parachute on the floor and take a step away. "'Circumference' is the outside edge of a circle like that seam that goes around the edge of the parachute. Jerome, walk the 'circumference' of the parachute." (He walks around the edge on top of the parachute.) Other children take turns walking the circumference. "'Diameter' is a line that goes all the way across the parachute, like one of these seams going from one side all the way to the other side. Tara, walk the diameter and then walk it back to your place." Other children take turns walking the diameter. "'Radius' is a line that goes from the outside edge just to the middle, like this seam. Naomi, walk the radius into the middle and back." Each child then has a turn walking either the "circumference," "diameter," or "radius." (Check that the children do not confuse diameter and radius.)

The next time we work on "circumference," "diameter," and "radius," I have the words printed on large cards. Each child has to read the word I present and then walk the appropriate line.

I do not spend too much time with these lessons, mainly because the children are anxious to do other parachute activities. Two or three 15 minute lessons will generally suffice to make these 3 words clear and useful.

COMPUTATIONS

GROUP DIVISIONS AND THE FOAM JUMP
Good for: 1) Division, addition, and subtraction skills.
2) Teaching words.

There are 2 math activities I do regularly: group dividions and the foam jump. These are done without special emphasis; the academic results come from using them often.

When I ask a class to divide into groups, ready to move across the diagonal, I follow this procedure: I ask for a certain group division, for example, "Get into groups of 4." (When the term "sets" was popular it was "sets of 4.") *Only* those children who are in groups of 4 can line up. If the class divides up evenly, I say, "Wow, this class divides evenly into 4's." Pointing to the groups as I (and the children once they catch on) count: "4, 8, 12, 16, 20, 24, 28, 32." If the class did not divide evenly, the remaining children stand aside. Let us say there are 2 children left. I shake their hands: "Congratulations, you 2 children are the *remainders*." Speaking to the class as well, "Remainders are very lucky. They get to pick any group they want. You 2 pick 2 separate groups to join. How many children will be in those groups?" "Five," they conclude. If the remainder had been 3 children, I would have also congratulated them and said they would have a smaller group of 3 together.

This whole procedure (having the children divide into certain size groups, counting by that number, and distinguishing the remainders) takes under 5 minutes. It can be done with any group size. I do it almost every time I use the Diagonal Structure, which is almost every movement class. By the end of the year, the children are very familiar with the word and the idea of "remainder," and some catch on to counting by 2's, 3's, 4's, and 5's as well. Further, since we all have to be remainders some times, it is nice to take the stigma out once in a while.

The other simple procedure I do often is mathematical foam jump. This is useful for kindergarten to 3rd grade. I have 10 pieces of 2 feet by 2 feet by 4 inches foam rubber stacked one on top of the other. When a child is ready to jump, he tells me how many pieces of foam he wants and what computation I must do to get that number. For example, the first child might want to jump 5 foams. Since I have all 10 stacked in the middle of the room, he says, "I want 5; take away 5." The next child might want 8 foams: "I want 8; add 3." If the next child wants to jump the same number as the child before him, he says, "I want 8; leave them the same."

This "computation jumping" takes about twice as long as regular jumping (see page 114). But the extra time, when we have it, is certainly well spent. What I especially like about this math work is that it is visible, personal, and real.

SUMS
    Good for: 1) Addition skills.
                   2) Control.

"Do 4 jumps...Add 2 steps...The 'sum' of both movements is what? Now do the 4 jumps and the 2 steps while I count the sum, 1, 2, 3, 4, 5, 6. On what count do you change from jumping to stepping? Great! Hop 7 times...Add 9 skips...Add 1 jump...What is the 'sum' of all those movements? Do them while I count the sum...Walk 14 steps... Add 29 gallops...What is the 'sum' of those 2 movements? Can we do them? Take 1 jump...Add 2 jumps...Add 3 jumps...Add 4 jumps...Add 5 jumps...What is the 'sum' of all those jumps? Let's do them...Great!"

If the lesson is kept light and short, sums are fun. They can be slipped in whenever the children are doing locomotor movements.

PATTERNING

PATTERNING SKILLS
Seeing and creating patterns is important to both math and language development. It is a form of mental discipline that helps children think clearly and logically. The ability to recognize patterns is often tested in IQ tests and in scholastic achievement tests.

NAME SYLLABLE PATTERNS
Good for: 1) Syllable division.
           2) Coordination.
           3) Sequencing and memory skills.

This is an excellent name learning activity for the beginning of the year. In this activity we pick names and accent their syllables in one of 3 ways: clapping hands, slapping thighs, and snapping fingers.

The class sits near me on the floor. I pick a name at random and we clap the syllables: "Har/ry" (2 claps). We pick a different name and slap the syllables: "John" (one slap on the thighs). We pick a 3rd name and snap the syllables: "Mar/gar/ite" (3 snaps of the fingers). Then we put them all together: "Har/ry--hands clap twice; John--hands slap thighs once; Mar/gar/ite--fingers snap 3 times. Ideally there is no break between name changes: clap-clap-slap-snap-snap-snap. Once everyone has the pattern, we pick 3 different names and repeat the process.

These name syllable patterns provide good practice in coordination and rhythm. This is as far as I go with kindergarten and first grades. We do one pattern of 3 names at the beginning of each class for about a month and then throughout the year occasionally review the process.

For older classes we add body movements to the hand movements. For example: Har/ry--clap, clap and walk, walk; John--slap and jump; Mar/gar/ite--snap, snap, snap and hip thrust side, side, side. The children do the body movements *with* the hand movements. This is very difficult. Other examples:

1) Ta/ra--clap, clap and jump, jump: Hen/ry--slap, slap and hop, hop, Sha/ron--snap, snap and step, step.

2) Kim--clap and hop; Le/ti/cia--slap, slap, slap and skip, skip, skip; Jack--snap and contract.

3) Ran/dy--clap, clap and jazz walk, jazz walk; Da/vid--slap, slap and jump, jump; Cyn/thi/a--snap, snap, snap and swing, swing, swing.

BEGINNING LINEAR PATTERNS--COLOR PAPER SQUARES
Good for: 1) Problem solving.
           2) Coordination.
           3) Control.
           4) Memory skills.

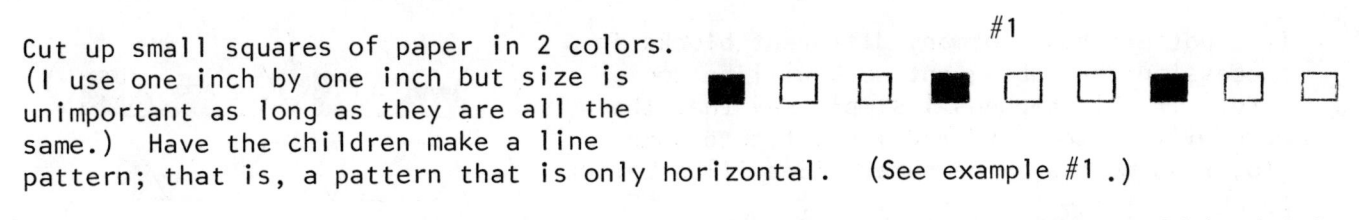

Cut up small squares of paper in 2 colors. (I use one inch by one inch but size is unimportant as long as they are all the same.) Have the children make a line pattern; that is, a pattern that is only horizontal. (See example #1.)

"If we give these colors letter names, starting with 'A' this pattern would be A-B-B-A-B-B-A-B-B. What other letters could stand for this pattern?" With some help the children will think of all sorts of letter possibilities: X-Y-Y-X-Y-Y-X-Y-Y, B-O-O-B-O-O-B-O-O, and so forth. "What number patterns could represent this colored paper?" Possible answers: 1-2-2-1-2-2-1-2-2, 18-300-300-18-300-300-18-300-300. We go on to represent the colored papers in all sorts of ways: food: apple-cookie-cookie...; toys: skate board-bike-bike...; nature: flower-tree-tree...

Finally we come to movement: "How could we represent the paper pattern in movement?" Possible answers: jump-step-step...; hop-jump-jump...; step-swing-swing...We practice these movement patterns until we can do them precisely.

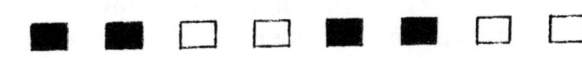

The next step, at a later lesson, is for the class to divide into groups and create their own linear patterns. They paste the pattern on a large sheet of paper and underneath represent it with letters, numbers, food, toys, and movement. The groups practice their movement patterns and show them to the class. For sample pattern #2, the children create patterns such as the following: M-M-P-P-M-M-P-P, 3-3-7-7-3-3-7-7, steak-steak-potato-potato-steak-steak-potato-potato, train-train-doll-doll-train-train-doll-doll, and twist-twist-jump-jump-twist-twist-jump-jump.

OTHER PATTERNING POSSIBILITIES
Once the children are accustomed to seeing patterns, almost anything can be used to create movement patterns.

    PATTERN BLOCKS
       Good for: 1) Problem solving.
                    2) Coordination.
                    3) Control.
                    4) Memory skills.

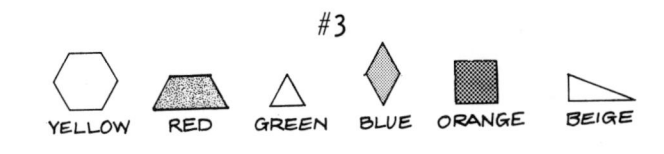

Pattern blocks are wooden blocks in 6 different shapes and colors that fit together to form beautiful designs. If pattern blocks are available, that is great; if not, any different shaped blocks will do. (See sample colored blocks in illustration #3.)

After some free exploration play*, the children divide into groups and design one linear, repeatable pattern. (See sample patterns in illustration #4.)

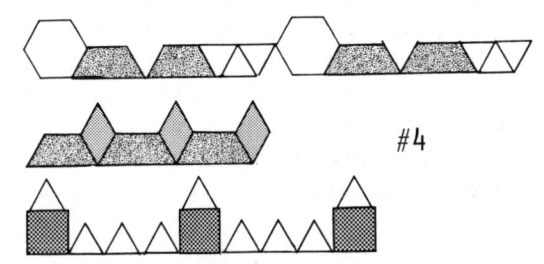

------

* The children need time for free exploration play with the blocks before they are ready for a lesson. If they have not had time to "fool around" with them, they will not want to structure their patterns.

If a pattern has too many different blocks in succession the subsequent work will be too hard. If this happens I simply say that the work will be too hard and I substitute some blocks so more are the same. (See illustration #5 .)

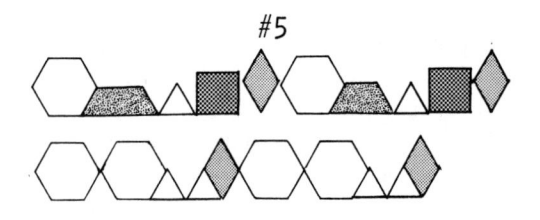

As with the colored papers, the children pick movements that represent their patterns. The block shapes may stand for any movements as long as the same blocks have the same movement and they are done precisely the number of times shown. The children practice their movement patterns until they can do them "perfectly" without looking at the blocks. (See illustration #6 for some sample block movement patterns.)

Here are some other patterning incentives: 1) Stripes on a shirt. Pick a child's shirt that has a strong repetitive stripe and designate each stripe a different movement. 2) Furniture. Arrange tables, desks, and chairs in a pattern and find corresponding movements. 3) Books. Arrange the books on a bookcase in a linear pattern and find corresponding movements. 4) On a walk. Look for accidental patterns in arrangements of fence posts, buildings, cars, cracks in sidewalks, leaves, and trees.

Obviously patterns can be found almost everywhere. The children like to surprise me with hidden patterns: "Look, our shoes make the pattern of gym shoe-gym shoe-boot-gym shoe-gym shoe-boot." The trick with patterning is to do it *less* than the children want to. If kept light and game-like, patterning is fun. If done too often or too intensely, patterning can become overwhelming and dull.

CONCLUDING

THE ACADEMIC SPIRIT
   Traditional physical education classes have usually been mindlessly strenuous. Strenuousness I approve of, mindlessness I do not. Progressive dance classes are often fun but chaotic. Fun is great but chaos is unworkable. It is hard to reach a happy medium with movement. Children love it and get exhuberant. If the teacher structures too much, the class gets rigid; and if not enough, it gets wild. The solution (yes, I will venture a solution) comes from 2 ingredients necessary for academic growth: goals and expectations.

   GOALS
      The key to an effective use of movement is considering it a subject with clearly defined goals. A subject with goals makes the class purposeful and directed.

Certainly there will be side tracks and activities that are "just for fun," just as in any subject, but there will also be direction and achievement.

EXPECTATIONS

Further, the expectations within the class need to be clear and of high standard. Just as we do not accept slipshod reading and incorrect math, we must know what we want from a movement study and get it. If the children are to stop in the middle of the room and they run 3/4's of the way across, it is incorrect and needs to be done again. If they are to shake for 4 beats and they shake for 5, it needs to be corrected. Corrections are best done nicely, even gently, but they need to be firmly done.

We need to know what we want in movement class, what is great and what is not so good, what is acceptable and what is not. Our expectations need to be clear both behaviorally and academically. Movement is an invaluable tool as long as we make it of the highest quality.

PART 10
ADVANCED WORK

WHAT CONSTITUTES ADVANCED WORK

THE CRUX OF ADVANCED WORK
We have come a long way. The children know the fundamental language of movement: they are at ease with locomotor and nonlocomotor movements, levels, directions, and floor patterns. They have enjoyed working with props and they have used movement to reinforce some academic skills. Most importantly, the children are becoming at ease with their bodies and with the basic movement vocabulary.

We are ready to move on. It is time to attempt more difficult physical challenges, time to incorporate new and difficult concepts, time for longer and harder patterns. The crux of more advanced work, however, is not any particular element. It is a quality of richness, a playfulness of movement. Studies are no longer simply geared to teach an idea or practice a step (although they still do); they now become a form of communication; they become dances.

MORE DIFFICULT PHYSICAL CHALLENGES
The body is extended by demanding more strength, flexibility, and endurance in addition to greater coordination and control.

MORE DIFFICULT CONCEPTS
There are a number of possible advanced concepts. I will touch on focus, dynamic quality, falls, and balance. These concepts are advanced because they require more concentration and control. Introducing these concepts is not initially difficult; what makes them difficult is where they lead and how they combine with other concepts.

MORE DIFFICULT PATTERNS
Teacher taught patterns are made more difficult in 4 ways: 1) making them longer, 2) using challenging physical problems, 3) using complicated rhythmic structures, and 4) using a fewer number of any one movement. (One skip, one jump, one leap is much more difficult than 2 skips, 2 jumps, 2 leaps, which is more difficult than 4 skips, 4 jumps, 4 leaps.)

Teacher structured problems are made harder by using less structure. The more freedom a child has, the more difficult it is to make up a pattern. Here are some very advanced group studies: 1) Pick a piece of music and make up a pattern to it. 2) Pick a poem and make up a pattern to it. 3) Do any floor pattern in exactly 32 beats. 4) Pick a prop and do a dance with it. 5) Make up a dance.

ADVANCED PHYSICAL CHALLENGES

WARM-UP

Advanced warm-up activities are similar to those in beginning classes; the difference is that I speed up the pace. By including more movements, the children are vigorously active for the entire 10 to 15 minute warm-up period. This is excellent for building up strength and endurance as well as reviewing a great deal of movement vocabulary.

Here are 3 examples of advanced warm-ups:

1) Alternating locomotor and nonlocomotor movements.

Locomotor	Nonlocomotor
A) Skip forward, backward, sideways, turning; one-legged skip with the right leg bent in front, then the left leg bent in front; one-legged skip with the right leg straight in back, then the left leg straight in back.	A) Contract, stretch, go limp, change levels. Repeat about 5 times.
B) Jump forward, backward, sideways, turning; hop; hop alternating legs every 4 beats; hopscotch.	B) Swing, swing, shake, balance, change levels. Repeat about 5 times.
C) Jazz walk; waltz walk; waltz walk turn.	C) Bend, straighten, twist, change levels. Repeat about 5 times.
D) Jog, run, run and leap.	

2) Balls with partners.

   A) Pass the ball by rolling it: sitting level, knee level, standing level, air level.

   B) Bounce pass the ball and move at the same time (both children move at all times): jump, hop, hopscotch, jog, waltz walk, skip, gallop, side-slide, leap, run.

3) Teacher structured Free Traveling pattern. Swing, swing, contract, stretch, go somewhere, go somewhere, stop. Repeat about 10 times going faster and faster.

EXERCISES

As the children get older and more experienced, the exercises we do in Perfect Spots change in 2 ways: 1) they become more strenuous and 2) they become more pure exercise as opposed to rhythmic games and stories.

Here is an example of an advanced exercise sequence:

1) Body wave warm-up, see page 78.

2) Flex and point feet. Start sitting down, legs straight ahead, torso held erect. Feet pull up then point down vigorously 16 times. This is essentially Hello and Goodbye with grown-up words.

3) Leg stretches. Start sitting down, right leg straight to the side and left leg bent forward (see illustration #9c5 on page 77 and note that the leg positions are reversed). Bounce over the straight leg, shoulders parallel to the floor: bounce 8 times with the foot pointed and 8 times with the foot flexed. Stretch over the same leg with the torso open to the front: bounce 8 times with the foot pointed and 8 times with the foot flexed.

   Swing to the left, place the left hand near the seat and lift to the left knee (one fluid movement); swing back to the right leg (see illustration #2m3b on page 73). Repeat 6 times.

   Repeat these exercises to the other side.

   Stretch both legs wide and bounce forward while flexing and pointing toes. Strive to go farther and farther, hold the last reach.

4) Stomach contractions. Start lying down on back. Contract stomach muscles and lift back and legs so that the body is balanced on the seat. Hold a second and lower the body with control. Start with 20 repetitions; work to 50 or 60. At the end, push into a bridge to stretch the stomach muscles out.

"RAISING OUR STANDARDS" SPEECH

Of course movement class must be appropriately strenuous. Children need to be developed rather than pushed. Ideally this development results from the *child's* inner drive. Sometimes this drive needs to be activated: "Lie down and close your eyes. Picture the olympic atheletes. Do you think the track stars stop running when they feel a little tired? Can you picture how hard a gymnast practices stretching? How many stomach contractions do you think atheletes do every day? Hundreds, probably. We have to raise our standards. We might not be olympic athletes, but let's get as close as we can!"

COORDINATION AND CONTROL

In addition to developing the body, more difficult physical challenges present themselves in difficult movements. What makes a movement difficult is how much coordination and control is required to execute it and how it fits in with other movements. More difficult movements will be covered in the following sections, "Advanced Concepts," (especially falls and balances) and "Advanced Patterns."

ADVANCED CONCEPTS

FOCUS
   Good for: 1) Teaching concept.
              2) Lengthening attention span.
              3) Concentration.

"Focus" means directing and controlling the eyes. As I tell the children, "'Focus' means looking at something hard." Focus is easy to understand and difficult to do.

What makes focus difficult is the concentration needed to control one's eyes. It is somewhat like controlling one's breathing. We are accustomed to breathing and looking unconsciously; we must concentrate to do so consciously.

I gather the children on the floor and ask if anyone has heard of the word "focus."

"What you do to a camera." "How you fix the TV." "You twist it (the focusing mechanism) on the binoculars." "When the focus is out, you call the (TV) repair man."

"Good. All the ways you have used 'focus' have to do with seeing clearly. In movement there is 'focus' too, and it is like seeing clearly. 'Focus' means to look at something hard." As I say this, I focus on one child and point with my finger: "I am focusing on Andrew." I focus on and point at several different children.

I then ask the children to focus on (and point at) different objects and people. At this beginning stage, pointing is important because it helps the children remember what they are doing, and it helps you to see if they are focusing on what they think they are focusing on. For example, if the children are told to focus on the ceiling, often their fingers will point up while their heads look straight ahead. It is a funny sight and fun to show them what they look like.

Once the children understand what focus is, we practice changing focus while remaining stationary. "Focus on me...Focus on the ceiling...Focus on the floor...Focus on the clock...Focus on the piano...Focus on your neighbors eyes (giggles)...Focus on your own tummy...Focus on your own big toe."

The next step is to focus while doing locomotor movements. I ask the children to get into small groups (usually 3) ready to move on the diagonal. I place something bright and colorful in the middle of the room. One of my favorite props is a bunch of bright paper flowers sprayed with cologne.* I ask each group to focus (eyes and fingers) on the flowers, walk to them, smell them, and continue walking to the end of the diagonal. They are *never to lose their focus*. This is not easy. From the middle to the end of the diagonal, the children will either have to walk backwards or turn their heads sharply back. (See illustration at right.)

I ask the children who are waiting for their turn to help me check the focus of the children who are moving. After focusing on a central object and walking across the diagonal, we try the exercise jumping, skipping, hopping, galloping, and running.

I do not do this, or any focus problem, for very long. It takes a lot of concentration to focus for even a few minutes. I think it is better for children to succeed in focusing while moving across the diagonal twice, than to do it several times and lose their attention. This is good exercise to review often.

Once the children are relatively at ease moving across the diagonal while focusing on a central object, we go on to harder focus problems:

---

* If you are planning to work with a prop later that day, you can use that prop as a focus point; for example, if you are going to play with the parachute later, put the parachute in the middle of the room, if you are going to work with scarves, dump the whole box of scarves in the middle of the room.

1) I stand at one corner of the diagonal: "Focus on me as you side-slide on the diagonal...Focus on me as you side-slide, *changing sides*, on the diagonal." The children like to focus on me; I ham it up and make faces at them. Also it is easier for me to see if they are doing it right and to make a commotion if they are not: "Hey, here I am, look at me!"

2) Focus on the ceiling as you tip-toe to the middle of the room; focus on the floor as you low-walk (bent knee walk) from the middle to the end of the diagonal. Later, use a quicker change of focus by having 4 beats of tip-toe walk with the focus on the ceiling, and 4 beats of low-walk with the focus on the floor. Then ask for 2 beats of each.

3) Have interesting objects in the corners of the diagonal in which the children are *not* moving, that is, objects "A" and "B" in the diagram at right.

   The children hopscotch on the diagonal; they focus on object "A" for their jump and on object "B" for their hop. Therefore, the focus changes every beat. Past the middle, they have to do it backwards or turn their heads, but do not worry, if they can do it just to the middle, that is great. This is extremely difficult.

4) Place an interesting object (like yourself) at the end of the diagonal. The children focus on the object and turn. I allow any kind of moving turn. This is the dance technique called "spotting": the head turns as much as possible to keep the focus on the object and then snaps around to regain the focus without "seeing" anything else. You might mention to the children that it is this technique of spotting that allows dancers to do those endless turns without getting dizzy.

5) Focus is fun to do with a partner. a) Partners stand facing each other holding hands; they focus on each other's eyes and side-slide. b) Partners lie down on their stomachs opposite each other and hold both hands; they focus on each other's eyes and roll. c) Partners stand facing each other holding both hands; they lean back a little and spin while keeping the focus on each other's eyes.

6) Focusing on one's own body while moving is a good coordination problem and provides interesting results. a) "Focus on your own hand. Let your hand take you on a trip to the end of the diagonal. Your hand goes around you, above you, and under you; all the while your eyes never lose sight of your hand." b) "Focus on your own big toe as it leads you across the diagonal." c) "Focus on your tummy, seat, elbow, or hip as it leads you across the diagonal."

7) Finally, include directed focus within a study. Pick a study the children have already learned. Incorporate several focus changes within the pattern. Later, pick one pattern and have the children individually decide where to include focus changes. It is very interesting to see the same pattern done with different focus changes.

There is a direct correlation between the ability to focus and attention span. Both result from self-discipline: they require an inner force to selectively pay attention and to ignore distractions. These are the very qualities that are necessary for any type of concentration. Children begin school unequal in their ability to focus, but focus is a skill that can be taught and developed in all children.

DYNAMIC QUALITY
   Good for: 1) Teaching concepts.
              2) Coordination.
              3) Concentration.

Dynamic quality is the type of force that controls a movement. I distinguish 3 dynamic qualities: percussive, sustained, and limp.

"'Percussive' means to move quickly and sharply; it is a burst of activity followed by a freeze." I call out several movements and the children do them percussively: contract, stretch, twist, strike, jump. The children then improvise their own percussive movements. Watch that the children's percussive movements are clear and sharp and that they hold their ending positions for a few seconds; it is easy for percussive movements to degenerate into a series of jerks.

"'Sustained' means to move slowly and smoothly but with intensity." I call out several movements and the children do them with a sustained quality: contract, stretch, bend, straighten, turn, step, fall. They then improvise their own sustained movements.

"Both percussive and sustained qualities use a lot of energy: percussive movements burst with energy, and sustained movements flow with a strong constant force. 'Limp' quality is different in that the movements use as little energy as possible." Again the children try out movements I call out, doing them with a limp quality, and then improvise their own movements.

We are now ready to use dynamic qualities in studies.

1) Teach a pattern that has specified dynamic qualities. For example, start standing and circle the arms with a sustained quality, beats 1 to 4; contract in a series of percussive contractions, beats 5 to 8; drop limply to the floor, beat 9 hold 10; balance on one knee and hand and stretch one arm and one leg with a sustained quality, beats 1 to 4; in that position, contract percussively, beat 5 hold 6; stretch percussively, beat 7 hold 8; contract percussively, beat 9 hold 10; stretch percussively, beat 11 hold 12; stand and turn limply, beats 13 to 16. The pattern is actually quite simple, but adding dynamic qualities requires an additional element to remember and control.

2) Teach a basic, rather simple, pattern and have the children add their own dynamic qualities. For example, start standing and reach up, contract, fall back to seat, rock back and then up to knee level, turn, and stand. The children must designate a specific dynamic quality for each movement.

3) Do a semi-structured improvisation using dynamic qualities. For example, do one movement percussively, do one movement sustained, do one movement limply, then go somewhere in no particular quality. The rhythm is percussive-sustained-limp; go somewhere, go somewhere, go somewhere, stop. Repeat several times.

4) Do a group study using dynamic qualities: Pick 3 percussive, 3 sustained, and 3 limp movements and put them together in a remembered sequence.

FALLS
   Good for: 1) Teaching concept.
              2) Coordination.
              3) Control.

"To 'fall' means to lower your body. In movement class it does not mean to plop down and hurt yourself. You must control the lowering so that you never get hurt. There is a secret to this control: whatever way your body is lowering, pull in the *opposite* direction." I then demonstrate this secret: "I am going to fall back. Which way should I pull? Right, my arms pull forward as I fall backwards...(I lower my seat to the floor and rock back.) If I want to fall to the right side, which way should I pull? Correct, I would pull to the left. (I do a side fall, reaching to the left and falling right.)...If I want to fall forward, which way should I pull? Correct, I should pull back. (I do a teeter-totter fall, falling forward while pulling back with one leg.)..."

This conceptual approach to falls opens up an enormous number of movement possibilities. The children try out their own ideas of possible falls under the condition that they absolutely cannot hurt themselves. The difficulty with falls is, of course, the control of energy. The child must stretch consistently throughout the movement or the body will collapse. If I see them getting sloppy, I instruct them to do their falls in slow motion.

After this general introduction the children are ready to learn specific falls. I usually introduce specific falls throughout the year, as I need them for particular patterns. The basic falls I teach are: 1) teeter-totter, 2) back fall, 3) side fall, 4) spiral twist fall, 5) one-leg side fall, and 6) lunge fall. A description of these falls is found in the "Catalog Of Nonlocomotor Movements," Part 5.

Beautiful studies result from combining falls.

1) Cat dance. This study is in 2 parts, each 12 beats long. Each 12 beat pattern can stand by itself or they can fit together.

    Children start in Perfect Spots, standing level. Jump and land in a crouched position, upbeat *and* (for the jump) beat 1 (for the landing); fall back onto the seat, beat 2; rock back to lowest level, beat 3; rock up to sitting level with right foot on the floor, left knee on the floor, beat 4; lift seat up, without using hands, weight on left knee, beat 5; lift to standing level, beat 6 (see illustration #1 for beats 3, 4, 5, and 6); teeter-totter fall, ending on the stomach, beats 7 to 10; pull seat back to ankles and lift body up to knee level, beats 11 and 12.

    On knee level, do a sidefall, beats 1 and 2; roll once toward the back of the room, beats 3 and 4; curl up to the knees, facing the front of the room, beats 5 and 6; side fall to the other side, beats 7 and 8; roll back once to the back of the room, beats 9 and 10; curl up to the knees facing the front of the room, beats 11 and 12.

2) Fall dance. Children start in Perfect Spots, standing level. Lift the left leg to a "T" balance (like the teeter-totter fall balance); contract while balanced on the right leg; shoot the left leg out into a low lunge position. (See illustration #2.)

Fall to the side and roll once (straighten the legs wide for a second while on the back) and end on the knees. Do a side fall; roll back once (straighten the legs for a second) and immediately push up to the knees and stand. Do a spiral fall; spin the seat and shoot the legs back as the torso falls forward, ending flat on the stomach. Lift up to standing like a reversed teeter-totter fall, ready to start again.

There are no counts. The exact movements are not as important as the feeling of fluidity. The pattern should flow like waves continuously rising, falling, and ebbing.

BALANCE
   Good for: 1) Teaching concept.
              2) Coordination.
              3) Control.

Like falls, I introduce "balance" conceptually before working with specific balances. Like falls, the difficulty with balance work is that it requires a great deal of control. Balance requires even more control than falls because it is a control of energy while still. To be in balance, the body must be centered and the weight pulled up. It is easier to exert energy while moving than while standing still.

"Balance means being steady, not falling. Some positions are easier to balance in than others. For example, standing on 2 feet is an easy way to balance; standing on one foot is a little harder; standing on half toe (the ball of the foot) is much harder." The children have some time to explore different ways of balancing. Ideally, the children have access to mats as well as cleared floor space, so that they can try some more dangerous balances, like head stands and hand stands.

After the children have had a chance to freely explore different balances, I like to guide them in 2 ways: with level changes and with numbers of body parts.

1) Levels. On lowest level, balance on just the tummy, or balance in a shoulder stand, if possible without using hands. (See illustration #3.)

   On sitting level, balance on just the seat, try just half a seat. (See illustration #4.)

   On knee level, balance on 2 knees and a head, one knee and one hand, just one knee. Standing level, balance on one foot and one hand, balance on tip-toes, balance on one foot with eyes closed, on half-toe.

2) Number of body parts. Balance on 7 parts of the body, on 4 parts of the body, on 3 parts of the body, 2 parts, 1 part, a half of a part.

We are then ready for studies using difficult balances. Here are a few teacher taught patterns:

1) One waltz walk, turn waltz walk, balance on half-toe for 3 beats, one-legged skip with the leg bent in front, one-legged skip with the leg straight back, run-run-run leap, hold the ending balance for 3 beats. Every movement gets 3 beats, therefore, the pattern is 7 measures of 3 beats.

2) Run very fast to the middle of the diagonal and immediately balance in a strange shape, hold; skip turning twice, then reach up and fall down to the floor, immediately balancing in a strange shape on the floor, hold.

3) Use tables or barres, if available, to practice this pattern. Stand on the left foot, contract the right leg, torso, and head. Stretch the right leg to the side while stretching the torso away, like a sideways "T" position. (See illustration #5.) Keep the right leg outstretched and still and lift the torso and head vertically. Put the right leg down and side-slide to the right. Turn once and repeat the pattern using the other leg.

After practicing this pattern using a table or barre, try it balancing without any help.

Difficult balances can also be used in teacher structured group studies:

1) Divide the class into groups of 4 and give each group 4 cards with the numbers 1, 2, 3, 4. Each group must have a different colored set of cards, that is, group one has 4 red cards, group 2 has 4 green cards, group 3 has 4 purple cards, and so on. The groups tape their cards in 4 different places throughout the room. They must then pick 4 difficult balances, one to do at each number card, and hold these balances for 10 seconds. In addition, they choose different locomotor movements to do to each balance point. Possible result: skip to card 1; balance on one foot for 10 seconds; leap to card 2; balance on half a seat for 10 seconds; side-slide to card 3; balance on one knee and one hand for 10 seconds; crab crawl to card 4; balance on one foot with the torso tilted for 10 seconds. Have each group show their own study, then have all the groups do their studies at the same time.

2) Divide into small groups. Have each group pick 4 to 7 difficult balances and put them together in a sequence.*

ADVANCED PATTERNS

THE PARTNER DANCE
   Verbal descriptions of movements are long, boring, and usually unclear. I will, however, describe my most favorite pattern, The Partner Dance, because the result is worth the effort.

---

* With this study I often introduce the idea of "transitions." The groups can make the transitions between their balances as long or as short as they want, but the transitions must be interesting and smooth.

This pattern is in 2 parts, each 16 beats long. The children need to learn all 32 beats perfectly in order to do the pattern as intended. It is especially important that they do each movement exactly at its specified count.

First part: The children start lying on their stomachs, facing the *back* of the room. The right leg bends and pulls the body (see illustration #6) up to a sitting position facing the *front* of the room while the legs bend into a triangle position, beats 1 and 2. The left hand is placed by the seat and the children push up onto their feet and left hand, the hips and the right hand reach up, beats 3 and 4. (See illustration #7.)

The children sit back down in the triangle position, beats 5 and 6. The children lie back down on their stomachs, facing the back wall, beats 7 and 8. They curl their toes under and push their seats up, like a high push-up position, beats 9 and 10. (See illustration #8.) Starting from this push-up position, the left leg crosses in back of the right leg while the left arm lifts up, so that the children are balanced on 2 feet and the right hand, beats 11 and 12. (See illustration #9.)

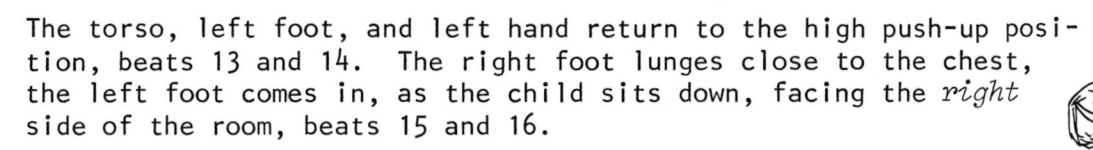

The torso, left foot, and left hand return to the high push-up position, beats 13 and 14. The right foot lunges close to the chest, the left foot comes in, as the child sits down, facing the *right* side of the room, beats 15 and 16.

Second part: The children start sitting, facing the right side of the room (this is the position in which the first part ended). They lower the torso so that they are lying down with their knees bent, beats 1 and 2. They push up into a bridge, beats 3 and 4. They lower the bridge one part of the body at a time (head, shoulders, back, seat) beats 5 to 8. (Watch that the children take all 4 beats to lower their bridges.) They push with their feet so that they are sliding backwards on their backs; meanwhile their hands reach up to the ceiling and pretend to tickle, beats 9 to 12. (See illustration #10.)

The children sit up and spin on their seats, beats 13 and 14. They lie down on their stomachs, facing the back of the room (starting position of the first part), beats 15 and 16.

The movements are not actually difficult or beautiful. What makes this pattern special is its execution. After the children know both parts very well it is time to put them together. Have the children divide into partners. One person lies down on his stomach facing the back of the room (starting position for the first part) while his partner sits on his right, facing the right side of the room (starting position for the second part).* The children do the first part and

---

* How far away should the sitting person be? Have the sitting person lie down so that his head touches his partner's hip and then sit up. That is the correct distance he needs to be.

the second part *at the same time*. If done correctly, the tickle section of the second part (beats 9 to 12) will slide under the partner's high lift. (See illustration #11.) When the partners have finished their respective parts, they should be in position to begin again doing the *other* part.

This pattern is difficult to teach at first because it is long and exacting. However, when the children realize how it fits together with a partner, they will take it over and practice until they have it.

PART 11
LESSON PLANS

FRAMEWORK

GENERAL STRUCTURE

Following are lesson plans for preschool/grades K and 1, 2 and 3, 4 through 6. There are 40 lessons for each grade grouping, one per week for a school year. The preschool/ K-1 lessons are presumed to be 30 to 45 minutes long; the other lessons are presumed to be 50 to 60 minutes long.

The basic framework of a lesson is this:

1) Warm-up.

2) Work in Perfect Spots.

3) Locomotor movements done on the diagonal.

4) Work with a prop.

Although I use this framework when I begin planning a lesson, the exceptions almost outnumber the rules.

The first time a concept or exercise appears in the plans it is in italics. Everything that is in italics is covered in the book.

VARIANCES WITH REALITY

The following lessons are unrealistic in 3 ways: 1) They are longer than what can usually be done with a typical public school class. 2) They do not repeat work enough. 3) They do not include some activities. I assume that teachers will cut down the lessons to suit their particular classes, and, who knows, some teacher may have an exceptionally bright class that can complete the lessons. I also assume that teachers will repeat work whenever necessary either by using these lessons for longer than a year, or, ideally, by having class more often than once a week. I have not included twirls, alignment, turn out, Are You Alive?, and stations. Twirls are for special occasions; alignment, turn out, and Are You Alive? are used when needed; and stations are used supplementally (see section on "Stations" at the end of Part 11).

USE OF PLANS

These lesson plans are intended for the first year of a movement program. There is a lot of similarity between the lessons for the 3 grade groups because all classes work with the basic concepts. However the plans can also work sequentially. A preschool/ kindergarten or first grade class that finishes their lessons will need the review provided in the next set of lessons. A beginning 4th to 6th grade class would start with the basic 2-3 grade lessons (except I would not use titles like Hello and Goodbye or Swordfish) and then move on to the next set. Only a very sophisticated or experienced older class would begin with the 4-6 grade lessons. I see these lesson plans not as doctrine but as examples of class progressions derived from the curriculum.

THE PLANS

PRESCHOOL/GRADES K-1

LESSON 1   PRESCHOOL/GRADES K-1

1) *Rocking Song* (p.29-31).
    a) Sing.
    b) Rock on different levels.
    c) Do various nonlocomotor movements: shake, spin, bounce, swing, jump.
    d) Do locomotor movements.
        1-Begin with jump then do walk, skip, hop, gallop, run.
        2-Do rhythm of song without singing.
    e) Do start and stop with different length sounds.
2) Begin work on *near* (p.10).
3) Gather together.
    a) Introduce *Hello and Goodbye* (p.14).
    b) *Rocking Song for relaxation* (p.120-121).

LESSON 2   PRESCHOOL/GRADES K-1

1) Repeat Rocking Song progression but do fewer of each.
2) Review near; introduce *far* (p.10).
3) Gather together.
    a) Hello and Goodbye.
    b) Introduce *Swordfish* (p.15-16).
    c) Rocking Song for relaxation.

LESSON 3   PRESCHOOL/GRADES K-1

1) Do start and stop to any sound, that is, *Free Traveling Structure* (p.25-27) with different locomotor movements: walk, jump, hop, skip, gallop, crawl, roll, run. (Insist on absolute freezes.)
2) Do some work on near; work hard on far. Introduce *Perfect Spots* (p.9-13).
    a) *Shake congratulations* (p.10).
    b) Hello and Goodbye--introduce *torso* (p.14-15) and include torso with Hello and Goodbye.
    c) Swordfish.

LESSON 4   PRESCHOOL/GRADES K-1

1) Quickly do a few locomotor movements in Free Traveling Structure.
2) Get Perfect Spots and shake congratulations.

a) Play *Firecracker* (p.13); see if most children can get spots in 10 seconds.
   b) In Perfect Spots.
      1-Hello and Goodbye.
      2-Swordfish, if time.
      3-Introduce *stage 1, Blast Off* (p.17).
3) Gather together and introduce word "*locomotor*" (p.23-24): do locomotor movements going from one side to the other, saying the word.

LESSON 5   PRESCHOOL/GRADES K-1

1) Review word "locomotor" and do locomotor movements in Free Traveling Structure, say word for some of the movements.
2) Get Perfect Spots.
   a) Add *face front* (p.11) component.
   b) Play Firecracker including face front.
   c) In Perfect Spots.
      1-Hello and Goodbye.
      2-All of *Blast Off* (p.16-18).
3) Do a locomotor movement study: 1 side of the room skip, 1 side jump, 1 side crab crawl, and 1 side run.
   a) Practice several times; see if they can do it without you saying.
   b) Half the class watch; switch.

LESSON 6   PRESCHOOL/GRADES K-1

1) Do a simple *obstacle course* (p.18-22).
2) Perfect Spots -- continuously check face front.
   a) Introduce *4 swings pattern* (p.63-64): front, cross, side, twist.
   b) Blast Off.
3) Introduce *diagonal* (p.27-29).
   a) Show picture and find diagonals on paper.
   b) Find diagonals in the room.
   c) Do a few locomotor movements on the diagonal moving individually.

LESSON 7   PRESCHOOL/GRADES K-1

1) Gather together and introduce word "*nonlocomotor*" (p.59).
   a) Teach word.
   b) Children do own movements.
   c) Alternate with locomotor movements; present shake, spin, swing. (Use Free Traveling Structure: piano = locomotor; drum = nonlocomotor.)
2) Review diagonal. (Just like introduction but fewer.)
3) Set up *Diagonal Structure* (p.27-29).
   a) Ask children to get into groups of 3 on side of room -- wait!
   b) Groups get ready at corner.
   c) Groups start when the group ahead reaches the end of the diagonal.
   d) Introduce *jump the foam* (p.166-167), if time.

LESSON 8   PRESCHOOL/GRADES K-1

1) Review nonlocomotor. Alternate locomotor and nonlocomotor: skip--swing; jump and then hop right and left--shake; run--introduce twist.
2) Perfect Spots.
   a) Hello and Goodbye.
   b) Introduce simple nonlocomotor study: swing--4 beats; shake going in air and falling down--4 beats; twist body like pretzel--4 beats.

            1-Practice with teacher calling out movements.
            2-Try it with just counts.
3) Diagonal Structure--groups of 3.
    a) Practice structure with basic locomotor movements: skip, gallop, jump, hop-scotch, run.
    b) Jump the foam.

LESSON 9   PRESCHOOL/GRADES K-1

1) Introduce *Partner Shake* (p.43-44): do individual locomotor movements alternated with different partner shakes: hands, feet, heads, seats.
2) Perfect Spots.
    a) Review 4 swings pattern (Lesson 6).
    b) Practice nonlocomotor study (Lesson 8)--if good enough, do it on the *stage* (p. 115).
3) Introduce *balls* (p.124-127).
    a) Free time.
    b) Few guided movements:
        1-Throw ball and run after.
        2-Sit and spin with ball in feet.
        3-Roll ball with just feet.
        4-Roll ball using no hands or feet.

LESSON 10   PRESCHOOL/GRADES K-1

1) *Partner work* (p.47-48): one partner for entire time.
    a) Hold hands and side-slide.
    b) Hold hands and spin.
    c) Sit down, hold ankles, and go somewhere.
    d) Hold hands and roll.
2) Keep partners and line up for the Diagonal Structure: do a few basic locomotor movements on the diagonal.
3) Balls.
    a) Short free time.
    b) Guided movements.
    c) Begin sequence:
        1-Throw ball and run after.
        2-Sit and spin with ball in feet.
        3-Roll ball without using hands or feet.
        4-Gently throw and catch ball while skipping.

LESSON 11   PRESCHOOL/GRADES K-1

1) Partner work: one partner for the entire time.
    a) Hold hands and side-slide; try it back to back.
    b) Stay back to back and sit down and up without hands.
    c) Stay back to back and spin on seat.
    d) Hold hands and roll.
2) Perfect Spots.
    a) 4 different swings.
    b) Introduce *levels* (p.53).
        1-Teacher demonstrates; class guesses meaning.
        2-Do levels up and down several times.
3) Balls
    a) Short free time.

b) Practice sequence: if good enough, show on stage.
  c) Go back to partners from first activity and carry ball without hands.

LESSON 12   PRESCHOOL/GRADES K-1

1) Alternate locomotor and nonlocomotor movements: Use different levels for the nonlocomotor movements, that is, swing changing levels, shake changing levels, twist changing levels.
2) Perfect Spots.
  a) Hello and Goodbye.
  b) 4 different swings.
  c) Introduce level pattern: air--jump, 4 beats; standing--swing, 4 beats; knee--contract and stretch, 4 beats; sitting--spin, 4 beats; lowest--*temper tantrum* (p.56), 8 beats.
3) Locomotor movements on diagonal: groups of 4.

LESSON 13   PRESCHOOL/GRADES K-1

1) Apply levels to locomotor movements and do some on all levels, Free Traveling Structure.
2) Gather together and introduce *contract and stretch* (p.64).
  a) Isolated parts: hands, arms, legs, torso, faces, necks.
  b) Whole body.
  c) Practice knee level contract and stretch (from level study, Lesson 12).
3) Perfect Spots.
  a) Practice level study.
  b) Do with just counts; if good enough, show on stage.
4) Locomotor movements on diagonal--groups of 4.
  a) Do some basic locomotor movements.
  b) Put middle marker and change levels in middle, for example:
      1-Air to middle; lowest from middle to end.
      2-Knee to middle; standing from middle to end.

LESSON 14   PRESCHOOL/GRADES K-1

1) Use mats for work on *"on" and "off"* (p.151-152).
  a) Shake "on"--run "off".
  b) Jump "on"--skip "off".
  c) Spin on seat "on"--gallop "off".
2) Introduce *floor pattern* (p.95-97).
  a) Gather together to see paper.
  b) Draw room representation.
  c) Draw a 3 or 4 line pattern.
  d) Do half the class at a time.
3) Perfect Spots--*Relaxation with Rocking Song fast then slow* (p.120-121).

LESSON 15   PRESCHOOL/GRADES K-1

(Class before Christmas vacation.)
1) Alternate locomotor and nonlocomotor movements, Free Traveling Structure.
2) Do floor pattern of star. (Can say it is a "Christmas star"--see drawing p.98.)
3) Perfect Spots.
  a) Be noodles; put in pot of boiling water and melt from bottom up.
  b) Drag children into a pile of *Spaghetti* (p.121-122).

LESSON 16   PRESCHOOL/GRADES K-1

(Class after vacation.)
1) Obstacle Course.
2) Review near; review far; review getting Perfect Spots (especially check for face front component).
    a) Hello and Goodbye.
    b) Swordfish.
    c) Blast Off.
3) Review diagonal and Diagonal Structure, groups of 3.
    a) Do basic locomotor movements on the diagonal.
    b) Jump the foam.

LESSON 17   PRESCHOOL/GRADES K-1

1) Review starting and stopping exactly with sound; practice locomotor movements in the Free Traveling Structure.
2) Perfect Spots.
    a) 4 different swings pattern.
    b) Introduce *Walk Down Your Front* (p.81-82).
    c) Introduce *Cops and Robbers* (p.86)--extend into work on side-slide.
3) Review floor patterns.
    a) Do a 4 or 5 line floor pattern or review the star--be sure to include one line a side-slide.
    b) Do the floor pattern in groups of 4.
4) If time, do some locomotor movements on the diagonal in the same groups of 4.

LESSON 18   PRESCHOOL/GRADES K-1

1) Quickly work on side-slide.
    a) Add changing sides.
    b) Get partners and side-slide holding both hands front to front, then back to back.
2) Perfect Spots.
    a) Walk Down Your Front.
    b) Introduce *Right and Left Bug* (p.85-86).
    c) Cops and Robbers.
3) Do a *helping floor pattern* (p.99).
    a) Children take turns putting the room representation straight.
    b) Children decide where lines go and what locomotor movements to use.
    c) Do the floor pattern half the class at a time.
4) Introduce *parachute--Ocean* (p.137-138).

LESSON 19   PRESCHOOL/GRADES K-1

(Borrow 6 older (5th and 6th grade) children for this lesson and the next one.)
1) Do another helping floor pattern--use 4 lines.
2) Children make own floor patterns.
    a) Divide into groups of 4.
    b) Assignment: Make your own floor patterns using 4 straight lines, each one a different locomotor movement.
    c) Older children walk around and help mainly with writing locomotor movement words.
    d) When groups are done, check patterns; children then practice.
    e) Keep the group work with the childrens' names on the back of the patterns.
3) Parachute.
    a) Ocean.
    b) Introduce *Whooshing* (p.138). (Have older children spread around the parachute among young ones.)

LESSON 20   PRESCHOOL/GRADES K-1

(Borrow 5 or 6 older children again.)
1) Return group floor patterns.
    a) Groups practice to be able to do it without the map (older children help).
    b) Each group performs own pattern.
2) Parachute.
    a) Whooshing--introduce *Hamburgers and French Fries* (p.138-139).
    b) Introduce *Lifting* (p.141).
    c) Introduce *Mushroom* (p.141).

LESSON 21   PRESCHOOL/GRADES K-1

1) Alternate locomotor and nonlocomotor movements.
2) Perfect Spots.
    a) Walk Down Your Front.
    b) Right and Left Bug.
    c) Work on *right* (p.84-85).
        1-Shake, bend and straighten, circle, contract and stretch, only right arm.
        2-Spin on different levels, freeze, and raise right arm.
3) Parachute.
    a) Alternate Ocean and *Merry-Go-Round* (p.139).
    b) Hamburgers and French Fries.
    c) Mushroom.

LESSON 22   PRESCHOOL/GRADES K-1

1) Do locomotor movement to sound; when stop, freeze and ask for right arm or leg to
   be raised.
2) Perfect Spots.
    a) Review work on right; alternate with left.
    b) Introduce *directions* (p.81).
    c) Do nonlocomotor movements using directions.
        1-Bounce torso: front, back, side, turning.
        2-Shake hands: front, back, side, all around.
        3-Jump: front, back, side, turning.
3) Parachute.
    a) Hamburgers and French Fries.
    b) Mushroom.

LESSON 23   PRESCHOOL/GRADES K-1

1) Introduce *directions in locomotor movements* (p.86-88).
2) Introduce *wiggly line, marker method* (p.103-104).
    a) Groups of 3 line up on one side of room.
    b) Place markers.
    c) Groups go around markers: skip, run, gallop, side-slide (see drawing p.103).
    d) Take away markers one at a time.
3) Jump the foam.

LESSON 24   PRESCHOOL/GRADES K-1

1) Locomotor movements using directions.
    a) Skip: forward, backwards, try sideways, turning.
    b) Hop: 4 directions.
    c) Crawl: 4 directions.

d) Run and leap: forward, try turning.
　　　e) Children's choice: 4 directions.
2) Review wiggly line.
　　　a) With markers.
　　　b) Without markers.
3) Introduce *scarves* (p.127-129).
　　　a) Free time.
　　　b) A few guided movements.
　　　　　1-Circle and gallop.
　　　　　2-Pick up with toes and shake while hopping; change legs.
　　　　　3-*Magic Scarf* (p.128).

LESSON 25   PRESCHOOL/GRADES K-1

1) Scarves.
　　　a) Short free time.
　　　b) Guided movements.
　　　c) Sequence.
　　　　　1-Gallop and circle scarf.
　　　　　2-Throw scarf in air and catch with different parts of the body.
　　　　　3-Spin changing levels.
　　　　　4-Pick scarf up in toes and shake while hopping (change feet).
　　　　　5-Magic Scarf.
2) Groups of 3 ready to go on the diagonal.
　　　a) Do simple direction study: run to middle of diagonal, stop, fall down and slide on back backwards.
　　　b) Introduce *wiggly line, conceptual method* (p.102-103)--go diagonally.
3) Do floor pattern using wiggly lines.

LESSON 26   PRESCHOOL/GRADES K-1

1) Groups of 3 on one side of the room.
　　　a) Introduce *spiral line* (p.105-106).
　　　b) At end of spiral, freeze in strange shapes touching one another.
2) Do cumulative floor pattern.
　　　a) (See drawings, p.107.)
　　　b) Add scarves while doing floor pattern.
3) Perfect Spots--relaxation with Rocking Song.

LESSON 27   PRESCHOOL/GRADES K-1

1) Introduce *"between"* (p.153-155): place objects in room, ask children to stand "between" 2 objects you call out.
2) Perfect Spots.
　　　a) Hello and Goodbye.
　　　b) Blast Off.
　　　c) 4 different swings.
3) Locomotor movements on the diagonal, groups of 3.
　　　a) Do a few basic locomotor movements.
　　　b) Do *"between" with locomotor movements* (p.153-154).
　　　　　1-*Carry* (p.153-154).
　　　　　2-*Galloping In A Basket* (p.154).
　　　　　3-*Directional Can-Can* (p.154).
　　　　　4-*The Stretcher* (p.154).

LESSON 28   *PRESCHOOL/GRADES K-1*

1) *In and Out Game* (p.154-155).
2) Perfect Spots.
    a) Hello and Goodbye.
    b) Introduce *teeter-totter fall* (p.75).
3) Locomotor movements on the diagonal, groups of 4.

LESSON 29   *PRESCHOOL/GRADES K-1*

1) Do masking tape *scooter line* (p.136-137) with different locomotor movements (not scooters).
2) Perfect Spots.
    a) Review teeter-totter fall.
    c) Introduce *Cat Dance* (p.178)--beats 1 to 12.
3) Introduce *scooters* (p.136-137).
    a) Free time.
    b) Do *line design with scooters* (p.136-137).

LESSON 30   *PRESCHOOL/GRADES K-1*

1) Obstacle course including a small line design done with scooters.
2) Perfect Spots--practice Cat Dance.
3) Locomotor movements on the diagonal.

LESSON 31   *PRESCHOOL/GRADES K-1*

1) Partner work--same partner throughout.
    a) Hold hands and spin.
    b) Leap frog.
    c) Hold 1 foot and hop; change legs.
    d) *Give Your Teacher A Heart Attack* (p.48).
2) *Scooters in partners* (p.137)--keep partners from first activity.
3) Perfect Spots.
    a) Practice Cat Dance, just counts.
    b) Rocking For Relaxation.

LESSON 32   *PRESCHOOL/GRADES K-1*

1) Introduce *Brain Catcher* (p.118-120)--music changes for each movement.
    a) 3 part sequence: run, shake, skip.
    b) 4 part sequences:
        1-Gallop, swing, side-slide, jazz walk.
        2-Contract and stretch, run and leap, jump, bend and straighten.
2) Perfect Spots.
    a) Perfect Cat Dance.
    b) Show on stage.
3) Introduce *Ms. Opposite* (p.162).
    a) Show and talk about "opposite".
    b) Do some with bodies.
4) Jump the foam.

LESSON 33   *PRESCHOOL/GRADES K-1*

1) Brain Catcher--no music differentiation.
    a) 4 part sequences:

                1-Twist, skip, teeter-totter falls, gallop.
                2-Side-slide, contract and stretch, side-slide changing sides, leap.
        b) Try a 5 part sequence: jump, swing, hop, shake, hopscotch.
2) Perfect Spots.
        a) Work on right and left.
        b) Formally introduce *bend and straighten* (p.66-67).
3) Groups of 4 lined up ready to move on the diagonal.
        a) Review the word "opposite".
        b) Introduce *Opposite Game* (p.162-163).
        c) Jump the foam--do *computation jumping* (p.167).

LESSON 34   PRESCHOOL/GRADES K-1

1) *Partner opposites* (p.162)--same partner throughout.
        a) High and low.
        b) Forward and backward.
        c) Crooked and straight.
        d) Fast and slow.
2) Perfect Spots.
        a) Work on right and left.
        b) Introduce bend and straighten study: bend and straighten right arm, beats 1 and
                2; left arm, beats 3 and 4; right leg, beats 5 and 6; left leg, beats 7 and 8;
                torso, beats 9 and 10; jump turn, beats 11 and 12.
3) *Balloons (blown)* (p.134-135).
        a) Free time.
        b) Start sequence:
                1-Jump and keep the balloon in the air.
                2-Move the balloon on the floor without touching it.
                3-Kick the balloon.
                4-Put the tied end in mouth and try to shake someone else's balloon out.

LESSON 35   PRESCHOOL/GRADES K-1

1) Partner opposites again.
2) Perfect Spots.
        a) Work on right and left.
        b) Perfect and show bend and straighten study.
3) Balloons.
        a) Free time.
        b) Perfect and show balloon sequence.

LESSON 36   PRESCHOOL/GRADES K-1

1) In and out Game.
2) *Name syllable patterns* (p.168): pick 3 names; clap syllables of first, slap thighs
        for syllables of 2nd, snap fingers for syllables of 3rd.
3) Locomotor movements done on the diagonal.
        a) Basic locomotor movements--work especially on hopscotch.
        b) Teach *one-legged skip* (p.36).
4) Spaghetti.

LESSON 37   PRESCHOOL/GRADES K-1

1) Alternate locomotor movements (include one-legged skip) and *nonlocomotor movements
        done with a partner* (p.44-45).
        a) One-legged skip--get partner, hold both hands and swing.
        b) Hopscotch--get different partner, hold one hand and shake.

c) Run and leap--get different partner and do contract and stretch in opposites.
2) Name syllable pattern.
3) Work on 1 letter, for example, "B".
    a) Children make "B's" individually.
    b) Children make "B's" with a partner.
    c) Make a floor pattern of a "B".

LESSON 38   PRESCHOOL/GRADES K-1

1) Partner letters: children in partners; each pair given a letter; they have to make that letter together; when completed they get a new letter.
2) Parachute.
    a) Hamburgers and French Fries.
    b) Introduce *Ms. Monster* (p.139-140).
3) Perfect Spots--Rocking Song relaxation.

LESSON 39   PRESCHOOL/GRADES K-1

1) Obstacle course.
2) Parachute (children's choice of activities).
3) Jump the foam--computation jump.

LESSON 40   PRESCHOOL/GRADES K-1

(Choose what activities class would like for last class. A typical outcome is:)
1) Balls.
2) Scooters.
3) Parachute.

GRADES 2-3

LESSON 1   GRADES 2-3

1) *Obstacle course* (p.18-22).
    a) Look at mental and physical level of class.
    b) Teach rules: shoes off, no gum, stage only used for perfect patterns.
    c) Example: (see drawing p.19).
2) Teach *near* (p.10); teach *far* (p.10)--end in *Perfect Spots* (p.9-13).
    a) *Shake congratulations* (p.10).
    b) *Hello and Goodbye* (p.14).
    c) *Rocking Song for relaxation* (p.120-121).

LESSON 2   GRADES 2-3

1) Review near; review far--end in Perfect Spots; shake congratulations.
    a) Hello and Goodbye.
    b) Introduce *Swordfish* (p.15-16).
2) Introduce *locomotor* (p.23-24): do locomotor movements going from side to side, saying word.

a) Walk.
   b) Jump.
   c) Hop.
   d) Skip.
   e) Gallop.
   f) Crawl.
   g) Roll and seat scoot.
   h) Run.
3) Introduce *Free Traveling Structure* (p.25-27).
   a) Isolated body parts move to sound and stop.
   b) Whole body moves stationary.
   c) Locomotor movements in Free Traveling Structure.
4) Back to Perfect Spots--rocking for relaxation.

LESSON 3   GRADES 2-3

1) Review Free Traveling Structure with locomotor movements: insist on absolute freezes!
2) Perfect Spots.
   a) Add *face front* (p.11) component.
   b) Practice Perfect Spots with game *Firecracker* (p.13).
   c) In Perfect Spots.
      1-Hello and Goodbye.
      2-Introduce *Blast Off* (p.16-18).
3) Introduce *diagonal* (p.27-29).
   a) Show picture and find diagonals on the paper.
   b) Find diagonals throughout the room.
   c) If time, do a few locomotor movements on the diagonal one at a time.

LESSON 4   GRADES 2-3

1) Locomotor movements done in the Free Traveling Structure. Introduce *hopscotch* (p.35) (one jump, one hop).
2) Perfect Spots: complete within 10 seconds or practice.
   a) Hello and Goodbye--teach *torso* (p.14-15) and use in Hello and Goodbye.
   b) Blast Off.
3) Review diagonal.
   a) Set up *Diagonal Structure* (p.27-29).
      1-Ask for groups of 3 and wait.
      2-Introduce *cause and effect starts* (p.28).
   b) Introduce *jump the foam* (p.114).

LESSON 5   GRADES 2-3

1) Begin partner work: *Shake a Partner* (p.43-44)--alternate individually done locomotor movements with shaking partner hands, feet, heads, backs.
2) Perfect Spots.
   a) Introduce *4 swings pattern* (p.63-64): front, crossed, side, twist. Swings done 4 times, 2 times and one time each.
   b) Blast Off.
3) Introduce *balls* (p.124-127).
   a) Free time.
   b) A few guided movements.
      1-Run and dribble.
      2-Move the ball with just feet.
      3-Move the ball, no hands or feet.
      4-Throw the ball in the air and catch while skipping.
4) Diagonal locomotor movements: groups of 4 (if time, jump the foam).

LESSON 6   GRADES 2-3

1) Partner work: one partner for entire time.
    a) Hold both hands and side-slide, front to front then back to back.
    b) Stay back to back, sit down and stand up.
    c) Sit facing partner, hold ankles and go somewhere.
    d) Hold both hands and roll.
    e) Hold one foot each and hop; change legs.
    f) Synchronized run and leap.
2) Perfect Spots.
    a) Introduce *levels* (p.53-58).
    b) Do shake, swing, and spin on all levels.
3) Balls
    a) Free time.
    b) Begin sequence:
        1-Run and dribble.
        2-Move ball with no hands or feet.
        3-Ball between legs and jump.
        4-Catch ball while skipping.
    c) Return to partner from first activity
        1-Roll ball back and forth.
        2-Catch ball while standing.
        3-Catch ball while jogging, then running.

LESSON 7   GRADES 2-3

1) Review levels and apply to locomotor movements, Free Traveling Structure.
2) Perfect Spots: introduce level pattern.
    a) Air level--jump, 4 beats.
    b) Standing level--cross swing, 4 beats.
    c) Knee level--spin, 4 beats.
    e) Lowest level--*temper tantrum* (p.56), 8 beats.
3) Balls: perfect sequence and show *audience and performers* (p.115).
4) Locomotor movements done on the diagonal, groups of 4.

LESSON 8   GRADES 2-3

1) Introduce *nonlocomotor* (p.59).
    a) Introduce word.
    b) Children's own movements.
    c) Alternate with locomotor movements: introduce spin, shake, and swing.
2) Perfect Spots.
    a) Review 4 swings pattern.
    b) Perfect level pattern: do only with counts. If ready, show on *stage* (p.115).
3) Locomotor movements done on the diagonal, groups of 3 or 4.
    a) Do a few basic: run, hopscotch, skip, gallop, etc.
    b) Teach *leap* (p.40).
    c) Divide diagonal in half with marker, do one level to the middle, a different
       level from the middle to the end (groups choose).
    d) Jump the foam.

LESSON 9   GRADES 2-3

1) Obstacle course (different from first).
2) Perfect Spots.

    a) Hello and Goodbye.
    b) Introduce *right* (p.84-85).
       1-Begin with right arm only: circle, shake, bend and straighten, etc., while saying "right".
       2-Practice finding right arm: twirl on different levels; face back.
    c) Introduce *Cops and Robbers* (p.86): work on side-slide.
3) Locomotor movements done on the diagonal.
    a) Basic: run, skip, jump, hop, hopscotch, etc.
    b) Side-slide: if good, introduce changing sides.
    c) Jazz walk.
    d) Leap.
    e) Jump the foam.

LESSON 10   *GRADES 2-3*

1) Alternate locomotor and nonlocomotor movements:
    a) Locomotor: skip forward, backward, turning; side-slide sideways.
    b) Nonlocomotor: introduce *contract and stretch* (p.64) for hands, arms, legs, face, neck, torso, whole body--all the while saying words.
    c) Locomotor: jump forward, backward, sideways, turning; hop right, left, hopscotch.
    d) Nonlocomotor: shake all levels.
    e) Locomotor: jazz walk, jog, run, run and leap.
2) Introduce *floor patterns* (p.95-97).
    a) Make a simple 4 line pattern.
    b) Do it in groups of 4.
3) Locomotor movements done on the diagonal, groups of 4 (same groups as did floor pattern).
    a) Run and leap to middle; roll from middle to end of diagonal.
    b) In middle, add contract lowest level and stretch knee level. Result: leap, contract and stretch, roll.
    c) Add shake from air level to lowest level after contract and stretch. Completed pattern: leap; contract and stretch; shake; roll.

LESSON 11   *GRADES 2-3*

1) Perfect Spots.
    a) 4 swings pattern: front, crossed, side, twist.
    b) Warm-up back: rock forward and back, bridge and contract--repeat several times.
    c) Introduce *one-knee back roll* (p.38): lie down, lift legs and seat, put one knee down, roll back onto knee.
    d) Add contract lowest level, stretch knee level to roll. Result: contract lowest; stretch knee; sit down and do one knee back roll.
2) Floor pattern.
    a) Teach star (see drawing p.98).
    b) Do it in groups of 4.
3) Introduce *parachute* (p.137).
    a) *Ocean* (p.137-138).
    b) *Whoosh* (p.138).

LESSON 12   *GRADES 2-3*

1) Perfect Spots.
    a) Warm-up backs: swings, rocking forward and back, bridge and contract.
    b) Review one-knee back roll.
    c) Teach *spiral twist fall* (p.66).

    d) Introduce complete nonlocomotor pattern: start standing, facing the back of the room.
        1-Spiral twist fall--counts 1 to 3.
        2-Spin on seat--4.
        3-Contract lowest level--5 to 6.
        4-Stretch knee level--7 to 8.
        5-One knee back roll--1 to 4.
        6-Sit down without using hands--5 to 6.
        7-Stand and turn--7 to 8.
2) Do a *helping floor pattern* (p.99), (stress connecting lines).
3) Parachute.
    a) Ocean.
    b) *Hamburger and French Fries* (p.138-139).
    c) *Mushroom* (p.141).

LESSON 13   GRADES 2-3

1) A few locomotor movements done in the Free Traveling Structure: skip, side-slide, hop, hopscotch, run, leap.
2) Perfect Spots: practice nonlocomotor pattern (from Lesson 12).
3) Floor patterns.
    a) Do another helping floor pattern but do not perform. Stress:
        1-Putting the room representation straight.
        2-Connecting lines.
    b) Own floor patterns.
        1-Get into groups of 4.
        2-Groups make one pattern using 4 straight lines, each a different locomotor movement.
        3-When done, teacher checks, then groups practice.
        4-Groups show their patterns.
4) Jump the foam.

LESSON 14   GRADES 2-3

1) Introduce *combining locomotor and nonlocomotor movements* (p.69-71).
    a) Talk about possibility; see if children can think of example.
    b) Do some:
        1-Nonlocomotor swing plus locomotor skip.
        2-Twist head "no" plus jump.
        3-Shake a leg plus hop; change legs.
        4-Contract and stretch plus roll.
        5-Clap hands plus leap.
2) Perfect Spots.
    a) Perfect nonlocomotor pattern (from Lesson 12).
    b) Show on stage.
3) Locomotor movements done on the diagonal.
    a) A few basic: run, skip, side-slide changing sides, leap.
    b) Kicks: front, back, sides. Pattern: kick front 2, back 2, side 4.
4) Parachute.

LESSON 15   GRADES 2-3

(Class before Christmas vacation.)
1) Combine locomotor and nonlocomotor movements.
    a) Circle arms + gallop.

      b) Contract and stretch + skip.
      c) Slap and clap + hopscotch.
      d) Wiggle hips + walk.
      e) Shake + run.
2) *Floor pattern of Christmas tree* (see drawing p.101).
3) Parachute.

LESSON 16   GRADES 2-3

(Class after vacation.)
1) Obstacle course.
2) Review near; review far; review finding Perfect Spots.
      a) Shake congratulations.
      b) Hello and Goodbye.
      c) Review nonlocomotor pattern (from Lesson 12).
3) Review diagonal and review Diagonal Structure, groups of 3.
      a) Run.
      b) Skip.
      c) Hopscotch.
      d) Side-slide, changing sides.
      e) Kick pattern from Lesson 14: front 2, back 2, side 4.
      f) Jazz walk.
      g) Leap.
      h) Jump the foam.

LESSON 17   GRADES 2-3

1) Introduce *Brain Catcher* (p.118-120): work to 5 part sequence said twice.
2) Perfect Spots.
      a) Work on right arm: shake, circle, contract and stretch while saying "right".
      b) Practice finding right in different positions: different levels, facing front and back of the room.
      c) Do *Walk Down Your Front* (p.81-82) and *Right and Left Bug* (p.85-86).
      d) Introduce *directions* (p.81): do bounces going front, back side, and turning.
3) Introduce *scooters* (p.136-137): free time.
4) Locomotor movements done on the diagonal.

LESSON 18   GRADES 2-3

1) Brain Catcher: no differentiation in music.
2) Perfect Spots.
      a) Review work on right; alternate with left.
      b) Review directions: front, back, side, turning.
      c) Do nonlocomotor movements using directions.
           1-Bounce: 8's in each direction, 4's, 2's, 1's.
           2-Kicks: 8's in each direction, 4's, 2's, 1's.
           3-Shake arms: front, back, side, all around.
           4-Push hips: forward, backward, sideways, all around.
      d) Pattern using directions: bounce front 4 beats, kick back 4 beats, shake hands to the right 4 beats, push hips out to the left 4 beats.
3) *Scooter line* (p.136-137).
4) If time, locomotor movements done on the diagonal or on the scooter line.

LESSON 19   GRADES 2-3

1) Partner work.
   a) Some of the activities from Lesson 6.
   b) In addition:
      1-Hold partner by both hands and spin.
      2-Sit back to back, link elbows and spin.
      3-Leap frog.
      4-*Give Your Teacher A Heart Attack* (p.48).
2) Stay with same partners--scooters in partners.
3) Perfect Spots.
   a) Review pattern using directions from Lesson 18.
   b) Do jumps forward, backward, sideways, turning: 4 times, 2 times, 1 time each.
4) Introduce directions in locomotor movements, Free Traveling Structure.
   a) Jazz walk: forward, backward, sideways, turning.
   b) Skip: 4 directions.
   c) Jump: 4 directions.
   d) Run: 4 directions.

LESSON 20   GRADES 2-3

1) Introduce *In and Out Game* (p.154-155).
2) Perfect Spots; begin pattern: *3 jumps forward, 5 steps backward, 4 side-slides to the right, 4 side-slides to the left* (p.91-92).
3) Locomotor movements done on the diagonal.
   a) Run forward to the middle; stop; skip backward from middle to the end.
   b) Side-slide to the middle; hopscotch backward to the end.
   c) Skip turning to the middle; run and leap forward to the end.

LESSON 21   GRADES 2-3

1) Review locomotor movements using directions, Free Traveling Structure.
2) Perfect Spots.
   a) Perfect 3/5/4/4 pattern: 3 jumps forward and 5 steps backward (total of 8 beats); 4 side-slides right and 4 side-slides left (total of 8 beats).
   b) Do counts in 8's.
3) Groups of 4 ready to move on the diagonal.
   a) Ask question: How can above pattern be done so that you get from the corner to the end of the diagonal? (Turn body.)
   b) Do the pattern on the diagonal.
   c) If time, do the pattern with groups starting 8 beats apart.
4) Jump the foam.

LESSON 22   GRADES 2-3

1) Locomotor movements done on the diagonal, groups of 4.
   a) Review 3/5/4/4 pattern.
   b) Do it with groups starting 8 beats apart.
   c) Teach *curved line* (p.104-105), like "c".
      1-Run.
      2-Skip.
      3-Side-slide.
2) Floor pattern using 3/5/4/4 pattern. (Break groups of 4 into 2's; if large class, do half the class at a time.) (See drawing p.92.)
   a) Do each group separately.

      b) Do each group starting 8 beats apart.
      c) Sing "Row, Row, Row Your Boat" while doing pattern.
3) Introduce *scarves* (p.127-128): free time.

LESSON 23   GRADES 2-3

1) Perfect Spots.
      a) Hello and Goodbye.
      b) Teach *teeter-totter fall* (p.75).
      c) Introduce *Cat Dance* (p.178).
2) Groups of 3 on one side of the room; introduce huge *wiggly line* (p.103-104)--marker method.
      a) With markers do the line run, skip, jazz walk, hopscotch.
      b) Take away the markers one by one: do one or 2 locomotor movements each time a marker is removed.
3) Scarves.
      a) Free time.
      b) Begin sequence:
            1-Gallop and circle scarf.
            2-Sit and spin with scarf in toes.
            3-Keep scarf in toes and hop.
            4-Throw scarf in air and catch with different parts of body.
            5-*Magic Scarf* (p.128).

LESSON 24   GRADES 2-3

1) Scarves.
      a) Free time.
      b) Perfect sequence and show.
2) Perfect Spots.
      a) Practice teeter-totter fall and practice knee-foot position.
      b) Review Cat Dance.
3) Groups of 3 on one side of the room.
      a) Review huge wiggly line: be able to do it without markers.
      b) Introduce *wiggly line, conceptual method* (p.102-103): have the wiggly line move on the diagonal.
      c) Introduce *spiral line* (p.105-106).
          1-Do one at a time.
          2-End in strange shapes holding on to each other.

LESSON 25   GRADES 2-3

1) Alternate locomotor and nonlocomotor movements: review levels and directions.
      a) Locomotor skip, backward direction; nonlocomotor spin changing levels.
      b) Locomotor run, sideways direction; nonlocomotor contract and stretch changing levels.
      c) Locomotor jazz walk turning directions; nonlocomotor twist changing levels.
2) Perfect Spots: perfect and show Cat Dance.
3) Groups of 4 on one side of the room.
      a) Teach how to do a *sharp angle* (p.106).
      b) Teach *zigzag line* (p.106).
4) Floor pattern using wiggly, zigzag, huge wiggly, and spiral lines (see drawings p.107).

LESSON 26   GRADES 2-3

1) Floor pattern.
    a) Perfect floor pattern from Lesson 25.
    b) Add scarves to the floor pattern.
2) Talk and show how a line can be a shape + a direction. Do some examples:
    a) Spiral line, skip, turning direction.
    b) Zigzag line, jump, backward direction.
    c) Wiggly line, side-slide, sideways direction.
3) Begin own floor patterns: groups of 4.
    a) Each group does one floor pattern using one straight, one wiggly, one zigzag,
       and one spiral line. (Work checked by teacher.)
    b) Add directions to floor patterns so that each line is a different direction:
       forward, backward, sideways, turning.

LESSON 27   GRADES 2-3

1) Partners: *Mirror and Shadow* (p.48).
2) Finish floor patterns from Lesson 26.
    a) Teacher check; if correct, practice so it can be done without the paper.
    b) Groups perform.
3) Locomotor movements on the diagonal.
    a) Basic locomotor movements.
    b) Work on *spelling* (p.163-164).
4) *Spaghetti* (p.121-122).

LESSON 28   GRADES 2-3

1) In and Out Game.
2) Perfect Spots.
    a) Hello and Goodbye.
    b) 4 swings pattern: front, crossed, side, twist--4 times, 2 times, 1 time each.
    c) Jump pattern:
        1-Feet together.
        2-Feet apart.
        3-One foot in front.
        4-Change so that the other foot is in front.
        5-Small jump to get ready.
        6-Jump turn.
        7-Jump and hit seat with heels.
        8-Jump with legs wide in air.
3) Locomotor movements done on the diagonal.
    a) Basic locomotor movements.
    b) Spelling.
    c) Jump the foam.

LESSON 29   GRADES 2-3

1) Balls.
    a) Free time.
    b) Harder "tricks":
        1-Ball between feet, jump and catch.
        2-Bounce ball, leg cross over.
        3-Throw ball in air and catch while leaping.
        4-Dribble with right hand, left, alternating hands.

    c) Groups of 4, create own ball sequence.
        1-Pick 5 different things to do with balls.
        2-Write ideas down and remember.
        3-Groups show sequences.
2) Perfect Spots: Introduce *8 + 8 pattern* (p.77-78).
    a) First practice running anywhere for 8 beats, returning exactly on count 8.
    b) Pattern: swing--1, swing back--2, shake lowering to sit--3 and 4, spin on seat--5, contract lowest level--6, stretch knee level--7 and 8, run anywhere returning by count 8--1 to 8.
3) If time, locomotor movements done on the diagonal.

LESSON 30   GRADES 2-3

1) Introduce *opposites* (p.162-163).
    a) Talk about opposites.
    b) *Partner opposites* (p.162): show examples then do:
        1-High and low.
        2-Fast and slow.
        3-Forward and backward.
        4-Straight and crooked.
2) Perfect Spots.
    a) Practice 8 + 8 pattern.
    b) Do it with half the class doing the 8 beats of running while the other half does the stationary 8 beats.
3) Introduce *linear pattern, color paper squares* (p.168-169).
    a) Show example of pattern: children represent pattern with letters, numbers, foods, etc.
    b) Do pattern in movement.
4) Locomotor movements done on the diagonal.
    a) A few basic locomotor movements.
    b) Introduce *Opposite Game* (p.162-163).

LESSON 31   GRADES 2-3

1) Opposites in partners (without examples).
    a) Pretty and ugly.
    b) Heavy and light.
    c) Contract and stretch.
    d) Frozen and moving.
    e) Boy and girl.
    f) Own example.
2) Groups of 4 create own color paper patterns.
    a) Teacher check; if OK, paste on to large sheet of paper.
    b) Represent pattern with letters, numbers, food, toys, nature, and movements.
    c) Each group shows movement pattern.
3) Locomotor movements done on the diagonal.
    a) Basic locomotor movements.
    b) Introduce *one-legged skip* (p.36).
    c) Work on leap.
    d) Do pattern: one-legged skip, one-legged skip, run-run-run-leap, hold a balanced shape at the end.
    e) Jump the foam.

LESSON 32   GRADES 2-3

1) Obstacle course.
2) Perfect Spots.
   a) Introduce *triangle position* (p.77) of legs.
   b) Introduce *first part of the Partner Dance* (p.181).
3) Groups of 3, pick any objects in room and create pattern, for example, books, blocks, chairs, pencils, shoes, etc.
   a) Represent the pattern with movements using locomotor and nonlocomotor movements.
   b) Groups show movement patterns.
4) Locomotor movements done on the diagonal, stay in same groups of 3.
   a) Talk about "between" person.
   b) Do *"between" with locomotor movements* (p.153-154).
      1-*Carry* (p.153-154).
      2-*Galloping in a Basket* (p.154).
      3-*Directional Can-Can* (p.154).
      4-*The Stretcher* (p.154).

LESSON 33   GRADES 2-3

1) Make *letters* (p.148-150).
   a) *Body shapes* (p.148-149): individually and with a partner.
   b) *Outlining* (p.149): using different parts of the body, different levels.
2) Perfect Spots.
   a) Hello and Goodbye.
   b) Practice first part of the Partner Dance.
   c) Introduce *second part of the Partner Dance* (p.181-182).
3) Floor pattern.
   a) Make a *floor pattern of a letter, for example, "B"* (p.149-150).
   b) Do it in groups of 4.
4) Spaghetti.

LESSON 34   GRADES 2-3

1) Review making letters in 3 ways, for example, "Make a 'B' with your body; outline a 'B' with your foot; do a floor pattern of a 'B' as big as the whole room."
2) Groups of 3, make own word pattern.
   a) Groups pick one word.
   b) Groups make each letter of the word a different way, that is, different body parts, levels, sizes.
3) Perfect Spots.
   a) Practice first and second part of Partner Dance.
   b) Teacher and one student show how parts fit together.
4) Introduce *balloons* (p.134-135).
   a) Free time.
   b) Guided movements:
      1-Keep the balloon in the air without hands.
      2-Move it on the floor without touching it.
      3-Kick the balloon.
      4-Balloon between feet and spin.
      5-Rub balloon on hair and see if it will stay on the wall.
      6-Put tied end in mouth and shake.

LESSON 35　　　　　　　　　　　　　　　　　　　　　　　　　　　　　　　　GRADES 2-3

1) Teach following sequence, Free Traveling Structure:
    a) Locomotor movements in air level for 8 beats.
    b) Locomotor movements on lowest level for 8 beats.
    c) Spin on seat for 8 beats. (Make sure the children know the sequence perfectly and can change exactly on the count of 1.)
2) Balloons.
    a) Free time.
    b) Do above sequence with balloons.
    c) Do it as a 2 part *Balloon Round* (p.135): divide class in half, 2nd half starts 8 beats late.
3) Go back to groups for word pattern from Lesson 34.
    a) Practice word pattern so that it is smooth.
    b) Groups show patterns, audience guesses words.

LESSON 36　　　　　　　　　　　　　　　　　　　　　　　　　　　　　　　　GRADES 2-3

1) Brain Catcher.
2) Perfect Spots.
    a) 4 different swings: front, crossed, side, twist.
    b) Practice thoroughly the first and 2nd parts of the Partner Dance. (Be able to do movements to counts with eyes closed.)
    c) Get partners and do Partner Dance together.
3) Scarves.
    a) Free time.
    b) Go back to partners from Partner Dance and do *Trust Walk* (p.129).

LESSON 37　　　　　　　　　　　　　　　　　　　　　　　　　　　　　　　　GRADES 2-3

1) Plan "show" of work done in movement class. (This can be as big or as small a production as you like.) Possible outcome:
    a) Level pattern (Lesson 7).
    b) Nonlocomotor pattern (Lesson 12).
    c) Cat Dance (Lesson 23).
    d) 8 + 8 pattern (Lesson 29).
    e) Partner Dance (Lesson 32 and 33).
    f) Ball sequence (Lesson 6).
    g) If *not* using stage, floor pattern using wiggly, zigzag, huge wiggly, and spiral line + scarves (Lesson 25 and 26).
2) Practice for show.
3) Parachute.

LESSON 38　　　　　　　　　　　　　　　　　　　　　　　　　　　　　　　　GRADES 2-3

1) Practice show.
2) Parachute: *Lifting* (p.141).

LESSON 39　　　　　　　　　　　　　　　　　　　　　　　　　　　　　　　　GRADES 2-3

(Invite another class, parents, etc., for show.)
1) Show.
2) Any extra time, parachute.
3) Decide what class wants for the last class. Probable outcome.....

LESSON 40   GRADES 2-3

1) In and Out Game.
2) Scooters.
3) Parachute.
4) Jump the foam.

GRADES 4-6
   For most 4th to 6th grade classes I would do the lessons planned for grades 2 to 3. The following lessons are appropriate for exceptionally sophisticated 4th to 6th graders or for children that have had movement class already.

LESSON 1   GRADES 4-6

1) *Obstacle course* (p.15-22).
2) Practice *near* (p.10) and *far* (p.10)--get *Perfect Spots* (p. 9-13).
   Teach simple but strenuous pattern. For example, start standing; jump and lie down on back--1 and 2; bridge--3 and 4; come down--5 and 6; balance on seat--7 and 8; rock back without using hands--9 and 10; sit up and spin--11 and 12; get up--13 and 14; jump turn--15 and 16.

LESSON 2   GRADES 4-6

1) Introduce *FreeTraveling Structure* (p.25-27).
   a) Isolated body parts.
   b) Whole body moving stationary.
   c) Introduce *locomotor* (p.23-24) and do locomotor movements in Free Traveling Structure: skip, run, jump, hopscotch, side-slide, leap.
2) Review near and far, get Perfect Spots.
   a) *4 different swings* (p.63-64): front, crossed, side, twist--4 times each, 2 times 1 time.
   b) Practice pattern from Lesson 1; if perfect, show on *stage* (p.115).
3) Set up *Diagonal Structure* (p.27-29).
   a) Practice finding diagonals on paper and throughout room.
   b) Get groups of 3 and set up Diagonal Structure.
   c) Do a few basic locomotor movements on the diagonal.

LESSON 3   GRADES 4-6

1) Review word "locomotor"; do locomotor movements Free Traveling Structure.
2) Perfect Spots.
   a) Add *face front* (p.11) component.
   b) Practice getting Perfect Spots quickly (like *Firecracker*, p.13, but do not call it that).
   c) 4 different swings pattern.
   d) Teach *teeter-totter fall* (p.75).
   e) Introduce *Cat Dance* (p.178).

205

3) Locomotor movements done on the diagonal.
    a) Double check the Diagonal Structure.
        1-*Cause and effect starts* (p.28).
        2-*Perfect corners* (p.28).
    b) Do some basic locomotor movements.
    c) Teach *leap* (p.40).

LESSON 4   GRADES 4-6

1) *Shake a Partner* (p.43-44): alternate individual locomotor movements with different partner shakes: hands, feet, elbows, backs.
2) Perfect Spots (if not done within 10 seconds, practice).
    a) Flex and point (like *Hello and Goodbye*, p.14, but do not call it that).
    b) 4 different swings.
    c) Practice teeter-totter fall. (Check that legs are straight and that the leg raises at the same time that the torso lowers.)
    d) Complete Cat Dance.
3) Introduce *balls* (p.124-127).
    a) Free time.
    b) Few guided movements.
        1-Move ball on floor without hands or feet.
        2-Move ball on floor with only feet.
        3-Fast dribble.
        4-Bounce ball, cross legs over.
        5-Throw and catch while skipping.
4) If time, locomotor movements on the diagonal.

LESSON 5   GRADES 4-6

1) Partner work: one partner for entire time.
    a) Side-slide hands in front, in back, stay back to back and sit down and get up, stay seated spin.
    b) Hold ankles and hop; change legs.
    c) Hold both hands and roll (try tucked roll).
    d) Syncronized leaps.
2) Perfect Spots.
    a) Flex and point; introduce *torso* (p.14-15) and use--up with flex and down with point.
    b) Perfect Cat Dance and show on stage.
3) Balls
    a) Free time.
    b) Harder guided movements.
    c) Sequence:
        1-Run and dribble.
        2-Roll ball with just feet.
        3-Roll ball with no hands or feet.
        4-Put ball between feet jump it up and catch.
        5-Throw and catch and leap.
    d) Partners place ball between them and move: foot to foot, back to back, any 2 parts.

LESSON 6   GRADES 4-6

1) *Balls with partners* (p.126): 1 ball per pair.
    a) Sit and roll.
    b) Kneel and bounce pass.

    c) Stand and bounce pass.
    d) Jump and bounce pass.
    e) Jog and pass.
    f) Run and pass.
2) Perfect Spots.
    a) Introduce *level* (p.53-58).
    b) Do level pattern:
        1-Air level--jump 4 beats.
        2-Standing--swing crossed 4 beats.
        3-Knee--contract and stretch 4 beats.
        4-Sit--spin 4 beats.
        5-Lowest--*temper tantrum* (p.56) 8 beats (if too "cool" for tantrum, ask for shake, lowest level).
3) Locomotor movements done on the diagonal.
    a) Basic locomotor movements.
    b) Practice leap.
    c) Introduce *one-legged skip* (p.36).
    d) Pattern: 1-legged skip, 1-legged skip, run-run-run-leap, balance.
    e) Jazz walk.
    f) Introduce *jump the foam* (p.114).

LESSON 7   GRADES 4-6

1) *In and Out Game* (p.154-155).
2) Perfect Spots.
    a) Flex and point.
    b) Introduce *body wave pattern* (p.78).
    c) Practice level pattern and show.
3) Introduce *linear patterns, color paper squares* (p.168-169).
    a) Show pattern and talk about representing it with letters, numbers, food, toys, nature.
    b) Do movement pattern.
4) Locomotor movements done on the diagonal.
    a) Basic locomotor movements.
    b) Practice 1-legged skip and leap pattern (Lesson 6).
    c) Childrens' choice.

LESSON 8   GRADES 4-6

1) Introduce levels in locomotor movements, Free Traveling Structure.
2) Groups of 3 make own color paper patterns.
    a) Represent pattern with letters, numbers, food, toys, nature, etc.
    b) Represent with movements; practice; groups show pattern.
3) Perfect Spots: introduce jump pattern.
    a) Feet together.
    b) Feet apart.
    c) One foot in front.
    d) Change foot in front.
    e) Get ready.
    f) Jump turn.
    g) Hit heels to seat.
    h) Jump with legs wide.
4) Locomotor movements done on the diagonal, groups of 3.
    a) Groups pick 3 different locomotor movements, each on a different level to do across the diagonal.
    b) Jump the foam.

LESSON 9   GRADES 4-6

1) Introduce *nonlocomotor* (p.59).
   a) Discuss possibilities--children's own movements.
   b) Alternate with locomotor movements, Free Traveling Structure: briefly present shake, spin, swing, twist.
2) Perfect Spot.
   a) Jump pattern.
   b) Introduce *8 + 8 pattern* (p.77-78).
      1-First do run anywhere for 8 beats, returning exactly on count 8.
      2-Stationary 8 beats (point out that the pattern uses several nonlocomotor movements), swing--1, swing back--2, shake to sitting--3 and 4, spin--5, contract lowest--6, stretch knee level--7 and 8.
3) Introduce *scooters* (p.136-137): free time.
4) Locomotor movements done on the diagonal.
   a) A few basic locomotor movements.
   b) *Spaghetti* (p.121-122).

LESSON 10   GRADES 4-6

1) Alternate locomotor and nonlocomotor movements, Free Traveling Structure.
   a) Introduce *contract and stretch* (p.64).
      1-Isolated body parts.
      2-Whole body.
      3-Whole body on different levels.
   b) Practice contract lowest level and stretch knee level.
2) Perfect Spots.
   a) Practice 8 + 8 pattern (check contract and stretch).
   b) Do pattern with half the class running while half does the stationary 8 beats-- repeat several times.
3) Scooters.
   a) Free time.
   b) *Scooter line* (p.136-137).
4) Introduce *floor pattern* (p.95-97); do *star* (p.98), groups of 4.
   a) Each group does the pattern alone.
   b) Groups start when the group ahead finishes the first line.

LESSON 11   GRADES 4-6

1) Alternate individual locomotor movements with *partner nonlocomotor* (p.44-45) movements.
   a) Skip, forward, backward, 1-legged; partner swing, *flip over* (p.47).
   b) Jump, hop, hopscotch; partner contract together like 1 ball, stretch apart on different levels.
   c) Run, run-leap, run-leap turning; partners hold on and shake changing levels.
2) *Scooters in partners* (p.137).
3) *Helping floor pattern* (p.99).
   a) Put room representation straight.
   b) Class makes floor pattern together, using 6 straight lines (stress connecting lines).
   c) Do the floor pattern, groups of 4.
4) Jump the foam.

LESSON 12   GRADES 4-6

1) Make another helping floor pattern but do not do it.
2) Groups of 4 make own floor patterns.

    a) Assignment: use 6 straight lines, each a different locomotor movement on a different level.
    b) Teacher check; groups practice.
    c) Groups show.
3) Perfect Spots.
    a) 4 different swings.
    b) Warm-up back: rock back and forth, bridge, contract--repeat several times.
    c) Introduce *1-knee back roll* (p.38).
4) Locomotor movements done on the diagonal.
    a) A few basic locomotor movements.
    b) Work on *spelling* (p.163-164) with locomotor movements.

LESSON 13   GRADES 4-6

1) Introduce *Brain Catcher* (p.118-120): work to 6 part sequence, music differentiates.
2) Perfect Spots.
    a) Warm-up back; rock back and forth, bridge, contract--repeat several times.
    b) Review 1-knee back roll.
    c) Introduce *spiral twist fall* (p.66).
    d) Introduce nonlocomotor pattern.
        1-Spiral sit--counts 1 to 3.
        2-Spin on seat--4
        3-Contract lowest level--5 and 6.
        4-Stretch knee level--7 and 8.
        5-One-knee back roll--1 to 4.
        6-Sit down without hands--5 and 6.
        7-Stand and turn--7 and 8.
3) Introduce *parachute* (p.137).
    a) *Ocean* (p.137-138).
    b) *Whoosh* (p.138).
    c) *Hamburgers and French Fries* (p.138-139).

LESSON 14   GRADES 4-6

1) Brain Catcher: 6 parts with no differentiation in music.
2) Perfect Spots.
    a) Review levels.
    b) Children pick own nonlocomotor movements to do on each level, 8 beats on each level.
    c) Practice nonlocomotor pattern from Lesson 13.
3) Introduce *homonym* (p.160-162, appropriate to language work in classroom) perhaps "*aisle*" *and* "*isle*" (p.161).
4) Parachute.
    a) Hamburgers and French Fries.
    b) *Merry-Go-Round* (p.139).
    c) *Mushroom* (p.141).

LESSON 15   GRADES 4-6

(Class before Christmas vacation.)
1) In and Out Game.
2) *Floor pattern of a Christmas tree* (p.101).
3) Parachute.
    a) *Lifting* (p.141).
    b) Childrens' choices.

LESSON 16 GRADES 4-6

(Class after vacation.)
1) Obstacle course.
2) Practice Perfect Spots for speed. (Double check face front component.)
    a) Flex and point.
    b) Practice nonlocomotor pattern from Lesson 14--show on stage.
3) Locomotor movements done on the diagonal.
    a) Review all basic locomotor movements.
    b) Review hopscotch, leap, 1-legged skip, jazz.
    c) Jump the foam.

LESSON 17 GRADES 4-6

1) Introduce *combining locomotor plus nonlocomotor movements* (p.69-71).
    a) Swing + skip.
    b) Twist + jump.
    c) Contract and stretch + roll.
    d) Contract and stretch + skip.
    e) Wiggle + walk.
2) Perfect Spots: strenuous warm-up.
    a) 4 different swings.
    b) Contract and stretch on each level.
    c) Jump pattern from Lesson 8.
3) Introduce *falls* (p.177-179).
    a) Talk about pulling the opposite direction of fall.
    b) Review teeter-totter fall and spiral twist fall.
    c) Children try out falls on their own (have mats available).
4) Introduce *scarves* (p.127-129): free time.

LESSON 18 GRADES 4-6

1) Locomotor plus nonlocomotor movements.
    a) Swing + side-slide.
    b) Shake leg + hop.
    c) Circle arms + gallop.
    d) Clap hands + leap.
2) Groups of 3 make up own fall pattern.
    a) Sequence 5 to 7 falls.
    b) Write down sequence.
    c) Practice.
3) Stay in groups of 3 and line up on one side of the room.
    a) Introduce *wiggly line--conceptual method* (p.102-103).
    b) Do all sorts of wiggly lines.
    c) *Put together in a pattern* (p.104).
4) Scarves.
    a) Free time.
    b) A few guided movements.

LESSON 19 GRADES 4-6

1) Scarves.
    a) Free time.
    b) Guided movements.
    c) Children individually pick 5 movements to do with their scarves; remember pattern.
    d) Children show pattern, 5 to 10 at a time.

2) Go back to group fall patterns (Lesson 18).
   a) Practice, especially transitions between falls.
   b) Show on stage.
3) Groups (same as above) line up.
   a) Review wiggly line.
   b) Introduce *sharp angle* (p.106).
   c) Introduce *zigzag line* (p.106).

LESSON 20   GRADES 4-6

1) Introduce *Machine* (p.106): one child makes a movement and noise of a machine; next child fits onto the first, adding his own movement and noise.
2) Line up individually on one side of the room.
   a) Introduce *spiral line* (p.105-106).
   b) Do floor pattern using wiggly, huge wiggly, zigzag, and spiral (see p.107).
   c) End in Machine (if class is large, do half the class at a time).
3) Perfect Spots.
   a) Introduce *directions* (p.81), front, back, side, and turning.
   b) Do one or 2 nonlocomotor movements: bounce--front, back, side, turning; hip thrust--front, back, side, around.

LESSON 21   GRADES 4-6

1) Introduce *directions in locomotor movements* (p.86-88).
   a) Jazz walk forward, backward, sideways, turning.
   b) Jump forward, backward, sideways, turning.
   c) Run forward, backward, sideways, turning.
2) Groups of 4 make own floor patterns.
   a) Assignment: use 4 different shaped lines, each a different locomotor movement.
   b) Teacher check.
   c) Talk about possibility of a line shape being done in different directions, for example, spiral line done with a skip turning.
   d) Children add 4 directions (forward, backward, sideways, turning) to their floor patterns.
   e) Practice.
3) Spaghetti.

LESSON 22   GRADES 4-6

1) Locomotor movements, line shapes, plus directions, for example:
   a) Jump a zigzag line, backward direction.
   b) Skip a spiral line, turning direction.
   c) Run a wiggly line, sideways direction.
2) Return own floor patterns from Lesson 21.
   a) Groups practice; be able to do it without the map.
   b) Show.
3) Break above groups of 4 into 2's: give each pair 1 *rope* (p.130-131).
   a) Free time.
   b) *Twirl* (p.131).
   c) *Moveable Maze Jump* (p.131).

LESSON 23   GRADES 4-6

1) *Partner Opposites* (p.162).

    a) Talk about possibilities.
    b) Do high and low, fast and slow, forward and backward, contract and stretch, crooked and straight, boy and girl.
2) Perfect Spots: Introduce *first part of the Partner Dance* (p.181).
3) Locomotor movements done on the diagonal.
    a) Work on fewer movement combinations, for example:
        1-4 skips and 4 gallops; 2 skips and 2 gallops; 1 skip and 1 gallop.
        2-8 kicks front, 8 kicks back, 16 kicks side; 4 front, 4 back, and 8 side; 2 front, 2 back, and 4 side.
        3-4 jumps, 4 hops, and 4 side-slides; 2 jumps, 2 hops, and 2 side-slides; 1 jump, 1 hop, and 1 side-slide.
    b) Introduce *Opposite Game* (p.162-163).

LESSON 24   GRADES 4-6

1) Introduce *bend and straighten* (p.66-67): do Free Traveling pattern: bend and straighten, contract and stretch, go somewhere, go somewhere, go somewhere, stop. Repeat several times.
2) Perfect Spots.
    a) Review first part of Partner Dance.
    b) Introduce *second part of Partner Dance* (p.181-182).
    c) Show how it fits together.
3) Locomotor movements done on the diagonal.
    a) A few basic locomotor movements.
    b) More work on locomotor patterns, stress precision.
        1-Do some from Lesson 23.
        2-Do 2 walks, 2 jumps, 2 gallops, 2 leaps.
        3-One-legged skip, 1-legged skip, run-run-run leap.

LESSON 25   GRADES 4-6

1) *Mirror and Shadow* (p.48).
2) Perfect Spots.
    a) Practice first and second parts of Partner Dance.
    b) Put the Partner Dance together (partners from first activity).
3) Groups of 4 (combine 2 partners) do a *number floor pattern* (p.165)
    a) Assignment: pick a number; use that number for the number of locomotor movements.
    b) Example: a "3" done with 3 jumps-3 skips-3 hops repeated as necessary to do the floor pattern.
    c) Practice and show.

LESSON 26   GRADES 4-6

1) Talk and work with different ways of forming *letters* (p.148-150).
    a) *Body shape* (p.148-149): on different levels, alone or with a partner, using different body parts.
    b) *Outlining* (p.149): on different levels, with different body parts, sizes, tempos, planes.
    c) *Floor pattern* (p.149-150): sizes, different locomotor movements.
2) Perfect Spots.
    a) Body wave pattern.
    b) Practice Partner Dance and show.
3) Create own letters pattern.
    a) If class is small (under 20), "Dance Your Name" individually.
    b) If class is large (over 20), get into groups of 3 or 4, pick one word, dance each letter of the word.

LESSON 27   GRADES 4-6

1) Practice letters pattern from Lesson 26.
    a) Check transitions; strive to make each letter flow into the next.
    b) Show.
2) Perfect Spots.
    a) Review levels.
    b) Talk about "rock shapes" and do shapes on every level.
    c) Do "1, 2, 3, change": change rock shape and level quickly.
3) Parachute.
    a) Spend a few minutes working on *circumference, diameter, and radius* (p.166).
    b) *Fly* (p.140) the parachute.
    c) Do *Rocks and Waves* (p.140-141).

LESSON 28   GRADES 4-6

1) Brain Catcher using *concept combinations* (p.70-71, 89-90), for example:
    a) Locomotor movement, backward direction, sitting level.
    b) Nonlocomotor movement changing levels.
    c) Locomotor movement, sideways direction, air level.
2) Perfect Spots.
    a) Flex and point.
    b) Body wave pattern.
    c) Children pick 4 different nonlocomotor movements, each on a different level.
       Each movement gets 6 beats. Repeat several times.
3) Parachute.
    a) Review "circumference, diameter, and radius".
    b) Do Rocks and Waves so that everyone has had a turn being the waves.
        1-Rocks are individual children.
        2-Partner rocks.
        3-Group rock.
    c) Other parachute activities, children choose. (Pick a group of 3 to 5 children
       to set up obstacle course for next week.)

LESSON 29   GRADES 4-6

(Children set up obstacle course before class arrives; try it out for feasibility.)
1) Obstacle course.
2) Introduce *focus* (p.175).
    a) Gather around and talk about focus.
    b) Change focus while remaining stationary.
3) Locomotor movements done on the diagonal, groups of 3.
    a) Some basic locomotor movements.
    b) Put flowers in the middle of the diagonal--keep focus on the flowers the entire
       diagonal line.
        1-Walk.
        2-Jump.
        3-Skip.
        4-Children pick movement.
    c) Jump the foam.

LESSON 30   GRADES 4-6

1) Alternate locomotor and nonlocomotor movements.
    a) Skip forward, backward, sideways, turning; introduce *strike* (p.65) with arms,
       legs, torso, and hips.
    b) Jump, hop, hopscotch; contract and stretch changing levels.

c) Jog, run, run and leap; twist.
2) Review focus.
3) Locomotor movements done on the diagonal, groups of 4.
   a) Do some *focus problems* (p.175-176).
      1-Side-slide keeping the focus on a corner object.
      2-Turn, keeping the focus on a corner object.
      3-Hopscotch changing the focus every beat.
   b) Divide groups of 4 into 2's, do *partner focus* (p.176).
      1-Side-slide keeping the focus on each other's eyes.
      2-Roll keeping the focus on each other's eyes.
4) *Trust Walk* (p.129), same partners as focus.

LESSON 31   GRADES 4-6

1) Introduce *symmetry and asymmetry* (p.111-112).
   a) Alternate locomotor movements and shapes, that is, locomotor movements, stop, get a shape that has symmetry, now a shape that has asymmetry.
   b) Get partners and together show a shape that has symmetry.
2) Floor pattern.
   a) Teacher makes a symmetrical floor pattern (see p.111-112). Each line is a different locomotor movement and gets a specific number of beats.
   b) Do the floor pattern either in partners (from first activity) or, if class is large, in 4's, 2 children on each side.
3) Partners begin *lifting* (p.48-50).
   a) Do stage 1 lifting.
   b) Teacher show stage 2 lifting.

LESSON 32   GRADES 4-6

1) Alternate locomotor movements with partner symmetrical shapes.
2) Review symmetrical floor pattern but do not do it.
3) Partners make own symmetrical floor patterns (if class is large, have groups of 4).
   a) Each line must be a different locomotor movement.
   b) Each line must be a specific number of beats.
   c) Urge use of different levels and directions.
   d) Stop 15 minutes before end of class even if not done (make sure children have names on back on floor patterns).
4) Partner lifting.
   a) Stage 1.
   b) Stage 2.

LESSON 33   GRADES 4-6

1) Finish symmetrical floor patterns.
   a) Practice.
   b) Show.
2) Perfect Spots.
   a) Flex and point.
   b) Introduce *fraction jump turns* (p.68): quarter, half, and whole.
3) Locomotor movements done on the diagonal, groups of 4.
   a) Basic locomotor movements.
   b) Introduce *Kick the Habit* (p.40).
4) Lifting again.

LESSON 34   GRADES 4-6

1) Introduce *Chinese jump ropes* (p.130-131).
    a) Individual ropes: free time.
    b) Groups of 3: one rope per group.
        1-Make a square--go somewhere.
        2-Make a hexagon--go somewhere.
        3-Make a circle--go somewhere.
        4-Tangle.
        5-Two horses and 1 driver (switch so that everyone has a turn driving).
2) Perfect Spots.
    a) Practice fraction jump turns to the right and left.
    b) Introduce *balance* (p.179-180): "How many different ways can you balance?" Use different levels and different parts of the body.
3) Locomotor movements done on the diagonal, groups of 3.
    a) A few basic locomotor movements.
    b) Practice Kick the Habit.
    c) *"The Sting" pattern* (p.41): step-hop, step-kick, step-turn; step-hop, step-kick, step-leap. (Goes to Scott Joplin's music.)

LESSON 35   GRADES 4-6

1) Alternate locomotor movements with balances on different number of body parts, for example:
    a) Skip; balance on 2 different body parts.
    b) Side-slide changing sides; balance on 7 body parts.
    c) Leap; balance on a half of a body part.
2) Groups of 3 make up own balance pattern.
    a) Pick 5 different, difficult balances; hold each for 10 seconds.
    b) Alternate with different locomotor movements.
    c) Practice and show.
3) Locomotor movements done on the diagonal, groups of 3. Practice "The Sting" pattern from Lesson 34.

LESSON 36   GRADES 4-6

1) Introduce *chairs* (p.144).
    a) Use for going "over, under, around, and through".
    b) Use for contract and stretch on different levels.
2) Groups of 5 make up own chair pattern.
    a) Pick sequence of contract and stretch on different levels.
    b) Practice and show.
3) Locomotor movements done on the diagonal.

LESSON 37   GRADES 4-6

1) Pick patterns for show. (Patterns can be done by small groups of children or by the whole class.) Possible outcome:
    a) Nonlocomotor pattern (Lesson 13).
    b) Cat Dance (Lesson 3).
    c) Partner Dance (Lesson 24).
    d) Letters patterns (Lesson 26).
    e) Balances patterns (Lesson 35).
    f) Rocks and Waves (Lesson 27).
    g) Symmetrical floor patterns (Lesson 32).
    h) "The Sting" pattern (Lesson 34).

2) Practice.

LESSON 38   GRADES 4-6

1) Practice show.
2) Decide who to invite: parents, another class, principal, etc. (invite for next week).

LESSON 39   GRADES 4-6

1) Show.
2) Decide what activities children want for the last class. Possible outcome....

LESSON 40   GRADES 4-6

1) In and Out Game.
2) Scooters.
3) Parachute.
4) Jump the foam.

STATIONS

USE OF STATIONS

DEFINITION OF STATIONS
   Stations are separate activities that are used by individual or small groups of children. They can be used as an addition to classroom work, for example, "When you finish your math papers you can go to the reading or puzzle stations." Or they can be used with the entire class. When using stations with a whole class, the room is divided into a number of activity areas (I like 5 areas); each activity is used by 6 or 7 children. The children rotate activities approximately every 10 minutes so that everyone has a turn with every activity.

   Movement activities can be used in stations, even in a small sized room. The most common stations I use are balance beam, tumbling, jump-hop, scooter line, and some form of eye-hand practice. The set up is similar to an obstacle course; instead of moving immediately from one activity to the next, the children complete a series of tasks at each activity area. (See diagram of sample station set up.)

WHEN AND HOW LONG
   The trick with stations is to know how long to keep them. The children need to have the same stations repeated often enough that they master most of the tasks, but the stations can not be used so much that the class gets bored and sloppy. How long to keep the stations

varies enormously with individual classes. In general, I keep them no less than 4 weeks and no longer than 8 weeks.*

Many movement programs use stations as their main format. Stations are excellent for physical development: coordination, strength, agility, balance, and perceptual awareness. However stations do not lend themselves to work with concepts. Because my program is based on a conceptual approach, I use stations only as a supplement.

I introduce stations the 2nd year I have a class because there are too many basics to teach the first year. Most often I use them in January or February. At that time of year regular work seems dull and the children (and teachers) are ready for something different. We do stations for about 6 weeks and then go back to general movement classes.

NOTES ON USING STATIONS
1) For young children (k-1) you will need 2 or more helpers. Older children are fine for this. For 2nd grade on up, helpers are nice but not essential.
2) Have written charts posted for each station. Examples will follow.
3) Teach every item on every chart.
4) Sometimes have the children do the charts in the reverse order so that they get to practice all the tasks.
5) Establish a sound (drum, bell, etc.) that means "freeze exactly where you are."

STATION CHARTS

BALANCE BEAM
The balance beam is perfect for station work because 1) it takes very little space, 2) the children need little supervision, (group members can help each other), and 3) almost all children benefit from work on the balance beam. On the beam children improve balance, control, coordination, and perceptual awareness. This work is crucial for children with motor problems and is beneficial for coordinated children. Also the balance beam is wonderful because it is self-corrective. No one needs to tell a child he fell off the beam; by the same token, it is clear when a child has mastered a task.

Here are some movement possibilities for the balance beam. Young children do items 1 to 10.

1) Walk forward.
2) Walk backward.
3) Walk sideways, right side leading.
4) Walk sideways, left side leading.
5) Grapevine (step side, cross the other leg in front, step side, cross the other

---
* An exception to this is when using stations for children with motor problems. An ideal arrangement is to have these children twice a week. Once a week they participate in movement class with their class and another time during the week they return for "special work." Stations are perfect for this "special work" because 1) it is easy to work with individual children, and 2) the children get the repeated practice they need. When accompanying general movement classes, stations can be used throughout the year.

leg in back).
6) Walk turning.
7) Walk on the balance beam while balancing a bean bag on the head.
8) Walk to the middle of the balance beam; stoop and pick up 2 bean bags from the floor; stand and walk the rest of the way.
9) Walk forward on the balance beam while bouncing a ball on the floor.
10) Crawl.
11) Jump over the balance beam. (Young children or children with motor problems jump forward over the beam; other children jump sideways.)
12) Hop on the right foot.
13) Hop on the left foot.
14) Skip.
15) Leap.
16) Walk to the middle of the balance beam; balance on one foot for 10 seconds; walk to the end of the beam.
17) Walk to the middle of the balance beam and step over obstacle (yardstick held at knee level).
18) Walk to the middle of the balance beam and stoop under an obstacle (yardstick held at shoulder level).
19) Move any way you want on the balance beam.

TUMBLING

Tumbling is another essential station. Like the balance beam, it does not require too much space and almost all children benefit from tumbling practice. On the mats children improve strength, agility, coordination, and control. In addition, work on tumbling often promotes children's feelings of self-worth. Somersaults, cartwheels, head stands, and hand stands are scary. A child who even partially conquers these tasks glows with pride.

However, tumbling does require careful supervision. When I work alone I position myself by the tumbling mats and keep an eye on the whole room. If I have helpers, I still supervise the tumbling station. Watch closely the rolls that go over the head; the children must *round their necks* so that they do not get hurt.

Following are possible movements to include on a tumbling chart. Young children do 1 to 6.

1) Log roll. (Stretch straight and roll. If the children are angling off the mats it is probably because they are not stretching their arms and legs equally; most likely they are not stretching their legs enough.)
2) Cat roll. (The knees are kept together, close to the chest, while rolling.)
3) Baby crawl. (Crawl on hands and knees. Make sure the hands and knees are opposite, that is, right hand steps with left knee.)
4) Spider crawl. (Crawl on hands and feet. Again make sure the hands and feet are opposite.)
5) Inch worm crawl. (The feet remain frozen while the hands walk forward as far as possible; the hands then remain frozen while the feet catch up.)
6) Forward roll or somersault. (See "Catalog Of Locomotor Movements," Part 2, for method of teaching the forward roll. Advanced classes do the roll with legs in different positions: piked, straddle, and lunge.)
7) Backward roll.
8) Cartwheel.
9) Bridge walk. (The children push into a bridge position and "walk" down the mats; to rest the back, follow with a cat roll.)

10) Head stand, forward roll.
11) Hand stand, forward roll.

In addition the mats can be used for work on jumping and hoping.

12) Jump down the length of the mats.
13) Hop on the right foot all the way down and up the mats.
14) Hop on the left foot all the way down and up the mats.
15) Jump backwards the length of the mats.
16) Hop on the right foot backwards all the way down the mats.
17) Hop on the left foot backwards all the way down the mats.

JUMP-HOP

99% of children with motor problems need work on jumping and hopping. Most of these children do not push equally with both feet while jumping and most have trouble hopping, at least on one side. Even coordinated children gain a great deal of strength and agility from practice with jumping and hopping.

Set up a hula hoop pattern or a line of bicycle tires. The line can be straight (easier) or can wiggle (harder). Have the tires or hoops touching one another and tape them together. See sample patterns below.

1) Jump in all the hoops (or tires).
2) Hop on the right foot in all the hoops.
3) Hop on the left foot in all the hoops.
4) Alternate jump and hop.
5) Jump backwards in all of the hoops.
6) Hop on the right foot backwards in all the hoops.
7) Hop on the left foot backwards in all the hoops.
8) Bounce a ball and jump in all the hoops.

If you can make a pattern out of different sized tires or different colored hula hoops, the children conclude with the pattern, for example, jump in the blue hoops, hop in the yellow, step in the red.

SCOOTER LINE

If you have 3 or 4 scooters available this is a nice station to include because the children like it and it is a good break from the control needed in the other stations. A scooter line is excellent for work on perceptual awareness. Even simple play on the scooters promotes balance, coordination, and strength.

Set up a small scooter line with tape or paint. See diagram of sample scooter line at right.

Two rules: 1) The children start when the child ahead has gone through the "tunnel." 2) Under no condition can a child stand on a scooter. Here are some ideas for a scooter line:

1) With the scooter, on tummy.
2) With the scooter, on knees.
3) With the scooter, on seat.
4) With the scooter, on back (for older children).
5) Skipping.
6) Galloping.
7) Running.
8) Jumping.
9) Hopping. (Change feet at midway mark.)
10) Any locomotor movement you want.
11) Any way you want using the scooter (except standing).
12) With a partner pushing or pulling the scooter.

EYE-HAND WORK

Eye-hand work means practice in placing an object where the eyes direct it. There are a number of ways to practice this skill.

The most easily controlled eye-hand work is a bean bag toss station. The children simply practice tossing bean bags into a container. If you can make a stand up receptacle, it is more fun. See sample bean bag targets.

Children can also get partners and toss the bean bags to each other.

If you have enough room, the eye-hand station can use balls:

1) Toss the ball into a container.
2) Bounce and catch the ball with 2 hands.
3) Dribble with the right hand.
4) Dribble with the left hand.
5) Roll the ball with the feet. (This is obviously eye-foot work.)
6) Bounce and catch the ball off the wall.
7) Throw the ball into the air and catch it.
8) Partners pass the ball.

Some schools have small bowling sets and these are good fun. (When using a bowling set, tape X's where the pins should stand so that the children do not spend their entire time arranging pins.) Other possibilities for eye-hand practice are a ring toss game and, for mature classes, a game of marbles.

Because children need general practice rather than specific repetition with eye-hand work, I like to vary this station often.

OTHER POSSIBLE STATIONS

JUMP ROPES

Ideally, have enough ropes for one per child at the station. Give children a goal to shoot for, for example, "See if you can get to 500 today; if you step on the rope, keep going." Note: Concrete floors are very hard on the feet. If possible, use mats or, if you have a wooden floor on the stage, use that for the jump rope station.

PATTERNING STATION

This station is for 2nd grade on up. Have pattern blocks or color paper squares available. The children create a pattern and represent it in letters, numbers, food, toys, and movement. They practice the movement patterns and ideally show their patterns to the teacher or the rest of the class before moving on to the next station.

SMALL MUSCLE COORDINATION STATION

Here are a few of the many possible small muscle coordination activities:

1) Sort beans with tweezers. Have 3 or 4 different kinds of beans on a small plate. The child sorts the beans using a hand tweezer.*
2) Use an eye dropper to count how many drops of colored water fit in different sized containers.*
3) Trace the inside of a form. Tracing a form with the pencil pushing against an outline is easier than the pencil pushing in. An easily available form is a plastic puzzle where the pieces lift out of the frame. For this activity the child uses the frame; for the next activity the child uses the puzzle pieces.
4) Trace a puzzle piece form.
5) Make a design out of pattern blocks. The child traces and colors each block in the design and then *recreates* his design with the paper forms.

---

* These 2 wonderful ideas came from Jan Dederick.

INDEX

ABSTRACTING MOVEMENTS, 145-146
ACADEMIC SKILLS, 1-2, 148-171
   Attention span, see "FOCUS"
   Computations, 166-167
   Geometry, 130, 165-167
   Language development, 148-164
   Letters, 98, 105, 148-150
   Logic problems, 59, 91, 110-111
   Map reading, see "FLOOR PATTERNS"
   Math, 164-167
   Measuring, 93
   Memory, see "BRAIN CATCHER"
   Numbers, 98, 105, 164-165
   Patterning, 168-170
   Spelling, 163-164
   Ways movement can be used, 148
   Word comprehension, 150-163
ACADEMIC SPIRIT, 170-171
   Expectations, 171
   Goals, 170-171
ACCIDENTS, 26-27, also see "ARE YOU ALIVE?"
ACTIVE TEACHING, 5
ADVANCED CONCEPTS, 172, 174-180
ADVANCED PATTERNS, 79, 172, 176, 178-182
ADVANCED PHYSICAL CHALLENGES, 172-174
AISLE and ISLE, 161
ALIGNMENT, 115-116
   Rocketship straight, 17
ALTERNATING LOCOMOTOR AND NONLOCOMOTOR MOVEMENTS, 44-45, 60, 61, 173
ANTONYMS, 162-163
   Ms. Opposite, 162
   Opposite Game, 162-163
   Partner opposites, 162
ARE YOU ALIVE?, 113-114
ARTWORKS (FLOOR PATTERNS), 108
ASYMMETRY, 111-112
   Floor patterns, 112
   Introducing, 111
   Own floor patterns, 112
AUDIENCE, 115
BACK FALL, 75, 177-178
   One-knee back fall, 75
   Sitting back fall, 75
BAG A PARTNER, 46
BAG THEM UP, 139
BAGS, 46, 143-144
BALANCE, 179-180
   Body parts, 179
   Definition, 179

    Introducing, 179
    Levels, 179
    Studies, 179-180
BALANCE BEAM STATION, 210
BALLOON POP, 13
BALLOON ROUND, 135
BALLOONS, 133-135
    Blown, 134-135
    Blown, free time, 134
    Blown, guided movements, 134-135
    Blown, studies, 135
    Round, 135
    Unblown, 133-134
    Unblown, fly, 133
    Unblown, guided movements, 133
    Unblown, studies, 134
BALLS, 124-127, 220
    Eye/hand work, 220
    Free time, 125
    Guided movements, 125-126
    Partner work, 126-127, 173
    Passing them out, 124-125
    Studies, 126
    What kind, 124
BEAN BAGS, 220
BEHIND, 153
    In the "In and Out Game", 154-155
BEND AND STRAIGHTEN, 66-67, 73-74
    Definition, 66
    Difference with contract and stretch, 67
    Full body, 67
    Introducing, 66-67
    Isolated, 67
    Study, 67
BENEFITS AND DANGERS OF PROPS, 123
BESIDE, 153
    In the "In and Out Game", 154-155
BETWEEN, 153-155
    In the "In and Out Game", 154-155
    With locomotor movements, 153-154
BLAST OFF, 16-18
    Stage one, 17
    Stage three, 17-18
    Stage two, 17
BLIND MAN'S SPOT, 13
BODY SHAPE LETTERS, 148-149, 150
BODY SHAPE NUMBERS, 164, 165
BODY WAVE, 72
BODY WAVE PATTERN, 78
BOTH, 158-159
BRAIN CATCHER, 118-120
  Introducing, 119
  Parts of the body, 120
  To reinforce directions, 120
  To reinforce levels, 120
  To reinforce locomotor and nonlocomotor, 119

    To reinforce tempo and size, 120
    Using combined locomotor and nonlocomotor movements, 70, 120
    Using concept combinations, 71
BRIDGE, 17
BRIDGE CRAWL, 34
CAN'T, 18
CAT DANCE, 178
CATALOG OF LOCOMOTOR MOVEMENTS, 32-40
CATALOG OF NONLOCOMOTOR MOVEMENTS, 71-77
CARRYING, 51, 154
    The Stretcher, 154
    To work on "between," 153-154
CAUSE AND EFFECT STARTS, 28
CHAIRS, 144
    Free time, 144
    Guided movements, 144
    Studies, 144
CHINESE JUMP ROPES, 130-131
CHOREOGRAPHY, also see "STUDIES"
    Criticizing, 146-147
    With moveable props, 145-146
CHRISTMAS TREE FLOOR PATTERN, 101
CINCH APPROACH, 95
CIRCLE SWING, 72
CIRCLE TURNS, 68
CIRCUMFERENCE, DIAMETER, AND RADIUS, 166
COLOR PAPER SQUARES, 168-169
COMBINING LEVELS AND DIRECTIONS WITH PARTNERS, 46
COMBINING LOCOMOTOR PLUS NONLOCOMOTOR MOVEMENTS, 69-71
    Examples, 70
    In Brain Catcher, 120
    Introducing, 69-70
    Used for, 70-71
COMFORTABLE, 156-157
COMPUTATIONS, 166-167
    Counting by two's, three's, etc., 166-167
    Foam jump, 167
    Group division, 166-167
    Remainder, 167
    Sums, 167
CONCEPT COMBINATIONS, 70-71, 89-90
CONCEPT REVIEW
    Ms. Monster, 139-140
    Twirls, 118
CONCEPTS, DIFFICULT, 172, 174-180
    Balance, 179-180
    Dynamic quality, 177
    Falls, 177-179
    Focus, 174-176
CONCEPTUAL APPROACH, 2-3, 178
CONCEPTUAL METHOD OF TEACHING THE WIGGLY LINE, 102-103
CONNECTING LINES (IN FLOOR PATTERNS), 99
CONTRACT AND STRETCH, 44-45, 64-65, 73, 144
    Definition, 64
    Difference with bend and straighten, 67

    Including limp, 65
    Introducing, 64
    Isolated, 64
    Putting energy into, 65
    Study, 65
    Using chairs, 144
    Using levels, 53-54, 64
    With a partner, 44-45, 65
COPS AND ROBBERS, 86
COSTUMES, 145
COUNTERPOINT, 154
COUNTING BY TWO'S, THREE'S, ETC., 166-167
CRAWL, 34
    Bridge, 34
    Crab, 34
    Inch worm, 34
    Spider, 34
CRITICISM, 146-147
CROSSED SWING, 63, 72
CRUX OF ADVANCED WORK, 172
CURVED LINES, 104-105
DANCE, 69
DANCES, see STUDIES
DANGEROUS ACTIVITIES, 20
DESIGNS, 109-110
DIAGONAL STRUCTURE, 3-4, 27-29
    Cause and effect starts, 28
    Definition, 27
    Group work, 28-29
    Perfect corners, 28
    Setting up, 28
    Teaching diagonal lines, 27
DIRECTION PROBLEMS, 90
    Combined with room directions, 110-111
DIRECTIONAL CAN-CAN, 154
DIRECTIONAL RUNNING, 154
DIRECTIONAL SKILLS, 81
DIRECTIONAL SKIPPING, 154
DIRECTIONS, 80-92
    Definition, 80
    Difference between floor pattern, 80
    Difficult locomotor movements, 88
    Directional skills, 81
    Introducing directions, 81
    Locomotor movements, 86-88, 90
    Nonlocomotor movements, 82-84
    Preparing for locomotor movements, 86
    Problems, 90, 110-111
    Studies, beginning, 88-89; full scale, 91-92
    Used in concept combinations, 70-71, 89-90
DIRECTIONS IN PARTNERS, 45-46
DRAGGING, 47
DYNAMIC QUALITY, 177
    Definition, 177
    Studies, 177

EIGHT PLUS EIGHT PATTERN, 77-78
EMOTION WORDS, 159-160
EQUIPMENT, 6-7, 210-213, also see PROPS
EVERYBODY, 159
EYE/HAND WORK STATION, 212
   Balls, 212
   Bean bag toss, 212
   Other, 212
FACE FRONT COMPONENT, 11
FALLING CHILDREN, 26-27, also see ARE YOU ALIVE?
FALLS, 75-76, 177-179
   Back falls, 75
   Cat Dance, 178
   Definition, 178
   Fall Dance, 178
   Introducing, 178
   Lunge fall, 76
   One-knee back fall, 75
   One-leg side fall, 76
   Side fall, 75
   Sitting back fall, 75
   Spiral twist sit, 66, 74, 75
   Teeter-totter fall, 75
FAN SWING, 72
FAR, 10
FEATHERS, 143
FIFTH POSITION, 76-77
FIGURE EIGHT SWING, 72
FIRECRACKER, 13
FIRST POSITION, 76
FLIP OVER, 47
FLOOR PATTERNS, 80, 94-112
   Artworks, 108
   Beginning lines, 96
   Beginning patterns, 96-97
   Christmas tree, 101
   Cinch approach, 95
   Definition, 80
   Designs, 109-110
   Difference between direction and floor pattern, 80
   Difficult patterns, 100-102
   Drawing the room representation, 95
   Geometric shapes, 165-166
   Helping floor pattern, 99
   Individual maps, 108
   Introducing, 95-97
   Letters, 98, 149-150
   Lines, 102-108
   Maps, 94-102
   Numbers, 165
   Organizing the class to see the map, 84-85
   Row, Row, Row Your Boat, 92
   Skills, 94
   Star, 98
   Starting point, 96

   Symmetrical and asymmetrical, 111-112
   Tumbling, 108-109
   Used in concept combinations, 71, 100-101
   Voice box, 109
FLYING
   Balloons, 133-134
   Parachute, 140
   With Rocks and Waves, 140-141
FOAM JUMP, 114, 166-167
FOCUS, 174-176
   Definition, 174
   Introducing, 175
   Locomotor movements, 175-176
   On own body, 176
   Partners, 176
   Problems, 175-176
   Within a study, 176
FOLDING LESSON, 129
FOOT
   Hello and Goodbye, 14
   Warm-up, 32, 114, 173
FORMULA FOR USING PROPS, 123-124
FOUL AND FOWL, 161
FOUNDATION OF MOVEMENT PROGRAM, 3-4, 113
FOUR DIFFERENT SWINGS PATTERN, 63-64
FOURTH POSITION, 76-77
FRACTION JUMP TURNS, 68
FREE TRAVELING STRUCTURE, 3-4, 25-27
   Definition, 3, 25
   Precision, 26
   Problems with, 26-27
   Teaching, 25-26
   Teaching very young children, 29-31
FRONT SWING, 63, 72
FUN, 147
GALLOP, 36-37
GALLOPING IN A BASKET, 154
GEOMETRY, 130, 165-166
GIVE YOUR TEACHER A HEART ATTACK, 48
GOAL OF THE BOOK, 2
GOAL OF THE FIRST CLASS, 8-9
GRAPEVINE, 33
GROUP CONTRACT AND STRETCH, 65
GROUP DIVISIONS, 166-167
GROUP STUDIES, TEACHER STRUCTURED, 42, 57, 79, 126, 130, 134, 135, 143, 144, 146, 149, 150, 160, 164, 165, 170, 172, 177, 180
GROUP WORK 28-29, 50-51
   Between, 153-154
   Chinese jump ropes, 130-131
   Group movements, 50-51
   Groupings for floor patterns, 97
   Ms. Monster, 139-140
   Necessity of, 50
   Ropes, 131
   Staying together, 50

GROUPING (FOR FLOOR PATTERNS), 97
GYMNASTICS
   Balance beam, 210
   Pyramid at end of spiral line, 106
   Tumbling, 37-38, 108-109, 210-211
HAMBURGERS AND FRENCH FRIES, 138-139, 142
   For putting the parachute away, 142
   Variation one, 138-139
   Variation two, 139
HELLO AND GOODBYE, 14
HELP FROM OLDER CHILDREN, 138
HELPING FLOOR PATTERN, 99
HOMONYMS, 160-162
   Aisle and isle, 161
   Fowl and foul, 161
   Pantomime, 161-162
   Row, row, and row, 161-162
   Skip, 160-161
HOP, 35
HOP-JUMP, 154
HOPSCOTCH, 35
   With focus, 176
HORIZONTAL AND VERTICAL, 156
HORSE IN THE CORRAL, 51
HOUSES (MATS), 152
HULA HOOPS, 132-133
   Individual prop, 132
   Patterning prop, 132-133
IN AND OUT, 152
   In the In and Out Game, 154-155
IN AND OUT GAME, 154-155
IN FRONT OF, 153
   In the In and Out Game, 154-155
INCLUSIVE AND EXCLUSIVE WORDS, 158-159
   Both, 158-159
   Everybody, 159
   Nobody, 159
   Only, 158
INDIVIDUAL MAPS, 108
INITIAL EXERCISES, 13-18
ISOLATED MOVEMENTS, 60-61, 62, 64, 65, 66, 67
   Bend and straighten, 67
   Contract and stretch, 64
   Definition, 60
   Only, 158
   Rotating, 68
   Shake, 62
   Strike, 65
   Swing, 62
   To expand nonlocomotor vocabulary, 60-61
   Twist, 66
JUGGLING PROCESS, 54
JAZZ WALK, 32
JUMP, 34-35
   Fraction jump turns, 68
   Straddle, 35
   Tuck, 35

JUMP-HOP STATION, 211
JUMP ROPE STATION, 213
JUMP THE FOAM, 114, 166-167
JUMP YOUR NAME, 9
KICK THE HABIT, 40
KICKS, 39-40
    Can-can, 40
    Hitch, 40
    Karate, 40
KNEE-FOOT POSITION, 77
LANGUAGE DEVELOPMENT, 148-164
    Letters, 148-150
    Spelling, 163-164
    Word comprehension, 150-163, 166
LATERALITY, 81-92
    Definition, 84
    Right and left, 84-86
LEAP, 40
    Stag, 40
    Teaching, 40
LESSON PLANS, 183
    Framework, 183-184
    Grades preschool-1, 184-193
    Grades 2-3, 193-205
    Grades 4-6, 205-216
LETTER AND NUMBER FLOOR PATTERNS, 98, 149-150, 165
LETTERS, 148-150
    Body shape letters, 148-149, 150
    Combining techniques, 150
    Floor pattern letters, 149-150
    Outlining letters, 149-150
LEVEL, 53-58
  As a way of expanding nonlocomotor vocabulary, 61
  Balance, 179
  Categorizing locomotor movements, 56-57
  Chairs, 144
  Contract and stretch, 53-54, 64
  Definition, 53
  Introducing, 53
  Locomotor movements, 56-57
  Nonlocomotor movements, 53-54
  Reinforced by Brain Catcher, 120
  Relaxation, 121
  Rising levels for Rocks and Waves, 140
  Rocking, 55
  Studies, 54-56, 57
  Swings, 64, 72-73
  Uncategorized levels, 56
  Use of, 58
  Used in a spiral line, 106
  Used in concept combinations, 70-71, 89-90
  With partners, 45, 46
LIFTING, 48-50
  Stage one, 49
  Stage two, 49-50

LIFTING (PARACHUTE), 141
LIMP, 65
  As a dynamic quality, 177
  In Spaghetti, 121-122
  With contract and stretch, 65
LINE DESIGN, 109-110
LINE SHAPES, 102-108
  Combining four line shapes, 107
  Curved lines, 104-105
  Looped lines, 107-108
  Spiral lines, 105-106
  Symmetrical and asymmetrical, 111-112
  Using new lines in floor patterns, 102
  Wiggly lines, 102-104
  Zigzag lines, 106
LINEAR PATTERNS, 168-169
  Color paper squares, 168-169, 213
  Other incentives, 170
  Pattern blocks, 169-170, 213
LOCOMOTOR MOVEMENTS, 23-42
  Alternating with nonlocomotor movements, 44-45, 60, 61, 173
  Catalog, 32-40
  Definition, 23
  For very young children, 29-31
  Introducing the concept, 23-24
  Introducing the term, 23
  Locomotor plus nonlocomotor movements, 69-71
  Reinforced by Brain Catcher, 119
  Structuring, 25
  Studies, 24-25, 41-42, 57, 88-89, 91-92
  To differentiate backward and reverse, 158
  To work on between, 153-154
  Used in concept combinations, 70-71, 89-90
  With focus, 175-176
LOCOMOTOR MOVEMENTS ON LEVELS, 56-57
  Locomotor level studies, 57
LOCOMOTOR MOVEMENTS USING DIRECTIONS, 86-89
  Cops and Robbers, 86
  Difficult, 88
  Introducing, 86
  Sideways, 87-88
LOCOMOTOR MOVEMENTS WITH PARTNERS, 46-48
LOOPED LINES, 107-108
LUNGE FALL, 76
MACHINE GAME, 106
MAGIC SCARF, 128
MAPS, 94-102
  Beginning floor patterns, 96-97
  Cinch approach, 95
  Drawing the room representation, 95
  First line, 96
  Helping floor pattern, 99
  Individual maps, 108
  Letter and number floor patterns, 98, 149-150, 165
  Organizing the class to see the map, 84-85

    Own patterns, 98-100
    Second line, 96
    Starting point, 96
    Subsequent changes, 97-98, 100-102
    Third line, 96
MARBLES, 143
MARKER METHOD OF TEACHING THE WIGGLY LINE, 103-104
MATH, 164-167
    Computations, 166-167
    Geometry, 130, 165-166
    Numbers, 164-165
MAYBE I DON'T, MAYBE I DO, 18
MEASURING, 93
MERRY-GO-ROUND, 139
MIDDLE, 92-94
    Introducing, 92-93
    Measuring, 93
    Of parts of the body, 93
    Of planes, 93
    Removing the middle marker, 94
MIRROR AND SHADOW, 48
MIRRORED MOVEMENTS, 84
MOTOR PROBLEMS, 1-2, 217-221
    Stations, 216-221
    Testing, 1
MOVEABLE MAZE JUMP, 131
MOVEABLE PROPS, 145-146
    Examples of choreography, 146
    Studies, 146
    What to use, 145
MOVEMENT EDUCATION
    Benefits, 1-13
    Definition, 1
MOVEMENT AS A SUBJECT, 8, 10, 11, 170-171
MS. MONSTER, 139-140
MS. OPPOSITE, 162
MUSHROOM, 141
NAME LEARNING ACTIVITIES
    Jump your name, 9
    Name syllable patterns, 168
    Shake a partner, 43-44
NAME SYLLABLE PATTERNS, 168
NEAR, 10
NEWSPAPERS, 143
NOBODY, 159
NONLOCOMOTOR MOVEMENTS, 59-79
    Alternating with locomotor movements, 44-45, 60, 61, 173
    Bend and straighten, 66-67, 70, 73-74
    Catalog, 71-77
    Combined with locomotor movements, 69-71
    Contract and stretch, 64-65, 70, 73
    Definition, 59
    Expanding the nonlocomotor movement vocabulary, 60-61
    Falls, 75-76, 177-179
    Introducing the concept, 59

    Introducing the term, 59
    On levels, 53-56
    Problems, 68-69
    Shake, 43-44, 62, 70, 71
    Spin, turn, or twirl, 67-68, 74-75
    Strike, 65, 70, 74
    Studies, 53-56, 62, 63, 64, 65, 66, 67, 68, 77-79, 83
    Swing, 62-64, 70, 72-73
    True nonlocomotor movements, 68-69
    Twist, 66, 70, 72-73
    With a partner, 44-45, 65
NONLOCOMOTOR MOVEMENTS USING DIRECTIONS, 82-84
    Bouncing torso, 82
    Combinations, 83
    Hip thrust, 82
    Jumping, 83
    Kicking, 82
    Looking, 82
    Patterns, 83
    Rolls, 83
    Shaking hands, 82
    Stretches, 83
    Strike, 83
    Tantrum legs, 83
NORMAL CHILDREN, 1
NUMBERS, 164-165
    Body shape numbers, 164, 165
    Floor pattern numbers, 165
    Outlining numbers, 165
OBSTACLE COURSE, 8, 18-22
    Additions, 21-22
    Beginning course, 19
    Childrens' own, 22
    Elaborate course, 19-21
    To teach relationship words, 151
    To teach reverse, 157-158
    Used for testing, 19
OCEAN, 137-138
ON AND OFF, 151-152
    In the In and Out Game, 154-155
    With in and out, 152
ONE-FOOT STANDING TWIRL, 67-68
ONE-KNEE BACK FALL, 75
ONE-KNEE BACK ROLL, 38
ONE-LEG SIDE FALL, 76
ONE-LEGGED SKIP, 36
ONLY, 158
OPPOSITE GAME, 162-163
OPPOSITES, 162-163
    Antonyms, 162-163
    Ms. Opposite, 162
    Opposite Game, 162-163
    Partner opposite, 162
    To work on between, 154
    To work on problem words, 156-157
ORGANIZATION OF THE FIRST CLASS, 8
    For very young children, 29-31

ORGANIZATION OF THE FIRST FOUR CLASSES, 9
ORGANIZING THE CLASS TO SEE THE MAP, 84-85
OUTLINING LETTERS, 149, 150
OUTLINING NUMBERS, 165
PANTOMIME, 161, 164
PARACHUTE, 137-142
   Bag Them Up, 139
   Children that stay under, 139
   Flying, 140
   For teaching circumference, diameter, and radius, 166
   Hamburgers and French Fries, 138-139, 142
   Introducing, 137
   Lifting, 141
   Merry-Go-Round, 139
   Ms. Monster, 139-140
   Mushroom, 141
   Ocean, 137-138
   Putting the parachute away, 142
   Rocks and Waves, 140-141
   Whooshing, 138
PARALLEL FEET, 76
PART ONE OF THE PARTNER DANCE, 181
PART TWO OF THE PARTNER DANCE, 181-182
PARTNER ACTIVITIES, 33, 35, 37, 39, 43-50, 65, 73
   Bag a Partner, 46
   Balls, 126-127, 173
   Chinese jump ropes, 130-131
   Combining level and direction, 46
   Contract and stretch, 44-45, 65, 73
   Directions, 45-46
   Floor patterns, 92, 101-102, 104, 111-112
   Focus, 176
   Levels, 45
   Lifting, 48-50
   Mirror and Shadow, 48
   Nonlocomotor movements, 44-45, 65
   Opposites, 162
   Parachute, 140-141
   Partner Dance, 180-182
   Ropes, 130-131
   Scooters, 137
   Shake, 43-44, 71
   Slide ride, 39
   Strictly Partner Movements, 46-48
   Symmetry and asymmetry, 111-112
   Trust Walk, 129
PARTNER DANCE, 180-182
PARTS OF THE BODY
   For outlining letters, 149
   In Brain Catcher, 120
   Right and Left Bug, 85-86
   Torso, 14-15
   With balance, 179
PATTERN BLOCKS, 169-170, 221
PATTERNING, 120, 132-133, 168-170, 221

    Color paper squares, 168-169, 221
    Hoops, 132-133
    Name syllable patterns, 168
    Pattern blocks, 169-170, 221
    Patterning incentives, 170
    Station, 221
PATTERNS, see STUDIES
PATTERNS, DIFFICULT, 79, 172, 176, 178-182
    Cat Dance, 178
    Fall Dance, 178-179
    Floor patterns, 100-102, 107-108
    Locomotor, 41-42, 57
    Nonlocomotor, 56, 79
    Partner Dance, 180-182
    The Sting, 41
    Using balance, 179-180
    Using dynamic quality, 177
    Using focus, 176
PERCUSSIVE, 177
PERFECT CORNERS, 28
PERFECT SPOTS, 3-4, 9-13
    Definition, 3, 9
    Difficulty with, 11
    Facing front, 11
    Games, 13
    Imperfect spots, 12
    Importance of, 11-12
    Initial exercises in, 13-18
    Introducing, 9-10
PLASTIC GARBAGE BAGS, 143-144
PLIES, 73-74, 116-118
POSITIONS OF THE BODY, 76-77
POSTURE, see ALIGNMENT
PRANCE, 33
PRECISION, 4-5, 11-12, 26, 28, 61, 115, 129, 171
    Expectations, 171
    For the stage, 115
    In folding scarves, 129
    In isolated movements, 61
PROBLEM WORDS, 156-158
    Comfortable and uncomfortable, 156-157
    Horizontal and vertical, 156
    Opposites, 156-157
    Physical objects, 157-158
    Progression, 156
    Reverse, 157-158
    Vignettes, 156-157
PROBLEMS WITH FREE TRAVELING STRUCTURE, 26-27
PROBLEMS WITH NONLOCOMOTOR MOVEMENTS, 68-69
PROGRESSION FOR PROBLEM WORDS, 156
PROPS, 6-7, 123-147, 216-221, also see EQUIPMENT and STATIONS
    Bags, onion and potato, 46
    Bags, plastic garbage, 143-144
    Balloons, 133-135
    Balls, 124-127, 173
    Benefits, 123, 147

   Chairs, 144
   Costumes, 145
   Dangers, 123
   Feathers, 143
   Formula for using, 123-124, 142
   Hula hoops, 132, 133
   Marbles, 143
   Newspapers, 143
   Parachute, 137-142
   Plastic garbage bags, 143-144
   Props that move, 145-146
   Ropes, 130-131
   Scarves, 127-129
   Scooters, 136-137, 219-220
   What can be used as a prop, 142
   What you need to start, 6-7
PUNS, 164
RAISING OUR STANDARDS SPEECH, 174
RELATIONSHIP WORDS, 151-155
   Behind, 153, 154-155
   Beside, 153, 154-155
   Between, 153-154, 154-155
   In and Out, 152, 154-155
   In and Out Game, 154-155
   In front of, 153, 154-155
   In general, 151
   On and Off, 151-152, 154-155
   With chairs, 144
RELAXATION, 120-121
   For older children, 121
   Rocking, 120-121
RELEASING ENERGY WITHIN A SWING, 64
REMAINDER, 167
REVERSE, 154, 157-158
RIGHT AND LEFT
   Combined with room directions, 110-111
   Cops and Robbers, 86
   In rooms, 110
   Nonlocomotor movements using directions, 82-84
   Right and Left Bug, 85-86
   Teaching, 84-85
   Walk Down Your Front, 81-82
RIGHT AND LEFT BUG, 85-86
ROCKING AS RELAXER, 120-121
   Fast and slow, 121
   Rising levels, 121
   Softer, 121
ROCKING SONG, 29
   For putting the parachute away, 142
   For relaxation, 120-121
   For teaching locomotor movements to young children, 29-31
ROCKING ON LEVELS, 55
   For relaxation, 121
ROCKS AND WAVES, 140-141
   For putting parachute away, 142

ROLLS, 37-38
  Backward, 38
  Cat, 37
  Fan, 72
  Log, 37
  One-knee back, 38
  Somersault or forward, 37-38
ROOM DIRECTIONS, 110-111
ROOM REPRESENTATION, 95, 97, 98-99
  Drawing, 95
  Putting it straight, 98-99
  Subsequent changes, 97
ROPES, 130-131, 221
  Chinese jump ropes, 130-131
  Jump rope station, 221
  Moveable maze jump, 131
  Straight ropes, 131
  Tangle, 131
  Twirl, 131
ROTATION TURNS, 68, 74
ROW, ROW, AND ROW, 161
ROW, ROW, ROW YOUR BOAT, 91-92
RUN, 33
SCARVES, 127-129
  Free time, 127
  Guided movements, 128
  Introducing, 127-128
  Magic Scarf, 128
  Partner work, 129
  Passing them out, 127
  Putting the scarves away, 129
  Studies, 128-129
  What kind, 127
SCOOTER LINE, 136-137, 219-220
SCOOTERS, 136-137
  Free time, 136
  Guided movements, 136
  Scooter line, 136-137, 219-220
  Station, 219-220
  What they are, 136
  With partners, 137
SEAT-SCOOT, 38-39
SECOND POSITION, 76
SELF DISCIPLINE, 11, 117, 176
SHADOW, 48
SHAKE, 43-44, 54, 62, 70, 71, 78
  Combined with locomotor movements, 70
  Initial study, 62
  Introducing, 62
  Using levels, 54
SHAKE A PARTNER, 43-44
SHAKE CONGRATULATIONS, 10
SHARP ANGLE, 106
SHOULDER STAND, 179
SIDE FALL, 75
SIDE-SLIDE, 37
  Cops and Robbers, 86

SIDE SWING, 63-64, 72
SITTING BACK FALL, 75
SIZE OF MOVEMENTS, 61
    As a way of expanding nonlocomotor vocabulary, 61
    Differentiated from tempo, 120
SKIP, 35-36
    One-legged, 36
    Teaching, 35
SKIP, 160-161
SLIDING ON THE FLOOR, 39
SMALL MUSCLE COORDINATION STATION, 221
SPAGHETTI, 121, 122
    At end of spiral line, 106
SPATIAL AWARENESS, 11, 80-112, also see FLOOR PATTERN
    Definition, 80
    Skills necessary for, 80
SPELLING, 163-164
    Connected to comprehension, 163
    Friend, 163
    Homonyms, 160-162
    Said, 163
    Strict memory, 163
    Thirteen colonies, 164
    Turn, 163
SPIN, 67-68, 74-75, also see TURN and TWIRL
    Definition, 67
    Group spin, 50
    Introduction, 67
    Partner spin, 47
    Studies, 54, 56, 67, 68, 78
SPIRAL LINE, 106-107
    Body size, 106
    Combined with other lines, 107
    Ending, 106
SPIRAL TWIST SIT, 66, 74, 75
SPOTTING, 176
STAGE, 115
STAGE ONE, BLAST OFF, 17
STAGE THREE, BLAST OFF, 17-18
STAGE TWO, BLAST OFF, 17
STANDARDS, 4-5, 174
STAR FLOOR PATTERN, 98
START AND STOP, see FREE TRAVELING STRUCTURE
STATIONARY LOCOMOTOR MOVEMENT SYNDROME, 61, 68-69
STATIONS, 216-221
    Balance beam, 217-218
    Definition, 216
    Eye/hand work, 220
    Jump-hop, 219
    Jump rope, 221
    Patterning, 221
    Scooter line, 219-220
    Small muscle coordination, 221
    Tumbling, 218-219
STING PATTERN, 41
STRETCHER, THE, 154

STRICTLY PARTNER MOVEMENTS, 46-48
STRIKE, 65, 74, 78
  Definition, 65
  Introducing, 65
  Study, 65, 78
STUDIES, also see FLOOR PATTERNS and PATTERNS, DIFFICULT
  Balance, 179-180
  Ball studies, 126
  Balloon, blown, 135
  Balloon Round, 135
  Balloon, unblown, 134
  Bend and straighten, 67
  Body shape letters, 149, 150
  Body wave pattern, 78
  Cat Dance, 178
  Chair, 144
  Chinese jump ropes, 130
  Contract, stretch, and limp, 54-56, 65, 149, 177, 180
  Direction studies, beginning, 88-89, full scale, 91-92
  Dynamic quality, 177
  Eight plus eight study, 77-78
  Emotion words, 159-160
  Fall Dance, 178
  Fluid Turns, 78
  Focus, 176
  Four different swings, 63-64
  Fraction jump turns, 68
  Horizontal and vertical, 156
  Hula hoops, 132-133
  In and out, 152
  Letters, combining techniques, 150
  Levels, 54-56, 57
  Locomotor studies, 24-25, 41-42, 57, 88-89, 91-92
  Locomotor level studies, 57
  Marbles, 143
  Nonlocomotor studies, 53-56, 62, 63, 64, 65, 66, 67, 68, 77-79, 83
  Nonlocomotor level studies, 53-56
  Nonlocomotor movements using directions, 83
  Number shapes, 164-165
  Partner Dance, 180-182
  Prop studies, 126, 128-129, 130, 132-133, 134, 135, 144, 145-146
  Rotation turns, 68
  Ropes, 130
  Row, Row, Row Your Boat, 91-92
  Scarves, 128-129
  Shake, 54-56, 78, 79, 114, 148
  Skip, 161
  Spin, turn, or twirl, 54, 56, 67, 68, 78
  Sting pattern, 41
  Strike, 65, 78, 79
  Swings, 54-56, 62, 63, 64, 77-78, 79
  Teacher structured group problems, 42, 57, 79, 126, 130, 134, 135, 143, 144, 146, 149, 150, 160, 164, 165, 170, 172, 177, 180
  Teacher structured patterns using Free Traveling Structure, 79, 173, 177
  The Monster Rises, 78

Three/five/four/four pattern, see Row, Row, Row Your Boat
To differentiate backward and reverse, 158
Twist, 66, 79
Vignettes, 157
SUMS, 167
SUSTAINED, 177
SWING, 62-64, 72-73
   Body wave, 72
   Circle swing, 72
   Crossed swing, 63, 72
   Definition, 62
   Fan swing, 72
   Figure eight swing, 72
   Four different, 63
   Front swing, 63, 72
   Introducing, 62
   Isolated swings, 62
   Levels, 54-56, 64, 72-73
   Releasing the energy within, 64
   Side swing, 63, 72
   Studies, 54-56, 62, 63, 64, 77-78, 79
   Twist swing, 63, 72
   Whole body swings, 63, 72-73
SWORDFISH, 15-16
SYMMETRY, 111-112
   Floor patterns, 111-112
   In Brain Catcher, 120
   Introducing, 111
   Mirror, 48
TANGLE, 131
TEETER-TOTTER FALL, 75
TEMPER TANTRUM, 56
TEMPO, 120
THIRD POSITION, 76-77
THIRTEEN COLONIES, 164
THREE/FIVE/FOUR/FOUR PATTERN, see ROW, ROW, ROW YOUR BOAT
TONE OF THE CLASS, 51-52
   Importance of, 51
   Promoting a good class atmosphere, 51-52
TORSO, 14-15
TOUCHING 43
   Reluctancy, 46
TRANSITIONS, 180
TRIANGLE POSITION, 77
TRUE NONLOCOMOTOR MOVEMENTS, 68-69
TRUST WALK, 129
TUMBLING
   In floor patterns, 108-109
   Rolls, 37-38
   Station, 210-211
TURN, 67-68, 74-75, also see SPIN and TWIRL
   Definition, 67
   Fraction jump turns, 68
   Introducing, 67
   One-foot standing turn, 67-68
   Rotation or circle turns, 68
   Studies, 54, 56, 67, 68, 78

TURN OUT, 116-118
   Definition, 116
   In plies, 73-74, 117-118
   In wide stride, 117
   Own true turn out, 117
TWIRL, see SPIN and TURN
TWIRL WITH ROPES, 131
TWIRLS, 118
TWIST, 66, 70, 74, 75
   Combined with locomotor movements, 70
   Definition, 66
   Introducing, 66
   Spiral twist sit, 66, 75
   Studies, 66, 79
TWIST SWING, 63, 72
UNCOMFORTABLE, 157
VIBRATION, 71
VIGNETTES, 156-157
VOICE BOX FLOOR PATTERNS, 109
WALK, 32-33
WALK DOWN YOUR FRONT, 81-82
WALTZ WALK, 32
WAVES, 55
WHEELBARROW, 47
WHOOSHING, 138
WIGGLY LINES, 102-104
   Combined with other lines, 104, 107
   Conceptual method of teaching, 102-103
   Marker method of teaching, 103-104
WORD COMPREHENSION, 150-163
   Connected to spelling, 163
   Emotion words, 159-160
   Homonyms and antonyms, 160-163
   Inclusive and exclusive words, 158-159
   Problem words, 156-158
   Relationship words, 151-155
ZIGZAG LINES, 106
   Combined with other lines, 107

MOVEMENT EDUCATION WORKSHOPS!

For information about workshops, teacher inservices, conferences, and school consultations contact the author directly.

Write:

Sheila Kogan
8 Highland Boulevard
Kensington, CA 94707

FREE PUBLISHER'S CATALOG!

Call toll-free or write for our free catalog of

INNOVATIVE CURRICULUM GUIDEBOOKS AND MATERIALS
for
Movement Education, Special Education, and Perceptual-Motor Development
(includes many equipment items used in this book)

Call Toll-Free:
1-800-524-9091

or call **1-510-634-5710** or write:

FRONT ROW EXPERIENCE
540 Discovery Bay Blvd.
Byron, CA 94514-9454